S0-BQB-341

THE LAST ABBOT OF GLASTONBURY
AND OTHER ESSAYS

THE LAST ABBOT OF GLASTONBURY

AND OTHER ESSAYS

BY

FRANCIS AIDAN GASQUET

BOOKS FOR LIBRARIES PRESS
FREEPORT, NEW YORK

First Published 1908
Reprinted 1970

BX
4705
.W5
G32
1970

INTERNATIONAL STANDARD BOOK NUMBER:
0-8369-5577-3

LIBRARY OF CONGRESS CATALOG CARD NUMBER:
72-137376

PRINTED IN THE UNITED STATES OF AMERICA

TO THE READER

A FEW words only seem necessary to introduce this volume of Essays to the public. The papers contained in a former volume of Essays were gathered together and published some ten years ago; and this edition having been now for some time out of print, I was urged to issue it in a cheaper form. Whilst this matter was under consideration, it was further suggested to me that while republishing the first series, I might add a second volume of collected papers, articles, etc., which have appeared since the publication of the first volume.

In regard to the Essays here presented in this second collection, it may be well to make the following remarks. The first item: *The Last Abbot of Glastonbury*, was published in 1895 as a small book for a special occasion. It gathers together memorials of the destruction of the great Benedictine abbeys of Glastonbury, Reading, and Colchester, and gives a brief sketch of the tragic deaths of the last abbots of those houses in the reign of Henry VIII. This volume has been for some years out of print; and as it is not too long to reprint as an essay, I have thought it better to include it in this present volume than to re-issue it separately.

Of the other papers, that on *St. Gregory and England* was written on the occasion of the thirteenth centenary of the death of that Pope some four years ago. It contains a sketch of what England owes to a Pope whom our

29463

forefathers loved to call the Apostle of our race. The paper on *English Biblical Criticism in the Thirteenth Century*, written ten years ago, seems to-day curiously to foreshadow the necessary work of preparing for a critical edition of the Vulgate which has been recently initiated by the present Pope, Pius X.

To some, no doubt, one or two of the papers in this present volume may appear too unimportant and slight to deserve preserving in a more permanent form than they enjoyed in the magazines in which they have already appeared. Such as they are, however, I have been advised to let them find a place in this collection, and therefore give them for what they are worth.

My thanks are in this instance due to Dom H. N. Birt in a very special manner. The whole work of preparing these papers for the press, correcting the proofs, and making the Index, has been undertaken by him.

Francis Aidan Gasquet.

CONTENTS

LIST OF ILLUSTRATIONS

VIEW OF GLASTONBURY AND THE TOR

(From Hollar's print)

[To face p. 1

I

THE LAST ABBOT OF GLASTONBURY

CHAPTER I

GLASTONBURY

THE prospect from the Roman camp of Masbury, on the Mendip hills of Somerset, is one to be remembered. The country presents itself to the view as in a map. In front a vast plain stretches out into the dim blue horizon across Dorsetshire to the shores of the English Channel. To the east the hills fall and rise like the swell of the sea in a series of vales and heights till they are lost in the distance. Westward the landscape is more varied, the ground, which at the spectator's feet had attained well-nigh to the dignity of a mountain, sinks away in a succession of terraces to the level country lying between it and the waters of the Severn sea. From the midst of this plain there rises clear and sharp against the sky, like a pyramid, a hill crowned with a tower, which forms from all points the most marked feature of the scene. Neither the glancing of the sunlight from the surface of the sea some fifteen miles away, nor the glimpse that is caught between the trees of the

B

grey towers and gables of the great cathedral church of
Wells, nor yet the sight of the spire of Doulting, calling
up as it does memories of Saint Aldhelm, can long
restrain the eye from turning once again to gaze on the
conical hill with its tower which stands out in the landscape. Remarkable alike in its contour and in its situation, these do not constitute its chief attraction, for it
speaks not only to the eye but to the mind also; it is
Nature's monument marking a spot of more than ordinary interest. The shadows of tradition seem still to
hover over the hill and recall a past which is lost in the
dimness of legend. More than all, however, the last
record which marks the place in the pages of history
brings to mind a deed of desecration and of blood perpetrated in the evil days which brought ruin to the most
famous sanctuary on English soil, for here suffered for
conscience sake Richard Whiting, last abbot of the far-
famed abbey of Glastonbury which nestled at its foot,
thus making a worthy close to a history without parallel
in the annals of our country.

The history of Glastonbury is the history of its abbey;
without its abbey Glastonbury were nothing.[1] Even among
those great ecclesiastical institutions, the Benedictine
abbeys of mediæval England, the history of Glastonbury
has a character all its own. I will not insult its venerable
age, says a recent historian, by so much as contrasting
it with the foundations of yesterday, which arose under
the influence of the Cistercian movement, for they play
but a small part indeed in the history of this church and
realm. Glastonbury is something more than Netley and
Tintern, Rievaulx and Fountains. It is something more
again than the Benedictine houses which arose at the

[1] The following is adapted from the late Professor Freeman.

bidding of the Norman Conqueror, of his race and of his companions; more than Selby and Battle, and Shrewsbury and Reading. It is in its own special aspect something more even than the royal minster of St. Peter, the crowning place of Harold and of William, which came to supplant Glastonbury as the burial place of kings. Nay, it stands out distinct even among the great and venerable foundations of English birth which were already great and venerable when this country fell into the hands of the Norman. There is something in Glastonbury which one looks for in vain at Peterborough and Crowland and Evesham, or even at Winchester and Canterbury; all these are the works of our own, our English people; they go back to the days of our ancient kingship, they go back—some of them—even to the days when Augustine preached, and Theodore fixed the organisation of the growing English Church; but they go back no further. We know their beginnings, we know their founders; their history, nay, their very legends do not dare to trace up their foundations beyond the time of the coming of Saxon and Angle into this island. At Glastonbury, and at Glastonbury alone, we instinctively feel that the name of England is not all, for here, and here alone, we walk with easy steps, with no thought of any impassable barrier, from the realm of Saxon Ina back to that of Arthur, the hero king of the British race. Alongside of the memory and the tombs of the West-Saxon princes, who broke the power of the Northmen, there still abides the memory of the British prince who checked for a generation the advance of the Saxon.

But at Glastonbury even this is a small matter. The legends of the spot go back to the very days of the Apostles. Here, and here alone on English soil, we are linked, not only to the beginnings of English Christianity, but to the beginnings of Christianity itself. We are met at the outset by the tradition that the spot was made sacred as the dwelling of a multitude of the just, and its soil hallowed by the bodies of numerous saints, " whose souls now rejoice," says an ancient writer, " in the possession of God in heaven." For here were believed to have found a resting place the twelve disciples of Philip the Apostle, sent by him to Britain, under the leadership of Joseph of Arimathea, who had buried our Lord. " We know not," continues our author in his simple style, " whether they really repose here, although we have read that they sojourned in the place for nine years; but here dwelt assuredly many of their disciples, ever twelve in number, who in imitation of them led a hermit's life until unto them came St. Patrick, the great Apostle of the Irish and first abbot of the hallowed spot. Here, too, rests St. Benen, the disciple of St. Patrick; here St. Gildas, the historian of the British; here St. David, bishop of Menevia, and here the holy hermit Indractus with his seven companions, all sprung from the royal race. Here rest the relics of a band of holy Irish pilgrims, who, returning from a visit to the shrines of Rome, turned aside to Glastonbury out of love to St. Patrick's memory and were martyred in a village named Shapwick. Hither, not long after, their remains were brought by Ina, our glorious king."

Such stories of the mediæval scribe, however little worthy of credit in point of detail, represent, there can be little doubt, a substantial truth. For as in later centuries there were brought hither even from far distant Northumbria the relics of Paulinus, and Aidan and Ceolfrid, of Boisil, of Benet Biscop and of others for security on the advance of the Danes, so too in earlier dangers there were carried to Glastonbury, to save them from the blind fury of the pagan Saxon, all that was most sacred and venerated in the churches of Christian Britain.

" No fiction, no dream could have dared," writes the historian, " to set down the names of so many worthies of the earlier races of the British Islands in the *Liber Vitæ* of Durham or of Peterborough. Now I do not ask you to believe these legends; I do ask you to believe that there was some special cause why legends of this kind should grow in such a shape, and in such abundance round Glastonbury alone of all the great monastic churches of Britain."

Though these Glastonbury legends need not be believed as the record of facts, still it has been well said that "the very existence of those legends is a very great fact." The simple truth is that the remoteness and isolation of Glastonbury preserved it from attack, until Christianity had won its way among the West Saxons. So that when at last the Teutonic conqueror came to Avalon, he had already bowed his head to the cross and been washed in the waters of Christian baptism. His coming was thus not to destroy, but to give renewed life to the already ancient monastic sanctuary. The sacred precincts, hitherto held by Britons only, now received monks of English race some time before King Ina, its new founder, following the example of his father, Cædwalla, after a reign of seven and thirty years, resigned his crown to journey to Rome, desiring to end his pilgrimage on earth in the near neighbourhood of the holy places, so that he might the more readily be received by the saints themselves into the celestial kingdom.

And when later the Danes overwhelmed the land, it was this hallowed spot that was destined to be the centre from which not merely a vigorous monastic revival spread throughout England, but whence the kingdom itself was raised by a great reformer to a new pitch of secular greatness; for it was here that Dunstan as a boy, brought by his father on a pilgrimage to the churches of St. Mary and St. Peter the Apostle, " built of olden time," passed the night in prayer. Overcome by sleep the boy saw in a dream an aged man, clothed in snowy vesture, leading him, not through the simple chapels and half-ruined buildings which then occupied the site, but through the fair alleys of a spacious church and comely claustral buildings, whilst he told him that thus was Glastonbury to be rebuilt by him, and that he was to be its future head. This, though but a dream, was yet a dream which must have been related by Dunstan himself in after years. The young daydreams of a strong nature have a tendency to realise themselves in later life, and this boyish vision of a renovated Glastonbury, the outward sign of a new monastic spirit, manifests the workings of a mind influenced, but prepared to be influenced, by the past memories and the present decay of the holy place. Nor did these early images pass away in view of the brilliant prospects that opened out before the young cleric, who had all the advantages of personal capacity and powerful connections, and so he betook himself to remote and solitary Glastonbury, to work out the realisation of his monastic ideals. Dunstan built up its walls with the essentially practical end of securing the primary requirements of monastic enclosure, and the buildings were just like those he dreamed of in his boyhood. He threw on his brother

INTERIOR VIEW OF ST. MARY'S CHAPEL, SHOWING THE
RUINS OF THE CHOIR THROUGH THE WEST
DOOR OF THE ABBEY CHURCH

[To face p. 6

Wulfric the entire temporal business and management of the estates, so that he, freed from the encumbrance of all external affairs, might build up the souls of those who had committed themselves to his direction. It was here at Glastonbury, under the care of St. Dunstan, that St. Ethelwold was formed and fashioned to be the chief instrument in carrying out his monastic policy. Here, too, St. Elphege the martyr, and a successor of Dunstan on the throne of Canterbury lived his monastic life. And from Avalon, too, about the same time, went forth the monk Sigfrid, as the evangelist of pagan Norway.

With such a history, such legends of the past, and such a renewal as the firm and lofty spirit of Dunstan effected in its refoundation, it is no wonder that the repute of Glastonbury drew to it a crowd of fervent monks and the ample benefactions of devout and faithful friends, so that from henceforward there was no monastic house in England which for splendour or wealth could compare with this ancient sanctuary. Through the later Middle Ages, to the people of England Glastonbury was a *Roma secunda*. Strangers came from afar to visit the holy ground, and pilgrim rests marked the roads which led to it. Foreigners coming in ships which brought their freight to the great port of Bristol, hardly ever failed to turn aside to visit this home of the saints, whilst memorials of the sanctuary were carried by the Bristol merchants into foreign lands.

Even now, as it lies in ruin, the imagination can conceive the wonder with which a stranger, on reaching the summit of the hill, still known as the *Pilgrim's Way*, saw spread out before him Glastonbury Abbey in all its vast extent, with its towers and chapels, its broad courts

and cloisters, crowned with the mighty church, the fitting
shrine of the sacred relics and holy memories which had
brought him thither.

CHAPTER II

RICHARD WHITING

NEVER, perhaps, was Glastonbury in greater glory than
at the moment when Richard Whiting was elected to
rule the house as abbot.

Richard Whiting was born probably in the early years
of the second half of the fifteenth century. The civil war
between the Houses of York and Lancaster was then at
its height, and his boyhood must have been passed amid
the popular excitement of the Wars of the Roses and the
varied fortunes of King Edward IV. It is not unimportant to bear this in mind, since the personal experience,
in his youth, of the troubles and dangers of civil strife
can hardly have failed to impress their obvious lesson
strongly upon his mind, and to influence him when the
wilfulness of Henry brought the country to the very
verge of civil war, with its attendant miseries and
horrors.

The abbot's family was west-country in its origin and
was connected distantly with that of Bishop Stapeldon,
of Exeter, the generous founder of Exeter College, Oxford. Its principal member was possessed of considerable estates in Devon and Somerset, but Richard Whiting
came of a younger branch of the family, numbered
among the tenant holders of Glastonbury possessions in

the fertile valley of Wrington. The name is found in the annals of other religious houses. About the time of Richard Whiting's birth, for example, another Richard, probably an uncle, was *camerarius*, or chamberlain, in the monastery of Bath,[1] an office which in after years, at the time of his election as abbot, the second Richard held in the Abbey of Glastonbury. Many years later, at the beginning of the troubles which involved the religious houses in the reign of Henry VIII, a Jane Whiting, daughter of John, probably a near relative of the Abbot of Glastonbury "was shorn and had taken the habit as a nun in the convent of Wilton;"[2] whilst later still, when new foundations of English religious life were being laid in foreign countries, two of Abbot Whiting's nieces became postulants for the veil in the English Franciscan house at Bruges.[3]

Nothing is known for certain about the childhood and youth of Richard Whiting; but it may be safely conjectured that he received his early education and training within the walls of his future monastic home. The antiquary Hearne says that "the monks of Glastonbury kept a free school, where poor men's sons were bred up, as well as gentlemen's, and were fitted for the universities."[4] And some curious legal proceedings, which involved an inquiry as to the Carthusian martyr, blessed Richard Bere, reveal the fact that, as a boy, he had been

[1] Reg. Beckington, f. 311.

[2] R. O. Chanc., *Inq. post mortem.*

[3] Oliver, *Collections illustrating the History of the Catholic Religion*, p. 135. This house returned to England on the French Revolution, and the high esteem with which it was regarded by English Catholics, persecuted at home or exiles abroad, still attends this venerable community, now established at Taunton.

[4] *History of Glastonbury*, preface.

"brought up at the charges of his uncle," Abbot Bere, in the Glastonbury school. The pleadings show that Richard Bere was probably the son of one of the tenants of the abbey lands, and among those who testify to the fact of his having been a boy in the school were "Nicholas Roe, of Glastonbury, gent," and "John Fox, of Glastonbury, yeoman," both of whom had been his fellow scholars "in the said abbey together,"[1] and Thomas Penny, formerly Abbot Bere's servant, who spoke to the nephew Richard as having been in the school at the monastery, whence, as he remembered, he afterwards proceeded to Oxford. What is thus known, almost by accident, about the early education of the martyred Carthusian, may with fair certainty be inferred in the case of Richard Whiting. The boy's training in the claustral school was succeeded by the discipline of the monastic novitiate: and it was doubtless in early youth, as was then the custom, that he joined the community of the great Benedictine monastery of the west country.

Glastonbury, with its long, unbroken history, had had its days of prosperity and its days of trouble, its periods of laxity and days of recovery, and when Whiting first took the monastic habit report did not speak too well of the state of the establishment. John Selwood, the abbot, had held the office since 1457, and under his rule, owing, probably in some measure at least, to the demoralising influence of the constant civil commotions, discipline grew slack and the good name of the abbey had suffered. But it would seem that, as is so often the case, rumour with its many tongues had exaggerated the disorders, since after a careful examination carried out

[1] *Downside Review*, vol. ix (1890), p. 162.

under Bishop Stillington's orders by four ecclesiastics unconnected with the diocese, no stringent injunctions were apparently imposed, and Abbot Selwood continued to rule the house for another twenty years.

From Glastonbury Whiting was sent to Cambridge,[1] to complete his education, and his name appears amongst those who took their M.A. degree in 1483.[2] About the same time the register of the university records the well-known names of Richard Reynolds, the Bridgettine priest of Syon, of John Houghton and William Exmew, both Carthusians, and all three afterwards noble martyrs in the cause of Catholic unity, for which Whiting was also later called upon to sacrifice his life. The blessed John Fisher also, although no longer a student, still remained in close connection with the university, when Richard Whiting came up from Glastonbury to Cambridge.

After taking his degree the young Benedictine monk returned to his monastery, and there probably would have been occupied in teaching. For this work his previous training and his stay at the university in preparation for his degree in Arts, would have specially qualified him, and in all probability he was thus engaged till his

[1] Probably to "Monks' College." Speed, speaking of Magdalen College, Cambridge, says it "was first an hall inhabited by monks of divers monasteries, and therefore heretofore called Monks' College, sent hither from their abbies to the universitie to studye. Edward Stafford, last Duke of Buckingham, &c., bestowed much cost in the repair of it, and in 1519 . . . . new built the hall, whereupon for a time it was called Buckingham College; but the Duke being shortly after attainted, the buildings were left imperfect, continuing a place for monks to study in, until the general suppression of monasteries by King Henry VIII."—Speed, *History of Great Britain*, 1632, p. 1053.

[2] Cooper, *Athenæ Cantabrigienses*, p. 71.

ordination to the priesthood, some fifteen years later. During this period one or two events of importance to the monks of the abbey may be briefly noted.

In 1493, John Selwood, who had been abbot for thirty-six years, died. The monks having obtained the king's leave to proceed with the election of a successor,[1] met for the purpose, and made their choice, without apparently having previously obtained the usual approval of the bishop of the diocese. This neglect was caused possibly by their ignorance of the forms of procedure, as so long a time had intervened since the last election. It may be also that in the long continued absence of the Bishop of Bath and Wells from his See they overlooked this form. Be this as it may, Bishop Fox, then the occupant of the See, on hearing of the election of John Wasyn without his approval, applied to the king for permission to cancel the election. This having been granted, he successfully claimed the right to nominate to the office, and on 20th January, 1494, by his commissary, Dr. Richard Nicke, Canon of Wells, and afterwards Bishop of Norwich, he installed Richard Bere in the abbatial chair of Glastonbury.[2]

In the fourth year of this abbot's rule, Somerset and the neighbourhood of Glastonbury were disturbed by the passage of armed men—insurgents against the authority of King Henry VII and the royal troops sent against them—which must have sadly broken in upon the quiet of the monastic life. In the early summer of 1497 the Cornish rebels who had risen in resistance to the heavy taxation of Henry, passed through Glastonbury and Wells on their way to London. Their number was

[1] Pat. Rot., 8 Henry VII, p. 2, m. 11.
[2] Reg. Fox Bath et Wellen, f. 48. Pat. Rot., 9 Henry VII, 26.

NORMAN DOORWAY OF ST. MARY'S
CHAPEL

EXTERIOR OF ST. MARY'S CHAPEL (COMMONLY CALLED ST. JOSEPH'S)
COVERING THE SITE OF THE OLD BRITISH CHURCH AND FORM-
ING THE ATRIUM OF THE MONASTIC CHURCH

[To face p. 12

estimated at from six to fifteen thousand, and the country for miles around was at night lighted up by their camp fires. Their poverty was dire, their need most urgent, and although it is recorded that no act of violence or pillage was perpetrated by this undisciplined band, still their support was a burden on the religious houses and the people of the districts through which they passed.

Hardly had this rising been suppressed than Somerset was again involved in civil commotions. Early in the autumn of 1497 Perkin Warbeck assembled his rabble forces—" howbeit, they were poor and naked "[1]—round Taunton, and on the 21st September the advanced guard of the king's army arrived at Glastonbury, and was sheltered in the monastery and its dependencies. The same night the adventurer fled to sanctuary, leaving his 8,000 followers to their own devices; and on the 29th of this same month Henry himself reached Bath and moved forward at once to join his other forces at Wells and Glastonbury. With him came Bishop Oliver King, who, although he had held the See of Bath and Wells for three years, had never yet visited his cathedral city, and who now hurried on before his royal master to be enthroned as bishop a few hours before he in that capacity took part in the reception of the king. Henry had with him some 30,000 men, when on St. Jerome's day he entered Wells, and took up his lodgings with Dr. Cunthorpe in the Deanery.[2] The following day, Sunday, October 1, was spent at Wells, where the king attended in the Cathedral at a solemn *Te Deum* in thanksgiving for his bloodless victory. Early on the

[1] B. Mus. Cott. MS. Vit. A. xvi, f. 166b.
[2] *Historical MSS. Report*, i, p. 107.

Monday he passed on to Glastonbury, and was lodged by Abbot Bere within the precincts of the monastery.

The abbey was then at the height of its glory, for Bere was in every way fitted for the position to which the choice of Fox had elevated him. A witness in the trial spoken of above describes Abbot Bere as "a grave, wise and discreet man, just and upright in all his ways, and for so accounted of almost all sorts of people." Another deposes that he "was good, honest, virtuous, wise and discreet, as well as a grave man, and for those virtues esteemed in as great reputation as few of his coat and calling in England at that time were better accounted of." [1] On the interior discipline and the exterior administration of his house alike he bestowed a watchful care, and under his prudent administration the monastic buildings and church received many useful and costly additions. At great expense he built the suite of rooms afterwards known as "the King's lodgings," and added more than one chapel to the time-honoured sanctuary of Glastonbury. At the west end of the town he built the Church of St. Benen, now commonly known as St. Benedict's, which bears in every portion of the structure his rebus. His care for the poor was manifested by the almshouses he established, and the thought he bestowed on the prudent ordering of the lowly spital of St. Margaret's, Taunton. Beyond this, Bere was a learned man, as well as a careful administrator, and even Erasmus submitted to his judgment. In a letter written a few years after this abbot's death this great scholar records how he had long known the reputation of the Abbot of Glastonbury. His bosom friend, Richard Pace, the well-known ambassador of Wolsey in many difficult

---

[1] *Downside Review, ut sup.*, p. 160.

negotiations, had told him how to Bere's liberality he owed his education, and his success in life to the abbot's judicious guidance. For this reason, Erasmus, who had made a translation of the sacred Scriptures from the Greek, which he thought showed a "more polished style" than St. Jerome's version, submitted his work to the judgment of the abbot. Bere opposed the publication, and Erasmus bowed to the abbot's opinion, which in after years he acknowledged as correct.[1] Henry the Seventh, who ever delighted in the company of learned men, must have been pleased with the entertainment he received at Glastonbury, where the whole cost was borne by the abbot.[2] It is possible, by reason of the knowledge the king then derived of the great abilities of Bere, that six years afterwards, in 1503, he made choice of him to carry the congratulations of England to Cardinal John Angelo de Medicis, when he ascended the pontifical throne as Pius IV.

The troubles of Somerset did not end with the retirement of the royal troops. Though the country did not rise in support of the Cornish movement, it appears to have somewhat sympathised with it, and at Wells Lord Audley joined the insurgents as their leader. For this sympathy Henry made them pay; and the rebels' line of march can be traced by the record of the heavy fines levied upon those who had been supposed to have "aided and comforted" them. Sir Amyas Paulet—the first Paulet of Hinton St. George—was one of the commissioners sent to exact this pecuniary punishment, and

[1] Ep. lib. xviii, 46; Warner, *Glastonbury*, p. 213.
[2] The Wardrobe accounts show that while the king had to pay somewhat heavily for his stay at Wells, his entertainment at Glastonbury cost nothing.

from his record it would appear that nearly all in Somerset were fined. The abbots of Ford and Cleeve, of Muchelney and Athelney, with others, had extended their charity to the starving insurgents, and Sir Amyas made them pay somewhat smartly for their pity. Somehow Glastonbury appears to have escaped the general penalty; probably the abbot's entertainment of the king saved the abbey, although some of the townsfolk did not escape the fine.[1] This severe treatment must have had more than a passing effect. The generation living at the time of the suppression of the abbey could well remember the event. They knew well what was the meaning of the heavy hand of a king, and had felt at their own hearths what were the ravages of an army. This may go far to explain how it happened that in Somersetshire there was no Pilgrimage of Grace.

Meantime Richard Whiting had witnessed these troubles, which came so near home, from the seclusion of the monastic enclosure in which he had been preparing for the reception of sacred orders. The Bishop of Bath and Wells, Oliver King, had not remained in his diocese after the public reception of Henry. He was much engaged in the secular affairs of the kingdom, and his episcopal functions were relegated to the care of a suffragan, Thomas Cornish, titular Bishop of Tinos, also at this time Vicar of St. Cuthbert's, Wells, and Chancellor of the Diocese. From the hands of this prelate Dom Richard Whiting received the minor order of acolyte in the month of September, 1498. In the two succeeding years he was made sub-deacon and deacon, and on the 6th March, 1501, he was elevated to the sacred order of

[1] R. O. Chapter House, Misc. Box, 152, No. 24. See also *Somerset Archæological Society*, 1879, p. 70.

the priesthood.[1] The ordination was held in Wells by Bishop Cornish in the chapel of the Blessed Virgin, by the cathedral cloisters—a chapel long since destroyed, and the foundations of which have in recent years been discovered.

For the next five and twenty years we know very little about Richard Whiting.   It is more than probable that his life was passed entirely in the seclusion of the cloister and in the exercise of the duties imposed upon him by obedience.   In 1505, the register of the University of Cambridge shows that he returned there, and took his final degree as Doctor in Theology.   In his monastery he held the office of "Camerarius," or Chamberlain, which would give him the care of the dormitory, lavatory, and wardrobe of the community, and place him over the numerous officials and servants necessary to this office in so important and vast an establishment as Glastonbury then was.

CHAPTER III

RICHARD WHITING ELECTED ABBOT

IN the month of February, 1525, Abbot Bere died, after worthily presiding over the monastery for more than thirty years. A few days after his death, on the 11th of February, the monks in sacred orders, forty-seven in number, met in the chapter house to elect a successor. They were presided over by their Prior, Dom Henry Coliner, and on his proposition it was agreed that five

[1] Reg. O. King, Bath et Wellen ED.

C

days were to be left for consideration and discussion, and the final vote taken on the 16th. On that day, after a solemn mass *de Spiritu Sancto,* the " great bell " of the monastery called the monks into chapter. There the proceedings were begun by the singing of the *Veni Creator* with its versicle and prayer, and then Dom Robert Clerk, the sacrist, read aloud the form of citation to all having a right to vote, followed by a roll call of the names of the monks. The book of the Holy Gospels was then carried round, and each in succession laid his hand on the sacred page, kissed it, and swore to make choice of him whom in conscience he thought most worthy. After this, one Mr. William Benet, acting as the canonical adviser of the community, read aloud the constitution of the general council *Quia propter,* and carefully explained the various methods of election to the brethren. Then the religious with one mind determined to proceed by the method called " compromise " (*per formam compromissi*), which placed the choice in the hands of some individual of note, and unanimously named Cardinal Wolsey to make choice of their abbot.

The following day the Prior wrote to the Cardinal of York, begging him to accept the charge. Having obtained the royal permission, and after having allowed a fortnight to go by for inquiry and consideration, he, on March 3rd,[1] in his chapel at York Place, declared Richard Whiting the object of his choice. The Cardinal's commission to acquaint the brethren of his election was handed to a deputation from the abbey consisting of Dom John of Glastonbury, the cellarer, and Dom John Benet, the sub-prior, and the document spoke in the highest terms of Whiting. He was described, for ex-

[1] Hearne, *Adam de Domerham,* App. xcvii.

ample, as "an upright and religious monk, a provident
and discreet man, and a priest commendable for his life,
virtues and learning." He had shown himself, it declared,
"watchful and circumspect" in both spirituals and temporals, and had proved that he possessed [ability and
determination to uphold the rights of his monastery.[1]
This instrument, drawn up by a notary and signed by
the Cardinal and three witnesses, one of whom was the
blessed Thomas More, was handed to the two Glastonbury monks, who returned at once to their abbey.

They arrived there on the 8th of March, and met the
brethren in the chapter house, where they declared the
result of the Cardinal's deliberations. Then, at once,
Dom John of Taunton, the precentor, intoned the *Te
Deum*, and they wended their way, chanting the hymn
from the chapter to the church, leading the newly elect.
Meantime the news had spread throughout the town.
The people thronged into the church to hear the proclamation, and as the procession of monks with Richard
Whiting came from the cloisters we can well picture the
scene. The nave of the mighty church was occupied by
"a vast multitude" eager to do honour to him who was
henceforth to be their temporal and spiritual lord and
father. The glorious sanctuary of Avalon, enriched
during ten centuries by the generous gifts of pious benefactors, had received new and costly adornments at the
hands of the abbot so lately gone to his reward. The
vaulting of the nave, which then rang with the voices of
the monks as they sang the hymn of praise, was one of
his latest works. The new-made openings in the wall
marked the places where stood King Edgar's Chapel,
and those of Our Lady of Loretto, and the Sepulchre,

[1] Hearne, *Adam de Domerham*, App. xcvii.

more fitting monuments than was the plain marble slab that marked his grave, of his love and veneration for the ancient sanctuary of Glaston. And as the monks grouped themselves within the choir, the eye, looking through the screen which ran athwart the great chancel arch—the *porta cœli*—would have seen the glitter of the antependium of solid silver gilt studded with jewels, with which the same generous hand had adorned the high altar.

Into this noble sanctuary the people of Glaston crowded on that March morning in the year 1525 to hear what selection the great Cardinal had made. And as the voices of the monks died away with the last "Amen" to the prayer of thanksgiving to God for mercies to their House, a notary public, at the request of the Prior and his brethren, turned to the people, and from off the steps of the great altar proclaimed in English the due election of Brother Richard Whiting. Then, as the people streamed forth from the church bearing the news abroad, the monks returned to chapter for the completion of the required formalities. And first, the free consent of the elect himself had to be obtained, and he as yet remained unwilling to take up the burden of so high an office. He had betaken himself to the guest-house, called the "hostrye," and thither Dom William Walter and Dom John Winchcombe repaired, as deputed by the rest, to win him to consent. At first he determined to refuse, and then demanded time for thought and prayer; but a few hours after, "being," as he declared, "unwilling any longer to offer resistance to what appeared the will of God," he yielded to their solicitations and accepted the dignity and burden.

Then on Richard Whiting's acceptance being notified

RUINS OF THE CHOIR OF GLASTONBURY ABBEY CHURCH, SHOWING THE WEST
DOORWAY OF THE NAVE IN THE DISTANCE

[To face p. 20

to the Cardinal, he sent two commissioners to conduct the required canonical investigations into the fitness of the elect for the office. On 25th March these officials arrived at the monastery, and early on the morning following, the Prior and monks came in procession to the conventual church; in the presence of the Prior and convent they made a general summons to all and any to communicate to them any facts or circumstances which should debar Whiting from being confirmed as abbot; after this the like obligation was laid in chapter on the monks. Once more, at noon, the decree was published to a "great multitude" in the church, and afterwards fixed against the great doors.

Three days later, as no one had appeared to object to the election, the procurator of the abbot, Dom John of Glastonbury, produced his witnesses as to age and character. Amongst them was Sir Amyas Paulet, of Hinton St. George, who declared that he had known the elect for eight-and-twenty years, which was just the time when Henry VII had visited Glastonbury, and Sir Amyas had been occupied in extracting from the people of Somerset the fines levied for their real or supposed sympathy with Perkin Warbeck and his Cornish rebels. The abbot's witnesses testified that he had always borne the highest character, not only in Somerset, but elsewhere beyond the limits of the diocese, and that none had ever heard anything but good of him. One who so testified was Dom Richard Beneall, who had been a monk at Glastonbury for nineteen years, and who declared that during all those years Richard Whiting had been reputed a man of exemplary piety.

When this lengthy and strict scrutiny was finished the Cardinal's commissioners declared the confirmation of the elect. Then, after the usual oath of obedience to the Bishop of the Diocese had been taken by the elect, he received the solemn blessing in his own great abbey church from Dr. William Gilbert, Abbot of Bruton and Bishop of Mayo in Ireland, at that time acting as suffragan to the Bishop of Bath and Wells.[1]

In the pages of ecclesiastical history Wolsey's name meets with scant favour. Writers of all parties, whether they look on him with friendly or unfriendly eye, have little to say of his devotion to the best interests of the Church. Whatever his defects, due credit has not been given him for the real and enlightened care which he bestowed on the true welfare of the religious orders. For the Benedictines and Augustinians he designed, and in part carried out, measures of renovation, the fruits of which were already visible when Henry suppressed the monastic houses. It is evident that he was not content with general measures, but he fully acquainted himself with details and with persons. The election of Abbot Whiting is a case in point, and it is by no means improbable that the keen eye of the ecclesiastical statesman had marked him out at the general chapter of the Benedictines at Westminster, over which the great Cardinal had himself presided.

Thus was inaugurated the rule of the last abbot of Glastonbury, amid the applause and goodwill of all who knew him. Hitherto his life had been passed, as the life of a monk should be, in seclusion and unknown to the world at large. He had clearly not been one to seek for power or expect preferment, and his election to the abbacy of Glastonbury, though causing his name and

[1] The account here given is from the official document in the Register of Bishop Clerke.

fame to be spread wider, would after all, in the ordinary course of events, have given him in the main a local repute, and one of its nature destined, after life's day well spent in the peaceful government of his monastery, to pass into oblivion. Of course his position as head of one of the greatest of the parliamentary abbeys (if the term may be used) obtained for him a place, and that no undistinguished one, in the roll of peers and in the House of Lords; and thus he would be brought naturally every year to the Court and the great deliberative assembly of the realm. But this was not a sphere which attracted a man of Whiting's temper and simple-minded religious spirit. His place was more fittingly found within his house, and in the neighbourhood which fell within the direct range of his special and highest duties. Here, then, he might have been best known and loved; and no further. But another lot was marked out for him in the designs of God. His life was to end in the winning of a favour greater than any which could be bestowed by an earthly power, for the crown of martyrdom was to be the reward of his devotion to daily duty. His fidelity to his state and trust issued in a final act of allegiance to Holy Church and to her earthly head which causes his name to be known and revered through all lands.

CHAPTER IV

TROUBLES IN CHURCH AND STATE

THE rule of Abbot Whiting over the vast establishment of Glastonbury had to be exercised in difficult times. Within a few months of his election Sir Thomas Boleyn was created Viscount Rochford, and this marked the first step in the king's illicit affection for the new peer's daughter, Anne, and the beginning of troubles in Church and State. For years of wavering counsels on the great matter of Henry's desired divorce from Katherine led in 1529 to the humiliation and fall of the hitherto all-powerful Cardinal of York.

Circumstances combined at this time to gather together in the social atmosphere elements fraught with grave danger to the Church in England. The long and deadly feud between the two " Roses " had swept away the pride and flower of the old families of England. The stability which the traditions and prudent counsels of an ancient nobility give the ship of State, was gone when it was most needed to enable it to weather the storm of revolutionary ideas. Most of the new peers created in the fifteenth and sixteenth centuries to take the place of the old nobles had little sympathy, either by birth or inclination, with the traditions of the past. Many were mere place-hunters, political adventurers, ready if not eager to profit by any disturbance of the social order. Self-interest prompted them to range themselves in the restless ranks of the party of innovation. Those who have nothing to lose are proverbially on the side of disorder and change. The "official," too, the special creation of the Tudor monarchs, was by nature unsettled and discontented, ever on the look-out for some lucky chance of supplementing an inadequate pay. Success in life depended, for men of this kind, on their attracting to themselves the notice of their royal master, which prompted them to compete one with the other in fulfilling his wishes and satisfying his whims.[1]

At the head of all was Henry VIII, a king of unbridled desires, and one whose only code of right and wrong was founded, at least in the second half of his reign, on considerations of power to accomplish what he wished. What he could do was the measure of what he might lawfully attempt. Sir Thomas More, after he had himself retired from office, in his warning to the rising Crumwell, rightly gauged the king's character. "Mark, Crumwell," he said, "you are now entered the service of a most noble, wise, and liberal prince; if you will follow my poor advice, you shall in your counsel given to His Grace, ever tell him what he *ought* to do, but not what he is *able* to do. For if a lion but knew his own strength, hard were it for any man to rule him."

Nor, unfortunately, were the clergy of the time generally fitted to cope with the forces of revolution, or hold back the rising tide of novelties. In the days when might was right, and the force of arms the ruling power of the world, the occupation of peace, to which the clergy were bound, excited opposition from the party who saw their opportunity in a disturbance of the existing order. The bishops were, with some honourable exceptions, chosen by royal favour rather than for a spiritual qualification. However personally good they

[1] See Friedmann, *Anne Boleyn*, i, p. 27, *seqq.*

may have been, they were not ideal pastors of their flocks. Place-seeking, too, often kept many of the lords spiritual at court, that they might gain or maintain influence sufficient to support their claims to further preferment.

The occupation of bishops over-much in the affairs of the nation, besides its evident effect on the state of clerical discipline, had another result. It created in the minds of the new nobility a jealous opposition to ecclesiastics, and a readiness to humble the power of the Church by passing measures in restraint of its ancient liberties. The lay lords and hungry officials not unnaturally looked upon this employment of clerics in the intrigues of party politics, and in the wiles and crafty business of foreign and domestic diplomacy, as trenching upon their domain, and as thus keeping them out of coveted preferment. Consequently, when occasion offered, no great difficulty was experienced in inducing them to turn against the clergy and thus enable Henry to carry out his policy of coercive legislation in their regard.

Five years after Abbot Whiting's election to rule over Glastonbury the fall of Cardinal Wolsey opened the way for the advancement of Thomas Crumwell, who may be regarded as the chief political contriver of the change of religion in England. On the fall of the old order he built up his own fortune. For ten years England groaned beneath his rule—in truth it was a reign of terror unparalleled in the history of the country. To power he mounted, and in power he was maintained by showing himself subservient to every whim of a monarch, the strength of whose passions was only equalled by the remorselessness and tenacity with which he pursued his aims. Crumwell fully understood, before entering on his new service, what its conditions were, and neither will nor ability was lacking to their fulfilment. Under his management, at once skilful and unscrupulous, Henry mastered the Parliament and paralysed the action of Convocation, moulding them according to his royal will and pleasure.

Having determined that the great matter of his divorce from Katherine should be settled in his own favour, he conceived the expedient of throwing off the ecclesiastical authority of the pope over the nation and constituting himself supreme head of the Church of England. Though the clergy struggled for a time against the royal determination, in the end they gave way; and on November 3rd, 1534, the "Act of Supremacy" was hurried through Parliament, and a second statute made it treason to deny this new royal prerogative.

The sequel is well known. The clergy caught in the cunningly-contrived snare of *premunire*, and betrayed by Cranmer, who, as Archbishop of Canterbury, had inherited Warham's office, but not his spirit, were at the king's mercy. With his hands upon their throats Henry demanded what, in the quarrel with Rome, was, at the time, a retaliation upon the pope for his refusal to accede to the royal wishes, the acknowledgment of the king as supreme head of the Church of England. Few among English churchmen were found bold enough to resist this direct demand, or who even, perhaps, recognised how they were rejecting papal supremacy in matters spiritual. As a rule, the required oath of royal supremacy was apparently taken wherever it was tendered, and the abbots and monks of Colchester, of Glastonbury, and probably also of Reading, were no exception, and on September 19th, 1534, Abbot Whiting and his community, fifty-one in number, attached their names to the required declaration.[1]

It is easy, after this lapse of time, and in the light of subsequent events, to pass censure on such compliance; to wonder how throughout England the blessed John Fisher and Thomas More, and the Observants, almost alone, should have been found from the beginning neither to hesitate nor to waver. It is easy to make light of the shrinking of flesh and blood, easy to extol the palm of martyrdom. But it is not difficult, too, to see how reasons suggested themselves at least for temporising. To most men at that date the possibility of a final separation from Rome must have seemed incredible. They remembered Henry in his earlier years, when he was never so immersed in business or in pleasure that he did not hear three or even five masses a day; they did not know him as Wolsey or Crumwell, or as More or Fisher knew him; the project seemed a momentary aberration, under the influence of evil passion or evil counsellors, and it was on the king's part "but usurpation desiderated by flattery and adulation;" these counsellors removed, all would be well again. Henry had at bottom a zeal for the Faith and would return by-and-by to a better mind, a truer self, and would then come to terms with the pope. The idea of the headship was not absolutely new: it had in a measure been conceded some years before, without, so far as appears, exciting remonstrance from Rome. Beyond this, to many, the oath of royal

[1] Deputy Keeper's *Report*, vii, p. 287. Mr. Devon, who drew up the report, says: "The signatures, in my opinion, are not all autographs, but frequently in the same handwriting; and my impression is, that the writer of the deed often added many names."

supremacy over the Church of England was never understood as derogatory to the See of Rome. While even those who had taken this oath were in many instances surprised that it should be construed into any such hostility.[1]

However strained this temper of mind may appear to us at this time, it undoubtedly existed. One example may be here cited. Among the State Papers in the Record Office for the year 1539 is a long harangue on the execution of the three Benedictine abbots, in which the writer refers to such a view:

" I cannot think the contrary," he writes, " but the old bishop of London [Stokesley], when he was on live, used the pretty medicine that his fellow, friar Forest, was wont to use, and to work with an inward man and an outward man; that is to say, to speak one thing with their mouth and then another thing with their heart. Surely a very pretty medicine for popish hearts. But it worked badly for some of their parts. Gentle Hugh Cook [the abbot of Reading] by his own confession used not the self-same medicine that friar Forest used, but another much like unto it, which was this: what time as the spiritualty were sworn to take the king's grace for the supreme head, immediately next under God of this Church of England, Hugh Cook receiving the same oath added prettily in his own conscience these words following: ' of the temporal church,' saith he, ' but not of the spiritual church.' "[2]

---

[1] Calendar, viii, Nos. 277, 387, etc., are instances of the temper of mind described above. No. 387 especially is very significant as showing the gloss men put on the supremacy oath, distinguishing tacitly between Church of England and Catholic Church, and *in temporalibus*, and *in spiritualibus*.

[2] R. O. State Papers, Dom., 1539, No. 207, p. 23.

Nor from another point of view is this want of appreciation as to the true foundation of the papal primacy a
subject for unmixed astonishment. During the previous
half-century the popes had reigned in a court of un-
exampled splendour, but a splendour essentially mun-
dane. It was a dazzling sight, but all this outward
show made it difficult to recognise the divinely ordered
spiritual prerogatives which are the enduring heritage of
the successors of St. Peter.

The words of Cardinal Manning on this point may be
here quoted:—" It must not be forgotten that at this
time the minds of men had been so distracted by the
great western schism, by the frequent subtraction of
obedience, by the doubtful election of popes, and the
simultaneous existence of two or even three claimants
to the Holy See, that the supreme pontifical authority
had become a matter of academical discussion *hinc inde*.
Nothing but such preludes could have instigated even
Gerson to write on the thesis *de auferabilitate Papæ*.
This throws much light on the singular fact attested by
Sir Thomas More in speaking to the jury and the judge
by whom he was condemned, when the verdict of death
was brought in against him: ' I have, by the grace of
God, been always a Catholic, never out of communion
with the Roman Pontiff; but I have heard it said at
times that the authority of the Roman Pontiff was certainly lawful and to be respected, but still an authority
derived from human law, and not standing upo n a
divine prescription. Then, when I observed that public
affairs were so ordered that the sources of the power of
the Roman Pontiff would necessarily be examined, I
gave myself up to a most diligent examination of that
question for the space of seven years, and found that the

authority of the Roman Pontiff, which you rashly—I will not use stronger language—have set aside, is not only lawful, to be respected, and necessary, but also grounded on the divine law and prescription. That is my opinion; that is the belief in which by the grace of God, I shall die.' "[1]

The lofty terms expressive of papal prerogatives might pass unquestioned in the schools and in common speech in the world, but from this there is a wide step to the apprehension, then none too common, of the living truths they express, and a yet further step to that intense personal realisation which makes those truths dearer to a man than life.

To some, in Whiting's day, that realisation came sooner, to some later. Some men, a few, seized at once the point at issue and its full import, and were ready with their answer without seeking or faltering. Others answered to the call at the third, or even the eleventh hour; the cause was the same, and so were the fate and the reward, though to the late comer the respite may perhaps have been only a prolongation of the agony.

It is of course impossible here to attempt even a sketch of the train of events which led to the destruction of Glastonbury and Abbot Whiting's martyrdom. The suppression of the monasteries has been described as simply "an enormous scheme for filling the royal purse."[2] As his guilty passion for Anne Boleyn is the key to half

---

[1] *Dublin Review*, January, 1888, p. 245.

[2] Dixon, *History of the Church of England*, i, p. 456. The last Abbot of Colchester, John Beche *alias* Marshal, is reported to Crumwell as saying: "The king and his council are drawn into such an inordinate covetousness that if all the water in the Thames were flowing gold and silver, it were not able to slake their covetousness." (R. O. State Papers, 1539, No. 207.)

of the extraordinary acts of the succeeding years of Henry's reign, so is the need of money to gratify his other appetites the key to the rest. From the seizure of the first of the lesser religious houses to the fall of Glastonbury, the greatest and most magnificent of them all, gain was the one thought of the king's heart. To this end every engine was devised, conscience was trodden under foot, and blood was spilled.

With the evident design of obtaining a pretext for falling on the religious houses, the oath of supremacy in an amplified form was tendered to their inmates.[1] "There was presented to them," writes a recent historian, "a far more severe and explicit form of oath than that which More and Fisher had refused, than that which the Houses of Parliament and the secular clergy had consented to take. They were required to swear, not only that the chaste and holy marriage between Henry and Anne was just and legitimate, and the succession good in their offspring," but "also that they would ever hold the king to be head of the Church of England, that the Bishop of Rome, who in his bulls usurped the name of Pope and arrogated to himself the primacy of the most High Pontiff, had no more authority and jurisdiction than other bishops of England or elsewhere in their dioceses, and that they would for ever renounce the laws, decrees and canons of the Bishop of Rome, if any of them should be found contrary to the law of God and Holy Scripture."[2] This scheme failed, "for the oath was taken in almost every chapter-house where it was tendered."

[1] Dixon, *History of the Church of England*, i, p. 213.
[2] *Ibid.*, p. 211.

CHAPTER V

RICHARD WHITING AS ABBOT OF GLASTONBURY

THE first years of Abbot Whiting's rule passed smoothly so far as the acts of his administration and his life at Glastonbury were concerned. He had of course to meet the troubles and trials incidental to a position such as was his. Moreover, for one who by his high office was called on to take a part, in some measure at least, in the great world of politics and public life, it could not be but that his soul must have been disturbed by anticipations of difficulties, even of dangers, in the not very distant future. Still, his own home was so far removed from the turmoils of the court and the ominous rumblings of the coming storm that he was able to rule it in peace. Discipline well maintained, a prudent and successful administration of temporals, and kindly relations with his neighbours, high and low, were certain evidences that the government of Abbot Richard Whiting was happy and prosperous. Under such circumstances the position which he occupied as a peer of Parliament and as master of great estates was one which, as the world might say, even from its point of view, was eminently enviable.

It is somewhat difficult in these days to form a just and adequate idea of the place held in the country by one who filled the abbatial chair of Glastonbury. For wealth and consideration, though not indeed for precedence, it may not unjustly be described as the most desirable ecclesiastical preferment in England. The revenues of the abbey exceeded those of the archbishopric

D

of Canterbury itself, whilst, although the abbot had to maintain a large community and a great household, still he was exempt from the vast burdens necessarily entailed on so lofty a position as that of Primate of England, who was *Legatus natus* of the Holy See and often a Cardinal. The annual value of the endowments of Westminster was, it is true, slightly greater, but the ecclesiastical position of an abbot of that royal monastery was singularly diminished by the presence in his near neighbourhood of two such great churchmen as the Archbishop of Canterbury and the Bishop of London, whilst in its worldly aspect Westminster was overshadowed by the splendour of the regal court at its doors. Glastonbury in the sixteenth century had no rival in its own district; the day was past when the aspiring Church of Wells could raise pretensions on that score. In the west country there was neither prince nor prelate, certainly since the fall of the Duke of Buckingham, to compare in position, all considered, with the Abbot of Glastonbury.

But withal there existed in the court of the abbot, for his household was regulated like that of a court, a simplicity befitting the monastic profession. His own house was large, its rooms were stately, but it did not pretend to the dimensions of a palace. He had a body of gentry to wait upon him and grace the hospitality he was ready to show to visitors the most distinguished and to the poorer classes who thronged the monastic guest-hall. To the great gate of the abbey, every Wednesday and Friday, the poor flocked for relief in their necessities, and as many as five hundred persons are said to have been entertained at times at the abbot's table. Still, a combined simplicity and stateliness characterised the whole rule of Abbot Whiting, and it is no wonder that, as we are told, during his abbacy some three or four hundred youths of gentle birth received their first training in the abbot's quarters.

It may be asked by some how in such a position as this, surrounded by all the world most ambitions, Abbot Whiting could still be a monk. The position was not of his making; he found it. But that he should ever remain a monk, that, as abbot, he should be a true guardian of the souls committed to him, the true father and pattern of his spiritual children, that was by God's grace still in his power. That he was all this, his very enemies have testified, and the explanation is simple. Raised to rule and command at an age when, as he knew, the grave could not be far distant, he was already a monk trained, disciplined, perfected in outward habit and in the possession of his soul by his long course of obedience. Tradition, which is often so true in matters of small moment, more than a century and a half after his death, still pointed out among the ruins of his house, in the abbot's simple chamber, Abbot Whiting's bed. It was " without tester or post, was boarded at bottom, and had a board nailed shelving at the head." This bedstead, according to the tradition of the place, was the same that Abbot Whiting lay on, and " I was desired," writes the visitor who describes it, " to observe it as a curiosity." The existence of the tradition is proof at least of an abiding belief, on the spot, in the simplicity of life of the last lord of that glorious pile, the vast ruins of which were evidence of the greatness of the monastery. It was possible even for an Abbot of Glastonbury to preserve the true spirit of poverty, and this was the secret of that excellent discipline which Dr. Layton to his bitter disappointment found to exist at Glastonbury. The abbot practised first what, as his duty imposed, he required from those entrusted to his care, that is, from his spiritual children, the monks of his house.

It was during these comparatively peaceful and happy times that Leland, the antiquary, on his journey through England in search of antiquities, and especially manuscripts, visited the abbey. He was introduced to the library by Abbot Whiting in person, " a man truly upright and of spotless life and my sincere friend " as he calls him.[1] He was filled with amazement at the treasures contained in the Glastonbury library. " No sooner did I pass the threshold," he writes, " than I was struck with awe and astonishment at the mere sight of so many remains of antiquity." He considered that the library had scarce any equal in all England, and spent some days in examining the shelves and the many wonderful manuscripts he found there.

With the conclusion of Henry's divorce case came the end of these peaceful years of Abbot Whiting's rule. Now began the anxious days which were to end for him in the death of the traitor, so far at least as the king's power could extend in death.

Within a year from the general oath-taking throughout England, and its failure to bring about the hoped-

---

[1] Hearne, *History of Glastonbury*, p. 67 ; *cf.* Walcott's *English Minsters*, ii, 129. Leland spoke of Abbot Whiting as " homo sane candidissimus et amicus meus singularis," and " though," says Warner (*History of Glastonbury*, p. 219) " the too cautious antiquary in after times passed his pen through this language of praise and kindness, lest it should be offensive to his contemporaries, yet happily for the abbot's fame the tribute is still legible and will remain for ages a sufficient evidence of the sacrifice of a guileless victim to the tyranny of a second Ahab."

for result, Crumwell, ever fertile in expedients, had organised a general visitation of religious houses. The
instruments he made choice of to conduct this scrutiny,
and the methods they employed, leave no doubt that
the real object was the destruction of the monasteries
under the cloak of reformation. The injunctions are
minute and exacting; in detail many were excellent;
as a whole, even in the hands of persons sincerely desirous of maintaining discipline and observance, they
were unworkable. In the hands of Crumwell's agents
they were, as they were designed to be, intolerable. It
was rightly calculated that under the pretence of restoring discipline they strike at the authority of religious
superiors by the encouragement given to a system of
tale-bearing. By other provisions the monasteries were,
with show of zeal for religion, turned into prisons and
reduced, if it were possible, to such abodes of misery
and unhappiness as the uninformed Protestant imagination pictures them to be.[1] The moral of this treatment
is summed up by John ap-Rice and Thomas Legh, two
of the royal visitors, in a letter to Crumwell:

" By this ye may see [they write] that they [the religious] shall not need to be put forth, but that they will
make instant suit themselves, so that their doing shall
be imputed to themselves and no other. Although I
reckon it well done that all were out, yet I think it were
best that at their own suits they might be dismissed to
avoid calumniation and envy,[2] *and so compelling them to
observe these injunctions ye shall have them all to do
shortly*, and the people shall know it the better that it

[1] *Henry VIII and the English Monasteries*, i, chapter vii, " The
Visitation of the Monasteries in 1535-6." Dixon, vol. i, p. 357.

[2] He means *invidia*, *i.e.*, public odium.

cometh upon their suit, if they be not discharged straight while we be here, for then the people would say that we went for nothing else, even though the truth were contrary."[1]

Armed with a commission to visit and enforce the injunctions, Dr. Richard Layton, the most foul-mouthed and foul-minded ribald of them all, as his own letters testify, came to Glastonbury on Saturday, August 21st, 1535. From St. Augustine's, Bristol, whither he departed on the following Monday, he wrote to Crumwell a letter showing that even he, chief among a crew who " could ask unmoved such questions as no other human being could have imagined or known how to put, who could extract guilt from a stammer, a tremble or a blush, or even from indignant silence as surely as from open confession "[2]—even Layton retired baffled from Glastonbury under the venerable Abbot Whiting's rule, though he covered his defeat with impudence unabashed. "At Bruton and Glastonbury," he explains, " there is nothing notable; the brethren be so straight kept that they cannot offend: but fain they would if they might, as they confess, and so the fault is not with them."[3]

At this period it would seem that Richard Layton

<hr />

[1] Gairdner, *Calendar of Papers Foreign and Domestic*, ix, No. 708. See also *Henry VIII and the English Monasteries*, i, p. 257.

[2] Dixon, i, p. 357.

[3] Wright, *The Suppression of the Monasteries*, p. 59. Godwin, the Protestant Bishop of Hereford, says that the monks, " following the example of the ancient fathers, lived apart from the world religiously and in peace, eschewing worldly employments, and wholly given to study and contemplation ;" and the editor of Sander, writing when the memory of the life led at Glastonbury was still fresh in men's minds, says that the religious were noted for their maintenance of common life, choral observance, and enclosure.

also spoke to the king in praise of Abbot Whiting. For this error of judgment, when some time later Crumwell had assured himself of the abbot's temper, he was forced to sue for pardon from both king and minister. "I must therefore," he writes, "now in this my necessity most humbly beseech your lordship to pardon me for that my folly then committed, as ye have done many times before, and of your goodness to instigate the king's highness majesty, in the premises."[1]

Hardly had the royal inquisitor departed than it was found at Glastonbury, as elsewhere, that the injunctions were not merely impracticable, but subversive of the first principles of religious discipline. Abbot Whiting, like so many religious superiors at this time, petitioned for some mitigation. Nicholas FitzJames,[2] a neighbour, dispatched an earnest letter to Crumwell in support of the abbot's petition.

"I have spoken," he writes, "with my Lord Abbot of Glastonbury concerning such injunctions as were given him and his convent by your deputy at the last visitation there. . . . To inform your mastership of the truth there be certain officers—brothers of the house—who have always been attendant on the abbot, as his chaplain, steward, cellarer, and one or two officers more, [who] if they should be bound to the first two articles, it should much disappoint the order of the house, which hath long been full honourable. Wherefore, if it may please your said good mastership to license the abbot to dispense with the first two articles, in my mind you

[1] R. O. *Crumwell Correspondence*, vol. xx, No. 14.
[2] Probably a relative of Chief Justice FitzJames, and grandfather of the first monk afterwards professed in the English Benedictine monastery of St. Gregory's, Douay (now at Downside).

will do a very good deed, and I dare be surety he will dispense with none but with such as shall be necessary. . . . Other articles there are which they think very straight, howbeit they will sue to your good mastership for that at more leisure; and in the meantime I doubt not they will keep as good religion as any house of that Order within this realm." [1]

A month after this letter of Nicholas FitzJames, Abbot Whiting himself ventured to present a grievance of another kind, affecting others than his community. The recent suspension by royal authority of the jurisdiction exercised by the abbey over the town of Glastonbury and its dependencies, had caused the gravest inconveniences. There are many " poor people," he writes, "who are waiting to have their causes tried," and he adds that he cannot believe that the king's pleasure has been rightly stated in Doctor Layton's orders.[2] What the result of this application may have been does not appear, but it was clearly the royal purpose to let inconveniences be felt, not to remove them.

The proceedings taken in 1536 in regard to the suppression of the lesser monasteries must have filled the minds of men of Whiting's stamp with deep anxiety, as revealing more and more clearly the settled purpose of the king. " All the wealth of the world would not be enough to satisfy and content his ambition," writes Marillac, the French ambassador, to his master, Francis I. To enrich himself he would not hesitate to ruin all his subjects.[3] The State papers of the period bear ample

---

[1] Wright, *Suppression of the Monasteries*, p. 64.
[2] R. O. *Crumwell Corr.*, xiii. f. 58.
[3] *Inventaire analytique. Correspondance politique de MM. Castillion et Marillac*, 1537-1542. Ed. J. Kaulek. No. 242.

witness to the justice of this sweeping statement.[1] The monasteries which were yet allowed to stand were drained of their resources by ever-increasing demands on the part of Henry and his creatures. Farm after farm, manor after manor was yielded up in compliance with requests that were in reality demands. Pensions in ever-increasing numbers were charged on monastic lands at the asking of those whom it was impossible to refuse.

Abbot Whiting was allowed no immunity from this species of tyrannical oppression. The abbey, for instance, had of its own free will granted to blessed Sir Thomas More a corrody or annuity. On his disgrace Crumwell urged the king's "pleasure and commandment" that this annuity should be transferred to himself under the convent seal. For a friend Crumwell asks (and for the king's vicegerent to ask was to receive) "the advocation of our parish church of Monketon, albeit that it was the first time that ever such a grant was made." A further request, for the living of Batcombe, Whiting was unable to comply with, since another of the king's creatures had been beforehand and secured the prize. In one instance an office which Crumwell had already asked for and obtained from the abbot, he a few months after demands for his friend " Mr. Maurice Berkeley ; " and because the place was already gone, he requests that the abbot will in lieu thereof give the rents of "his farm at Northwood Park." Abbot Whiting took an accurate view of the situation : "If you request it, I must grant it," he says; and adds, "I trust your servant will be content with the park itself, and ask no more."

The extant letters of Abbot Whiting, for the most

[1] The volumes of Crumwell's correspondence in the Record Office contain abundant evidence.

part answers to such like applications for offices or benefices in his gift, are marked by a courteous consideration and a readiness to comply up to the utmost limits of the possible. It is, moreover, evident that he had an intimate concern in all the details of the complex administration of a monastery of such extent and importance with its thousand interests, no less than a determining personal influence on the religious character of his community; and that public calls were never allowed to come between him and the primary and immediate duties of the abbot. He is most at home in his own country, among his Somersetshire neighbours, and in the "straight" charge of his spiritual children. Confident too in the affection with which he was regarded by the population, he had no scruples, whatever may have been his mind in subscribing to the Supremacy declaration of 1534, in securing for his monks and his townsfolk in his own abbey church the preaching of a doctrine by no means in accord with the royal theories and wishes on the subject. Thus on a Sunday in the middle of February, 1536, a friar called John Brynstan, preaching in the abbatial church at Glastonbury to the people of the neighbourhood, said "he would be one of them that should convert the new fangles and new men, otherwise he would die in the quarrel."[1]

By chance a glimpse is afforded of the popular feeling in the district by a letter addressed to Crumwell by one of his agents, always ready to spy upon their neighbours and report them to their master, in the hopes of gaining thereby the good graces of the all-powerful minister. Thomas Clarke writes that one John Tutton of Mere, next Glaston,—now by the way safely lodged in gaol—

[1] *Calendar*, x, 318.

had used seditious words against the king and had spoken great slander against Crumwell himself. The depositions forwarded with this letter explain how Tutton had called one Poole a heretic for working on St. Mark's day. Poole had replied that so the king had ordered, and upon this Tutton declared that they could not be bound to keep the king's command " if it was nought, as this was," and he added that " Lord Crumwell was a stark heretic." Nor did he stop here, for he continued in this strain; " Marry, many things be done by the king's Council which I reckon he knoweth little of, but that by such means he hath gathered great treasure together I wot well; there is a sort that ruleth the king of whom I trust to see a day when they shall have less authority than they have." [1]

Knowing doubtless what would be the nature of its business, Abbot Whiting, excusing himself on the plea of age and ill-health, did not attend the Parliament of 1539, which, so far as it could do, sealed the fate of the monasteries as yet unsuppressed. He awaited the end on his own ground and in the midst of his own people. He was still as solicitous about the smallest details of his care as if the glorious abbey were to last *in aevum*. Thus an interesting account of Abbot Whiting at Glastonbury is given in an official examination regarding some debt, held a few years after the abbot's martyrdom. John Watts, " late monk and chaplain to the abbot," said that John Lyte, the supposed debtor, had paid the money " in manner and form following. That is to say, he paid £10 of the said £40 to the said abbot in the little parlour upon the right hand within the great hall, the Friday after New Year's Day before the said abbot was attainted.

[1] Gairdner, *Calendar*, xi, No. 567.

The said payment was made in gold " in presence of the witness and only one other: " for it was immediately after the said abbot had dined, so that the abbot's gentle-men and other servants were in the hall at dinner." Also " upon St. Peter's day at midsummer, being a Sunday, in the garden of the said abbot at Glastonbury, whilst high Mass was singing," the debtor " made payment " of the rest. " And at that time the abbot asked of the said Master Lyte whether he would set up the said abbot's arms in his new buildings that he had made. And the said Master Lyte answered the said abbot that he would; and so at that time the said abbot gave unto the said Mr. Lyte eight angels nobles. And at the payment of the £30 there was in the garden at that time the Lord Stourton. I suppose," continues the witness, " that the said Lord Stourton saw not the payment made to the abbot, for the abbot got him into an arbour of bay in the said garden and there received his money. And very glad he was at that time that it was paid in gold for the short telling, as also he would not, by his will, have it seen at that time." [1] Thus too almost the last glimpse afforded of the last Abbot of Glastonbury in his time-honoured home shows him in friendly converse with his near neighbour, Lord Stourton, who was the head of an ancient race which popular tradition had justly linked for centuries with the Benedictine order, and which even in the darkest days of modern English Catholicity proved itself a firm and hereditary friend.

[1] R. O. Exch. Augt. Off. Misc. Bk., xxii, Nos. 13-18. In view of the circumstances of the time it seems likely that the witness was anxious to ward off any possibility of Lord Stourton being mixed up in the affair. This anxiety to save friends from embarrassing examinations is a very common feature in documents of this date.

Before passing on to the closing acts of the venerable abbot's life and to his martyrdom, it is necessary to premise a few words on suppression in its legal aspect. There seems to be abroad an impression that the monasteries were all, in fact, dissolved by order of Parliament, and accordingly that a refusal of surrender to the king, such as is found at Glastonbury, was an act which, however morally justifiable as a refusal to betray a trust, and even heroic when resistance entailed the last penalty, was yet in defiance of the law of the land. And, to take this particular case of Glastonbury, it is often stated, that when insisting on its surrender the king was only requiring that to be given up into his hands which Parliament had already conferred on him. However common the impression, it is false. What the Act (27 Hen. VIII., cap. 28) of February, 1536, did was to give to the king and his heirs such monasteries only as were under the yearly value of £200, or such as should within a "year next after the making of" the Act "be given or granted to his majesty by any abbot," etc. So far, therefore, from handing over to the king the property of all the monasteries, Parliament distinctly recognised, at least in the case of all save the lesser religious houses, the rights of their then owners, and contemplated their passing to the king's hands only by the voluntary cession of the actual possessors. How any surrender was to be brought about was left to the king and Crumwell, and the minions on whose devices there is no need to dwell. Before a recalcitrant superior, who would yield neither to blandishments, bribery nor threats, the king, so far as the Act would help him, was powerless.

For this case, however, provision was made, though but indirectly, in the Act of April, 1539 (31 Hen. VIII.,

cap. 13). This Act, which included a retrospective clause
covering the illegal suppression of the greater monasteries which had already passed into the king's hands,
granted to Henry all monasteries, etc., which shall here-
after happen to be dissolved, suppressed, renounced, re-
linquished, forfeited, given up or come unto the king's
highness. These terms seem wide enough, but there is also
an ominous parenthesis referring to such other religious
houses as " shall happen to come to the king's highness
by attainder or attainders *of treason.*" The clause did
not find its way into the Act unawares. It will be seen
that it was Crumwell's care how and in whose case the
clause should become operative. And with just so much
of countenance as is thus given him by the Act, with the
king to back him, the monasteries of Glastonbury, Reading and Colchester, from which no surrender could be
obtained, " were, against every principle of received law,
held to fall by the attainder of their abbots for high
treason." [1]

The very existence of the clause is, moreover, evidence
that by this time Crumwell knew that among the superiors of the few monasteries yet standing, there were
men with whom, if the king was not to be baulked of his
intent, the last conclusions would have to be tried. To
him the necessity would have been paramount, by every
means in his power, to sweep away what he rightly regarded as the strongholds of the papal power in the

---

[1] Hallam, *Constitutional Hist.*, i, 72. Harpsfield, *Pretended
Divorce*, ed. Pocock (Camden Society), p. 300, says: " Such as
would voluntarily give over were rewarded with large annual pensions, and with other pleasures. Against some other there were
found quarrels, as against Hugh Farindon, Abbot of Reading . . .
against Richard Whiting, Abbot of Glaston, etc."

country, and to get rid of these "spies of the pope."[1]
Such unnatural enemies of their prince and gracious lord
would fittingly be first singled out, that their fate might
serve as a warning to other intending evil-doers. Perhaps, too, Whiting's repute for blamelessness of life, the
discipline which he was known to maintain in his monastery and his great territorial influence may all have
conduced to point him out as an eminently proper subject to proceed against, as tending to show the nation
that where the crime of resistance to the king's will was
concerned there could be no such thing as an extenu-
ating circumstance, no consideration which would avail
to mitigate the penalty.

CHAPTER VI

THE BEGINNING OF THE END

IN the story of what follows we are continually ham-
pered by the singularly defective nature of the various
records relating to the closing years of Crumwell's administration. We are therefore frequently left to supply
links by conjectures, but conjectures in which, from the
known facts and such documentary evidence as remains,
there is sufficient assurance of being in the main correct.

Already, in 1538, rumour had spoken of the coming
dissolution; and the fact that all over the country even
the greatest houses of religion, one after another, were
falling into the king's hands by surrender, voluntary or
enforced, tended to give colour to the current tales.

[1] R. O., *Crumwell Correspondence*, xv, No. 7.

Henry's agents, it is true, had endeavoured to dissemble any royal intention of a general suppression of the monastic body. They not only denied boldly and unblushingly that the king had any such design, but urged upon Crumwell the advisability of putting a stop to the persistent reports on this subject. The far-seeing minister, fully alive to the danger, drafted a letter to reassure the religious superiors, and dispatched it probably in the first instance to Glastonbury.[1]

"Albeit," this letter runs, "I doubt not but (having not long since received the King's highness's letters wherein his majesty signified to you that using yourselves like his good and faithful subjects, his grace would not in any wise interrupt you in your state and kind of living; and that his pleasure therefore was that in case any man should declare anything to the contrary you should cause him to be apprehended and kept in sure custody till further knowledge of his grace's pleasure), you would so firmly repose yourself in the tenour of the said letters as no man's words, nor any voluntary surrender made by any governor or company of any religious house since that time, shall put you in any doubt or fear of suppression or change of your kind of life and policy." The king, however, feels that there are people who "upon any voluntary and frank surrender, would persuade and blow abroad a general and violent suppression;" and, because some houses have lately been

[1] The previous letter in the Cotton MS. Cleopatra E. iv. is endorsed: "The mynute of a letter drawn by Mr. Moryson to th'Abbot of Glastonbury." This endorsement is certainly wrong; but Mr. Gairdner (*Calendar*, xiii, No. 573 *note*) thinks the letters may possibly have always been together and the endorsement refers to the second.

surrendered, the king commands me to say " that unless there had been overtures made by the said houses that have resigned, his grace would never have received the same, and his majesty intendeth not in any wise to trouble you or to desire for the suppression of any house that standeth, except they shall either desire of themselves with one whole consent to resign and forsake the same, or else misuse themselves contrary to their allegiance." In this last case, the document concludes, they shall lose " more than their houses and possessions, that is, the loss also of their lives." Wherefore take care of your houses and beware of spoiling them, like some have done " who imagined they were going to be dissolved." [1]

This letter could scarcely have done much to reassure Abbot Whiting as to the king's real intentions, in view of the obvious facts which each day made them clearer. By the beginning of 1539, Glastonbury was the only religious house left standing in the whole county of Somerset. Rumours must have reached the abbey of the fall of Bath and Keynsham, shortly after the Christmas of the previous year, and of strange methods to which Crumwell's agents had resorted in order to gain possession of Hinton Charterhouse and Benedictine Athelney. At the former, the determination of the monks to hold to their house was apparently in the end broken down by a resort to a rigid examination of the religious on the dangerous royal-supremacy question, which resulted in one of their number being put in prison for " affirming the Bishop of Rome to be Vicar of Christ, and that he ought to be taken for head of the Church." This of itself must have prepared the mind of Abbot Whiting for the final issue which would have to be faced.

[1] B. Mus. Cott. MS. Cleop. E. iv, f. 68.

E

The short respite granted before conclusions were tried with him, could have been to all at Glastonbury little less than a long-drawn suspense, during which the abbot possessed his soul in peace, attending cheerfully to the daily calls of duty. They were left in no doubt as to the real meaning of a dissolution and had witnessed the immediate results which followed upon it. The rude dismantling of churches and cloisters, the rapid sales of vestments and other effects, the pulling down of the lead from roofs and gutters, and the breaking up of bells had gone on all around them; whilst homeless monks and the poor who had from time immemorial found relief in their necessities at religious houses now swept away must have all crowded to Glastonbury during the last few months of its existence. For eleven weeks the royal wreckers, like a swarm of locusts, wandered over Somerset, "defacing, destroying, and prostrating the churches, cloisters, belfreys, and other buildings of the late monasteries;" and the roads were worn with carts carrying away the lead melted from the roofs, barrels of broken bell-metal, and other plunder.

It was not till the autumn of the year 1539, that any final steps began to be taken with regard to Glastonbury and its venerable abbot. Among Crumwell's "remembrances," still extant in his own handwriting, of things to do, or matters to speak about to the king, in the beginning of September this year occurs the following: "Item, for proceeding against the abbots of Reading, Glaston and the other, in their own countries." [1] From this it is clear that some time between the passing of the Act giving to the Crown the possession of all dissolved or surrendered monasteries, which came into force in

[1] B. Mus. Cott. MS. Titus, B. i, f. 446a.

April, 1539, and the September of this year, these abbots must have been sounded, and it had been found that compliance in regard of a surrender was not to be expected.[1] By the sixteenth of the latter month Crumwell's design had been communicated to his familiar Layton, and had elicited from him a reply in which he abjectly asks pardon for having praised the abbot at the time of the visitation. "The Abbot of Glastonbury," he adds, "appeareth neither then nor now to have known God, nor his prince, nor any part of a good Christian man's religion."[2]

Three days later, on Friday, September 19th, the royal commissioners, Layton, Pollard and Moyle, suddenly arrived at Glastonbury about ten o'clock in the morning. The abbot had not been warned of their intended visit, and was then at his grange of Sharpham, about a mile from the monastery. Thither they hurried "without delay," and after telling him their purpose examined him at once "upon certain articles, and for that his answer

[1] In the spring of the year, Glastonbury, in common with other churches in England, was relieved of what it pleased the king to consider its "superfluous plate." Pollard, Tregonwell and Petre on May 2nd, 1539, handed to Sir John Williams, the keeper of the royal treasure-house, 493 ounces of gold, 16,000 ounces of gilt plate and 28,700 ounces of parcel gilt and silver plate taken from the monasteries in the west of England. In this amount was included the superfluous plate of Glastonbury. Besides this weight of gold and silver there were placed in the treasury "two collets of gold wherein standeth two coarse emeralds; a cross of silver gilt, garnished with a great coarse emerald, two 'balaces' and two sapphires, lacking a knob at one of the ends of the same cross; a superaltar garnished with silver gilt and part gold, called the great sapphire of Glastonbury; a great piece of unicorn's horn, a piece of mother of pearl like a shell, eight branches of coral" (Monastic Treasures, Abbotsford Club, p. 24).
[2] Ellis, *Original Letters*, 3rd Series, iii, p. 247.

was not then to our purpose," they say, " we advised him
to call to his remembrance that which he had forgotten,
and so declare the truth." [1] Then they at once took him
back to the abbey, and when night came on proceeded
to search the abbot's papers and ransack his apartments
" for letters and books; and found in his study, secretly
laid, as well a written book of arguments against the
divorce of the king's majesty and the lady dowager,
which we take to be a great matter, as also divers pardons, copies of bulls, and the counterfeit life of Thomas
Becket in print; but we could not," they write, " find
any letter that was material."

Furnished, however, with these pieces of evidence as
to the tendency of Whiting's mind, the inquisitors proceeded further to examine him concerning the " articles
received from your lordship" (Crumwell). In his answers appeared, they considered " his cankered and
traitorous mind against the king's majesty and his succession." To these replies he signed his name, " and so
with as fair words as " they could, " being but a very
weak man and sickly," they forthwith sent him up to
London to the Tower, that Crumwell might examine
him for himself.

The rest of the letter is significant for the eventual
purpose they knew their master would regard as of
primary importance:

" As yet we have neither discharged servant nor
monk; but now, the abbot being gone, we will, with as
much celerity as we may, proceed to the dispatching of
them. We have in money £300 and above; but the
certainty of plate and other stuff there as yet we know

[1] The whole of this account is from the letter of the commissioners to Crumwell, in Wright, p. 255.

not, for we have not had opportunity for the same;
whereof we shall ascertain your lordship so shortly as
we may. This is also to advertise your lordship that we
have found a fair chalice of gold, and divers other parcels
of plate, which the abbot had hid secretly from all such
commissioners as have been there in times past; and as
yet he knoweth not that we have found the same;
whereby we think that he thought to make his hand by
his untruth to his king's majesty."

A week later, on September 28th,[1] they again write
to Crumwell that they "have daily found and tried out
both money and plate," hidden in secret places in the
abbey, and conveyed for safety to the country. They
could not tell him how much they had so far discovered,
but it was sufficient, they thought, to have "begun a
new abbey," and they concluded by asking what the
king wished to have done in respect of the two monks
who were the treasurers of the church, and the two lay
clerks of the sacristy, who were chiefly to be held responsible in the matter.

On the 2nd October the inquisitors write again to
their master to say that they have come to the knowledge of "divers and sundry treasons" committed by
Abbot Whiting, "the certainty whereof shall appear
unto your lordship in a book herein enclosed, with the
accusers' names put to the same, which we think to be
very high and rank treasons." The original letter, preserved in the Record Office, clearly shows by the creases
in the soiled yellow paper that some small book or
folded papers have been enclosed. Whatever it was, it
is no longer forthcoming. Just at the critical moment
we are again deprived, therefore, of a most interesting

[1] Wright, p. 257.

and important source of information. In view, however, of the common sufferings of these abbots, who were dealt with together, the common fate which befell them, and the common cause assigned by contemporary writers for their death,—viz., their attainder " of high treason for denying the king to be supreme head of the Church," as Hall, the contemporary London lawyer (who reports what must have been current in the capital) phrases it—there can be no doubt that these depositions were much of the same nature as those made against Thomas Marshall, Abbot of Colchester, to which subsequent reference will be made. It is certain that with Abbot Whiting in the Tower and Crumwell's commissioners engaged in "dispatching" the monks " with as much celerity" as possible, Glastonbury was already regarded as part of the royal possessions. Even before any condemnation the matter is taken as settled, and on October 24th, 1539, Pollard handed over to the royal treasurer the riches still left at the abbey as among the possessions of "attainted persons and places." [1]

Whilst Layton and his fellows were rummaging at Glastonbury, Abbot Whiting was safely lodged in the Tower of London. There he was subjected to searching examinations. A note in Crumwell's own hand, entered in his "remembrances," says:

" Item. Certain persons to be sent to the Tower for the further examination of the Abbot of Glaston." [2]

At this time it was supposed that Parliament, which

---

[1] *Monastic Treasures* (Abbotsford Club), p. 38. These consisted of 71 oz. of gold with stones, 7,214 oz. of gilt plate, and 6,387 oz. of silver.

[2] B. Mus. Cott., MS. Titus, B. i, f. 441a.

THE PEGGED GRACE-CUP OF GLASTONBURY
ABBEY, NOW IN THE POSSESSION OF
LORD ARUNDELL OF WARDOUR

[To face p. 5.

ought to have met on November 1st of this year, would
be called upon to consider the charges against the abbot.
At least Marillac, the French ambassador, who shows
that he was always well informed on public matters,
writes to his master that this is to be done. Even when
the assembly was delayed till the arrival of the king's
new wife, Ann of Cleves, the ambassador repeats that
the decision of Whiting's case will now be put off. He
adds that "they have found a manuscript in favour of
queen Catherine, and against the marriage of queen
Anne, who was afterwards beheaded," which is objected
against the abbot.[1] Poor Catherine had been at rest in
her grave for four years, and her rival in the affections of
Henry had died on the scaffold nearly as many years,
before Layton and his fellow inquisitors found the
written book of arguments in Whiting's study, and
"took it to be a great matter" against him. It is hardly
likely that, even if more loyal to Catherine's memory
than there is any possible reason to suppose, Whiting
would stick at a point where More and Fish r could
yield, and would not have given his adhesion to the
succession as settled by Parliament. But as in their
case, it was the thorny questions which surrounded the
divorce, the subject all perilous of "treason," which
brought him at last, as it brought them first, to the
scaffold.

It is more than strange that the ordinary procedure
was not carried out in this case. According to all law,
Abbot Whiting and the Abbots of Reading and Colchester should have been arraigned before Parliament,
as they were members of the House of Peers, but no
such bill of attainder was ever presented, and in fact

[1] Kaulek, *Inventaire Analytique, ut sup*, No. 161.

the execution had taken place before the Parliament came together.[1]

The truth is, that Abbot Whiting and the others were condemned to death as the result of secret inquisitions in the Tower. Crumwell, acting as " prosecutor, judge and jury,"[2] had really arranged for their execution before they left their prison. What happened in the case of Abbot Whiting at Wells, and in that of Abbot Cook at Reading, was but a ghastly mockery of justice, enacted merely to cover the illegal and iniquitous proceedings which had condemned them untried. This Crumwell has written down with his own hand. He notes in his " remembrances ":[3] " Item. Councillors to give evidence against the abbot of Glaston, Richard Pollard, Lewis Forstell and Thomas Moyle. Item. To see that the evidence be *well sorted* and the indictments *well drawn* against the said abbots and their accomplices. Item. How the King's learned counsel shall be with me all this day, for the full conclusion of the indictments."

[1] According to Wriothesley's *Chronicle* they were arraigned in the " Counter." "Also in this month [November] the abbates of Glastonburie, Reding and Colchester were arrayned in the Counter." It is worthy of notice that whilst all trace or record of a trial has disappeared, the legal records are explicit as to a point of fact. Of course the king could only obtain the possessions of the monastery by the attainder of the abbot for high treason, and accordingly the official documents all speak of the attainder for high treason. For instance L. T. R. Memoranda Roll, 32 Henry VIII, m. 2, has : " Omnes libertates &c. dicti nuper abbatis Glaston sunt in manu dicti Regis nunc ratione attincturae praefati abbatis qui nuper de alta prodicione attinctus fuit." These presentments in the Counter or at Wells were evidently empty shows, intended to impress the populace.

[2] Froude, *Hist.*, iii, p. 432.

[3] B. Mus., Cott. MS., Titus, B. i, ff. 441 *a* and *b*.

And then, to sum up all: "Item. The Abbot of Glaston to be *tried* at Glaston, and *also executed* there." [1]

As Crumwell was so solicitous about the fate of the abbots as to devote the whole of one of his precious days to the final settlement of their case, in later times no less great was the solicitude of his panegyrist, Burnet, to "discover the impudence of Sander" in saying they suffered for denying the king's supremacy, and to prove that they did not. Even at a time when records were not so accessible as they now are, Collier, Burnet's contemporary, could see clearly enough where lay the truth. "What the particulars were (of the abbots' attainder) our learned church historian (Burnet) confesses 'he can't tell; for the record of their attainders is lost.' But, as he goes on, 'some of our own writers (Hall, Grafton) deserve a severe censure, who write it was for denying, &c., the king's supremacy. Whereas, if they had not undertaken to write the history without any information at all, they must have seen that the whole clergy, and especially the abbots, had over and over again acknowledged the king's supremacy.' But how does it appear our historians are mistaken? Has this gentleman seen the Abbot of Colchester's indictment or perused his record of attainder? He confesses no. How then is his

---

[1] The following is a transcript of the passages contained in the facsimile given on p. 59. "Item certayn persons to be sent to the Towre for the further examenacyon of the abbot of Glaston. Item letters to be sent with the copye of the judgement ageynst Sir John Sayntlow's men for the rape and burgalrye don in Somersetshyre unto lorde presedent Russell with a streyt commandement to procede to justyce. Item the abbot Redyng to be sent down to be tryed and executyd at Reding with his complycys. Item the abbot of Glaston to [be] tryed at Glaston and also executyd there with his complycys."

censure made good? He offers no argument beyond conjecture. He concludes the Abbot of Colchester had formerly acknowledged the king's supremacy, and from thence infers he could not suffer now for denying it. But do not people's opinions alter sometimes, and conscience and courage improve? Did not Bishop Fisher and Cardinal Pool, at least as this author represents them, acknowledge the king's supremacy at first? And yet it is certain they afterwards showed themselves of another mind to a very remarkable degree. . . . Farther, does not himself tell us that many of the Carthusians were executed for their open denying the king's supremacy, and why then might not some of the abbots have the same belief and fortitude with others of their fraternity?"[1] The real way of reaching them was through conscience, a way which, as we have seen, had just before been tried in the case of the Abbot Whiting's near neighbours, the Carthusians of Hinton. "To reach the abbots, therefore," continues Collier, "that other way, the oath of supremacy, was offered them, and upon their refusal they were condemned for high treason."[2]

But amidst these cares Crumwell never forgot the king's business, the "great matter," the end which this iniquity was to compass. With the prize now fairly within his grasp, he notes: "The plate of Glastonbury, 11,000 ounces and over, besides golden. The furniture of the house of Glaston. In ready money from Glaston, £1,100 and over. The rich copes from Glaston. The whole year's revenue of Glaston. The debts of Glaston, £2,000 and above.[3]

---

[1] *Eccl. Hist.*, ii, 173.   [2] *Ibid.*, p. 164.
[3] B. Mus., Cott. MS., Titus B. i, f. 446 *a*. The debts named here were evidently due to Glastonbury.

FACSIMILE OF PART OF CRUMWELL'S "REMEMBRANCES,"
COTTON MS., TITUS B. i, f. 441a.

Layton has borne witness to the state of spirituals in Glastonbury; Crumwell gives final testimony to the abbot's good administration of temporals. The house by this time had, according to Crumwell's construction, come to the king's highness by attainder of treason. It remained now to inaugurate the line of policy on which Elizabeth improved later, and after, in the secret tribunal of the Tower, condemning the abbot without trial for cause of conscience in a sentence that involved forfeiture of life and goods, to put him to death, so Lord Russell says, as if for common felony, for the "robbing of Glastonbury Church."

And now it only remains to follow the venerable man on his pilgrimage to the scene of his martyrdom.[1]

As we have seen under Crumwell's hand, Abbot Whiting's fate was already settled before he left the Tower. In the interrogatories, preliminary but decisive,

---

[1] The original edition of Sander simply says that the three abbots and the two priests, Rugg and Onion, "ob negatam Henrici pontificiam potestatem martyrii coronam adepti sunt." In the second and later editions this is cut out, another reason is assigned for their death, and an obviously legendary narrative about Whiting is inserted in the text. It is impossible to credit many of these oft-repeated statements. They seem to embody the gossip of half a century later; in some points running near enough to the truth, in others partaking of legend; such as the sensational scene, wanting alike in sense and probability, in the hall of the palace on the abbot's arrival at Wells; the assembly prepared to receive him, his proceeding to take the place of honour among the first, the unexpected summons to stand down and answer to the charge of treason, the old man's wondering inquiry what this meant, the whispered assurance that it was all a matter of form to strike terror —into whom or wherefore the story does not tell. These and later details are here entirely thrown aside, since they cannot be reconciled with the official documents of the time and private letters of the persons engaged in the act itself.

which he had there undergone, the abbot had come face to face with the inevitable issue. He knew to what end the way through the Tower had, from the time of More and Fisher to his own hour, led those who had no other satisfaction to give the king than that which he himself could offer.

It is not impossible, however, that hopes may have been held out to him that in his extreme old age and weakness of body he might be spared extremities; this supposition seems to receive some countenance from the narrative given below. But Henry and Crumwell had determined that Abbot Whiting should suffer before all the world the last indignity. And they designed for him the horrible death of a traitor in the sight of his own subjects who had known and loved him for many years, and on the scene of his own former greatness.

The following extract from an unknown but contemporary writer, in giving the only details of the journey homeward that are known to exist, manifests the abbot's characteristic simplicity and perfect possession of soul in patience, together with a real sense of what the end would certainly be:

" Going homewards to Glastonbury, the abbot had one Pollard appointed to wait upon him, who was an especial favourer of Crumwell, whom the abbot neither desired to accompany him, neither yet dared to refuse him. At the next bait, when the abbot went to wash, he desired Mr. Pollard to come wash with him, who by no means would be entreated thereunto. The abbot seeing such civility, mistrusted so much the more such courtesy was not void of some subtility, and said unto him: " Mr. Pollard, if you be to me a companion, I pray you wash with me and sit down; but if you be my keeper and I your prisoner, tell me plainly, that I may prepare my mind to go to another room better fitting my fortunes. And if you be neither, I shall be content to ride without your company.' Whereupon Pollard protested that he did forbear to do what the abbot desired him only in respect of the reverence he bore his age and virtues, and that he was appointed by those in authority to bear him company of worship's sake, and therefore might not forsake him till he did see him safe at Glastonbury.

" Notwithstanding all this the abbot doubted somewhat, and told one (Thomas) Horne, whom he had brought up from a child, that he misdoubted (him) somewhat, Judas having betrayed his master. And yet though (Horne) were both privy and plotter of his master's fall, yet did he sweare most intolerably he knew of no harm towards him, neither should any be done to him as long as he was in his company; wishing besides that the devil might have him if he were otherwise than he told him. But before he came to Glastonbury, Horne forsook, and joined himself unto his enemies." [1]

[1] B. Mus. Sloane MS. 2495. The passage in the text is taken from an early seventeenth-century life of Henry VIII. It is, however, a free translation of Arundel MS., 151, No. 62, which is a hitherto unnoticed account of the divorce, written somewhere about the year 1557, and dedicated to Philip and Mary. Some of the details agree with those given about Whiting by Le Grand (*Défense*, iii, p. 210), who may have drawn them from the same source.

CHAPTER VII

THE MARTYRDOM

THE venerable abbot thus journeyed home in the company of Pollard. It was this Pollard who had been Crumwell's agent in sending him to the Tower, who had weeks ago turned the monks out of the monastery and had begun the wrecking of Glastonbury Abbey, a house, which on his first arrival there he had described to his employer as "great, goodly, and so princely that we have not seen the like;" and in another letter he repeats the same assurance, adding that "it is a house meet for the king's majesty, and for no one else."[1]

Measures had already been taken to have all secure at Wells, although Abbot Whiting had evidently been left in ignorance of the fact that there was now no Glastonbury Abbey for him to return to. Crumwell's captive reached Wells on Friday, November 14th, and once safely brought back into his own country there was neither delay nor dissembling. The plan devised was rushed through without giving a soul among the unhappy actors in the scene time to reflect upon what they were doing —time to recover their better selves—time to avert the guilt which in some measure must fall upon them. In accordance with the wicked policy so often pursued in Tudor times, a jury—the people themselves—were made active agents in accomplishing the royal vengeance, the execution of which had been already irrevocably settled in London. John, Lord Russell, had for some time past

[1] Wright, *Suppression of the Monasteries*, pp. 256, 258.

been superintending the necessary arrangements in the county of Somerset itself. His business had been to get together a jury which he could trust to do, or perhaps in this case tacitly countenance, the king's will, and it was one part of his care, when all was over, to send to Crumwell their names with a view, doubtless, of securing their due reward. Unfortunately, although Russell's letter is preserved, the list enclosed has perished. But a letter from Pollard to Crumwell gives the names of some who distinguished themselves by their zeal, and who had been "very diligent to serve the king at this time." Among these, first of all is " my brother Paulet," for whom is bespoken " the surveyorship of Glaston," with the promise to Crumwell that " his lordship's goodness," showed in this matter, Paulet when he takes the prize "shall recompense to his little power." Other diligent persons whom Pollard specially names are John Sydenham and Thomas Horner, and finally Nicholas FitzJames, the same who, but a year or two before, had written to Crumwell in Abbot Whiting's behalf.

As is well known from the history of the Pilgrimage of Grace, jury-making had at this time been raised to an art,—an art so exquisitely refined that it aimed at making friends, kinsfolk, even brothers the accomplices by word of mouth in the legal or illegal murders which disgraced this reign. The minds of the men selected in this case to register the decrees of the kingly omnipotence, escape our means of inquiry, but Lord Russell has recorded " that they formed as worshipful a jury as were found here these many years," and of this fact he " ensured " his " good lord " Crumwell.

Russell's care, moreover, had been diligently exercised, not merely in assembling the jury, but in getting

GENERAL VIEW OF GLASTONBURY TOR

[To face p. 64

together an audience for the occasion. His efforts were successful, for he gathered at Wells such a concourse of people, that he was able to declare "there was never seen in these parts so great appearance as were here at this present time." He adds the assurance so tediously common in documents of that pre-eminently courtly age, that none had ever been seen "better willing to serve the king."¹

This was the scene which met Abbot Whiting's eyes in Pollard's company as he entered the city of Wells, where so often before he had been received as a venerated and honoured guest. Unfortunately we have no direct and continuous narrative of all that took place. If it was dangerous to speak it was still more dangerous to write in those days, except of course in one sense,—that which was pleasing to the court. Fortunately two letters survive, written by the chief managers of the business, John, Lord Russell, and Richard Pollard, one of the "counsel" who had been engaged in the Tower with Crumwell, for the careful drawing of the indictment against the abbot. Both were written on the Sunday, the day following the execution. An earlier letter by Pollard, written on the day itself and evidently giving more details, is wanting in the vast mass of Crumwell's papers. This, the earliest news of the accomplishment of the king's will, was not improbably taken by the ready minister to the king himself and left with his majesty. Fragmentary though the records that exist are, and only giving here a hint, there a mere outline of what took place, without order and without sequence, they in this form have a freshness and truthfulness which still enable us to realise what actually took place.

¹ Wright, *Suppression of the Monasteries*, p. 260.

F

On the abbot's arrival in the city of Wells, the business was begun without waiting to give the condemned man time for rest or for thought. Pollard was in charge of the indictment, over which Crumwell had spent his day, in the drafting of which so many counsel learned in the law had exercised their ingenuity, and which was the outcome of the secret examinations conducted during the abbot's two months' imprisonment in the Tower. But it was by no means intended that a drop of bitterness in the cup should be spared him; every successive stage of indignity was to be offered the venerable man till his last breath, and then to his lifeless body. He was to be struck in the house of his friends, and by his own dependents. From out the crowd there came forward new accusers, "his tenants and others," putting up "many accusations for wrongs and injuries he had done them:" not of course that it was in the least intended that there should be time for enquiry into their truth; the mere accusations were enough, and they were part of the drama that had been elaborated with such care.

But this was not the only business of the day. The venerable man was to be associated and numbered with a rabble of common felons, and to stand in the same rank with them. Together with the abbot of the great monastery of Glastonbury there were a number of people of the lowest class—how many we know not—who were accused of "rape and burglary." "They were all condemned," says Russell, and four of them "the next day, if not the same day, put to execution at the place of the act done, which is called the Mere, and there adjudged to hang still in chains to the example of others."

Of any verdict or of any condemnation of the abbot

and of his two monks nothing is said by Russell or Pollard, but they proceed at once to the execution.[1]

It is not impossible, seeing the rapid way in which the whole business was carried through, that had the scene of the so-called trial been Glastonbury in place of Wells, the abbot would have met his fate and gained his crown that very day. But the king and his faithful minister, Crumwell, had devised in the town of Glastonbury a scene which was to be more impressive than that which had taken place in the neighbouring city, more calculated to strike terror into the hearts of the old man's friends and followers.

After being pestered by Pollard with " divers articles and interrogatories," the result of which was that he would accuse no man but himself, nor " confess no more gold nor silver, nor anything more than he did before you [Crumwell] in the Tower," the next morning, Saturday, November 15th,[2] the venerable abbot with his two monks, John Thorne and Roger James, were delivered over to the servants of Pollard for the performance of what more had to be done. Under this escort they were carried from Wells to Glastonbury. Arrived at the entrance of the town the abbot was made to dismount.

[1] After a careful consideration of the evidence, my belief is that there was no trial of the abbot and his two companions at Wells. The sentence passed on them in London was probably published to the jury there, but there is nothing to show that it was asked to find any verdict.

[2] It is generally stated that the martyrdom took place on November 14th. The authority for this is a statement in the original edition of Sander, that the three abbots obtained the crown of martyrdom "ad decimum octavum kalendas Decembris." Mr. David Lewis in his translation has not noticed the error. It is certain from the original letters of Pollard and Russell that the true date is Saturday, November 15th.

And now all the brutal indignities and cruel sufferings attending the death of a traitor condemned for treason were inflicted upon him. And in truth, like many a true and noble Englishman of that day, Richard Whiting was, in the sense of Crumwell and Henry, a traitor to his king. The case from their point of view is well expressed by one of the truculent preachers patronised by the sovereign as his most fitting apologists.

"For had not Richard [1] Whiting, that was Abbot of Glastonbury, trow ye, great cause, all things considered, to play so traitorous a part as he hath played, whom the king's highness made of a vile, beggarly, monkish merchant, governor and ruler of seven thousand marks by the year? Trow ye this was not a good pot of wine? Was not this a fair almose at one man's door? Such a gift had been worth grammercy to many a man. But Richard Whiting having always a more desirous eye to treason than to truth, careless, laid apart both God's goodness and the king's, and stuck hard by the Bishop of Rome and the Abbot of Reading in the quarrel of the Romish Church. Alas! what a stony heart had (Richard) Whiting, to be so unkind to so loving and beneficent a prince, and so false a traitor to Henry VIII, king of his native country, and so true, I say, to that cormorant of Rome."

In this new meaning of treason, Abbot Whiting was adjudged the traitor's death. At the outskirts of his own town his venerable limbs were extended on a hurdle, to which a horse was attached. In this way he was dragged on that bleak November morning along the rough hard ground through the streets of Glastonbury, of which he and his predecessors had so long been the loved and

[1] The name in the MS. is John, but it is evidently a mistake.

SUMMIT OF TOR HILL

[To face p. 68

honoured lords and masters. It was thus among his own people that, now at the age of well nigh fourscore years, Abbot Whiting made his last pilgrimage through England's "*Roma Secunda*." As a traitor for conscience' sake he was drawn past the glorious monastery, now desolate and deserted, past the great church, that home of the saints and whilom sanctuary of this country's greatness, now devastated and desecrated, its relics of God's holy ones dispersed, its tombs of kings dishonoured, on further still to the summit of that hill which rises yet in the landscape in solitary and majestic greatness, the perpetual memorial of the deed now to be enacted.[1] For, thanks to the tenacity with which the memory of "good Abbot Whiting" has been treasured by generations of the townsfolk, the very hill to-day is Abbot Whiting's monument.

His last act was simple. Now about to appear before

[1] It has been suggested that the place of Abbot Whiting's martyrdom was not the Tor, but a smaller hill nearer the town, called Chalice Hill. The ground of this supposition is that the site of the abbey is not visible from the Tor, whilst it is from the latter hill. The steps by which the conclusion was arrived at that this consequently was the place of martyrdom, would appear to be that while the letters of Russell and Pollard state that the abbot was executed on the Tor hill, the Roman editor of Sander uses only a general expression, perfectly reasonable when writing for persons who were not acquainted with Glastonbury. The execution took place, he says, *ad montis editi cacumen qui monasterio imminet, i.e.*, overhangs, that is, *rises above* the monastery. This has been taken in the sense of *overlooking*, and next "overlook" in its strictest sense, as implying that the abbey was visible from the place of execution. It is only necessary, in order to refute a theory having no better basis than inaccuracy and misunderstanding, to refer to the simple assertion of the persons engaged in the execution of Abbot Whiting, who wrote at the very time it was taking place, and who knew perfectly well what Tor hill was.

a tribunal that was searching, just and merciful, he asks forgiveness, first of God, and then of man, even of those who had most offended against justice in his person and had not rested until they had brought him to the gallows amidst every incident that could add to such a death—ignominy and shame. The venerable abbot remains to the last the same as he always appears throughout his career; suffering in self-possession and patience the worst that man could inflict upon his mortal body, in the firm assurance that in all this he was but following in the footsteps of that Lord and Master in whose service from his youth upwards he had spent his life.

In this supreme moment, his two monks, John Thorne [1] and Roger James,[2] the one a man of mature age and experience, the other not long professed, showed themselves worthy sons of so good a father. They, too, begged forgiveness of all and "took their death also very patiently." Even Pollard seems moved for the moment,

[1] A comparison of the lists of monks qualified to take part in the election of Abbot Whiting in 1523 and the list appended to the acknowledgment of supremacy in 1534 seems to show that *John Arthur, treasurer* in 1523, is identical with *John Thorne, treasurer* in 1539, martyred with Abbot Whiting. This comparison also shows that the maker of the chair here illustrated, can be no other than *John Thorne*, the martyr. The lists of monks give only the Christian name and the name in religion (in this case Arthur). In the legal proceedings, for the religious name the family name, Thorne, is substituted.

The lists of 1523 and 1534 are noteworthy as showing how keen was the interest taken by the Glastonbury monks in the past of their house. Amongst the religious names occur: Abaramathea, Joseph, Arthur, Derivian, Gildas, Benen, Aidan, Ceolfrid, Indractus, Aldhelm, Dunstan, Ethelwold, Edgar, and other saints connected with Glastonbury.

[2] Roger James is evidently identical with Roger Wilfrid, who in the list of 1534 was the youngest monk of the house.

A GLASTONBURY CHAIR, DATING FROM THE TIME OF
ABBOT WHITING, AND PROBABLY MADE BY
HIS FELLOW MARTYR, JOHN THORNE
(From the Engraving in Warner)

[To face p. 70

for he adds with an unwonted touch of tenderness, "whose souls God pardon."

There is here no need to dwell on the butchery which followed, and to tell how the hardly lifeless body was cut down, divided into four parts and the head struck off. One quarter was despatched to Wells, another to Bath, a third to Ilchester, and the fourth to Bridgewater, whilst the venerable head was fixed over the great gateway of the abbey, a ghastly warning of the retribution which might and would fall on all, even the most powerful or the most holy, if they ventured to stand between the king and the accomplishment of his royal will.

All this might indeed strike terror into the people of the whole country, but not even the will of a Tudor monarch could prevent the people from forming their own judgment on the deed that had been done, and preserving, although robbed of the Catholic faith, the memory of the "good Abbot Whiting." It is easy to understand how, so soon after the event as Mary's reign, the inhabitants of the town and neighbourhood, with a vivid recollection of the past, were ready and even eager to make personal sacrifices for the restoration of the abbey. But even a hundred years later, and indeed even down to the present day, the name of Abbot Whiting has been preserved as a household word at Glastonbury and in its neighbourhood. There are those living who, when conversing with aged poor people, were touched to find the affectionate reverence with which his name was still treasured on the spot, though why he died and what it was all about they could not tell. That he was a good, a kind, a holy man they knew, for they had been told so in the days of their youth by those who had gone before.

CHAPTER VIII

ABBOT HUGH COOK OF READING

THE abbeys of Reading and Colchester, although of the first rank, seeing that their abbots were peers of Parliament, and Reading certainly among the most distinguished houses of the country, had no such position as that of Glastonbury. They were both Norman creations; Reading being founded by King Henry II and chosen by him as his burial place. By favour of its royal founder the commonalty of Reading recognised the abbot as their lord; the mayor of the city "being the abbot's mayor, &c.," as the diocesan, Bishop Shaxton, writes to Crumwell.

The history of the fall of Reading Abbey and of the execution of Hugh Cook, or Faringdon, the abbot, would be in its main features but a repetition of the story of Glastonbury and Abbot Whiting. The chief source of information about the Abbot of Reading is a paper, already referred to, which is still to be found among the public records, although it has remained unnoticed till a few years ago.[1] It was so decayed with age as to be almost dropping to pieces, but now encased in tissue paper it is fortunately legible almost in its entirety. The document in question is a virulent and brutal invective, evidently a sermon, drawn up for the approval of Crumwell, to be delivered in justification of the king's action in putting to death the three Benedictine abbots and their companions. It is unlikely that this proposed

---

[1] R. O. State Papers, 1539, No. 251.

sermon was ever delivered, for the deed was done, the abbots were dead, their property was now all in the king's hands, and from the point of view of the authors the less said about the matter the better. The draft was accordingly thrown by Crumwell into the vast mass of papers of all sorts accumulating on his hands, which on his attainder was seized by the king and transferred, as it stood, to the royal archives.

It seems not improbable that the author of the paper in question was Latimer. The harangue is brutal; it shows all his power of effective alliteration, and it is written quite in the spirit of the man who begged to be allowed to preach at the martyrdom of Blessed John Forrest, and to be placed near him that he might with better effect insult him in his death agonies. It is certainly written by a person fully acquainted with all the circumstances, and throws light on many matters which would be unintelligible without it. The paper is so far of the highest value; but in dealing with its statements it is to be remembered that the one object of the writer is to blacken the memory of the martyred abbots, to degrade them and to bring them by every means into contempt.

From the account of Abbot Cook's origin given by this writer, it would be gathered that he was born in humble circumstances. He thus apostrophises the abbot after his death: "Ah, Hugh Cook, Hugh Cook! nay, Hugh Scullion rather I may him call that would be so unthankful to so merciful a prince, so unkind to so loving a king, and so traitorous to so true an emperor. The king's highness of his charity took Hugh Cook out his cankerous cloister and made him, being at that time the most vilest, the most untowardest and the most miserablest monk that was in the monastery of Reading, born to nought else but to an old pair of beggarly boots, and made him, I say, ruler and governor of three thousand marks by the year." But the testimony of the writer on a point of fact such as this cannot be rated high.

It is probable that Abbot Cook belonged to that class from which the English monastic houses had been so largely recruited, "the devouter and younger children of our nobility and gentry who here had their education and livelihood."[1] There seems to be no doubt that he belonged to a Kentish family known to the heralds.[2] His election to the office of abbot took place in 1520. Grafton and Hall in their chronicles, in accordance with the practice common at the time, to depreciate falsely by any and every means, those who had fallen into the disfavour of the reigning tyrant, give him the character of an illiterate person. "The contrary," writes Browne

---

[1] Bodleian MS. Wood, B. vi. Woodhope's *Book of Obits*.

[2] It has been considered doubtful whether the name of the last abbot of Reading was Cook or Faringdon. He is sometimes called by one, sometimes by the other name. In the entry of his conviction for treason upon the Controlment Roll, usually very exact, he is called only by the name of "Cooke." As to the arms borne by the abbot, Cole, the antiquary, writes as follows:—"In a curious MS. Book of Heraldry, on vellum and painted, supposed to [be] written about 1520, contayning all ye arms of Persons who had a chevron in the same, is this entered: Hugh Faringdon, *alias* Cooke, Abbat of Reading. Gules a chevron lozenge sable and argent inter 3 Bezants each charged with a cinquefoil gules, on a chief argent a Dove inter 2 Flowers azure. This book belongs to my Friend Mr. Blomfield of Norwich.—W. C. 1748." (Note in Cole's copy of Browne Willis, *Mitred Abbeys*, i, p. 161, now in possession of the Earl of Gainsborough.) These arms, impaled with those of Reading Abbey, are also given in Coates' *Reading*, plate vii, engraved with a portrait of the abbot, from a piece of stained glass, formerly in Sir John Davis' chapel at Bere Court near Pangbourne. These are the arms of the family of Cook.

Willis, "will appear to such as will consult his *Epistles to the University of Oxford*, remaining in the register of that university, or shall have an opportunity of perusing a book entitled *The art or craft of Rhetorick*, written by Leonard Cox, schoolmaster of Reading. 'Twas printed in the year 1524, and is dedicated by the author to this abbot. He speaks very worthily and honourably of Faringdon on account of his learning." [1]

A letter written by Cook to the University in Oxford in 1530 is evidence of the abbot's intelligent zeal for the Catholic religion, which at that time was being attacked by the new heresies springing up on all sides. Among the monks of Reading Abbey was one Dom John Holyman, "a most stout champion in his preachings and writings against the Lutherans," who, "desirous of a stricter life had resigned his fellowship at New College, Oxford, and taken the cowl at Reading Abbey." When Holyman was to receive the doctorate, Abbot Cook asked that he might be excused from lecturing before

---

[1] Browne Willis, *Mitred Abbeys*, i, p. 161. For Leonard Cox consult *Dict. of National Biography*, xii, p. 136. Cox's preface, referred to, is printed in Coates' *Reading*. The whole is interesting, but it is too long to quote here. It may be gathered that Cox had been a protégé of the abbot, who bestowed much care in advancing the interest of promising youths, and that Greek was taught as well as Latin in "your grammar schole, founded by your antecessours in this your towne of Redynge." It may be worth while to mention here that in the years 1499 and 1500 a Greek, one John Serbopoulos, of Constantinople, was copying Greek MSS. in Reading. Two of these thick folios written on vellum now form MSS. 23 and 24 in the library of Corpus Christi College, Oxford. They were among Grocyn's books, and came to the college through the instrumentality of John Claymond, who was known and patronised by Abbot Bere, of Glastonbury. Grocyn himself was taught Greek by William Sellyng, Prior of Christ Church, Canterbury (see *Downside Review*, December, 1894).

the University, as the custom was, so that he might preach in London, where there was greater need of such a man, seeing that the city was already infected with Lutheranism, and where the great popularity which Holyman already enjoyed brought crowds to him whenever he appeared in the pulpit at St. Paul's.

On the visitation of Reading Abbey by Doctor London in 1535, the report was favourable as to the state of discipline. "They have," writes the Doctor, "a good lecture in Scripture daily read in their chapter-house both in English and Latin, to which is good resort, and the abbot is at it himself."[1] It is possible that at this time, in the Visitors' injunctions as in their report, Reading was lightly treated. It must have been known to them, as it evidently was to Crumwell, that the abbot was in high favour with the king.

At any rate this circumstance will explain the sharpness of a correspondence which took place at this time between Shaxton, Bishop of Salisbury, in which diocese Reading was situated, and Crumwell. The latter takes up the very unusual position as defender of an abbot, and administers a sharp reproof to the bishop for his meddlesome interference in matters in which, as Crumwell tells him plainly, he has no concern beyond a desire to obtain preferment for an unworthy dependent of his own.

It appears that the lecturer in Scripture at the abbey was one Dom Roger London, a monk of the house. In the usual encouragement given to tale-bearing at this time, some discontented religious had delated their teacher to Bishop Shaxton as guilty of heresy. "The matters were no trifles," says Shaxton, himself at that

[1] Wright, p. 226.

time a strong supporter of Lutheranism; and the four points of suggested heresy certainly run counter to the teaching of the German doctor. Shaxton examined him personally, "as favourably as I could do," he writes, "and found him a man of very small knowledge and of worse judgment." In the discussion which followed, the bishop failed to bring the monk to his mind, and this determined him to procure the appointment of a man after his own heart, one Richard Cobbes, who had been a priest and canon, but who was then "a married man and degraded." Shaxton applied to Crumwell for the appointment of Cobbes as lecturer to the monks in Dom Roger London's place, "with stipend and commons" at the expense of the monastery.[1]

Crumwell, on receipt of the bishop's letter, wrote to the abbot complaining that "the divinity lecture had not been read in the abbey as it ought to have been," and recommending Cobbes for the post of lecturer. Abbot Cook replied that he had already a fully qualified teacher, "a bachelor of divinity and brother of the house, who, by the judgment of others" better able to judge than himself, was "very learned in both divinity and humanities, profiting the brethren both in the Latin tongue and in Holy Scripture." He concludes by pointing out that this teacher read his lecture at far less charge than a stranger would do, and offers him to be examined by any whom Crumwell might appoint. As to the bishop's nominee, the abbot points out the condition of the man, and naturally declares him to be "a most dangerous man" to hold such a position in the monastery. Under these circumstances Abbot Cook refused to admit Cobbes

---

[1] Gairdner, *Calendar*, xiii, i, No. 143 (Jan. 26th, the Abbot of Reading to Crumwell).

into his house, and continued his monk, Dom Roger London in the lectureship.

Finding that he had not got his way, Shaxton at once proceeded to inhibit the monk from reading at Reading, and put a stop to the lectures altogether. The bishop had evidently expected that Crumwell would out of hand have appointed Cobbes to the post on his first representation; "the which thing, if it had come to pass, so should I not have needed to have inhibited the said monk his reading; but I bare with him," he writes, "to say his creed, so long as there was hope to have another reader there. But when my expectation was frustrated in that behalf, then was I driven to do that which I was loathe to do and which, nevertheless, I was bound to do."

No one could have been more in sympathy with Shaxton's views on this matter than Crumwell. With the exception of the Archbishop of Canterbury and the Bishop of Worcester—that is, Cranmer, and Latimer—no one was more according to the minister's mind in religious matters than Bishop Shaxton; for all of them were true Lutherans at heart. Two of these prelates, indeed, continued honest in the year 1539 when brought face to face with the king's "Six Articles," which extinguished the immediate hopes of the Lutherans in England. They resigned their Sees, whilst Cranmer, in accordance with his guiding principle, sacrificed his convictions and held to his archiepiscopal office.

In the matter of the Reading lectureship Shaxton had counted that his ground was safe; and so indeed it was, up to the one point of that personal caprice which, throughout his reign, Henry maintained as the most cherished point of his royal prerogative. Whatever be the cause or explanation of the bishop's failure in this matter, one thing is clear: Henry had a real affection for the Abbot of Reading, so far as his affection could go, and used, as the contemporary libeller reports, to call him familiarly " his own abbot."

Shaxton was intent on doing his duty as a good pastor of sound Lutheran principles. But Crumwell had that all-determining and all-varying factor to consider, the king's fancy. He accordingly wrote to the abbot to tell him that he need not pay any attention to the Bishop of Salisbury's inhibition. " I," writes Shaxton on hearing of this, " could not obtain so much of you by word or writing to have your pleasure, and the Abbot of Reading could out of hand get and obtain your letters to hinder me in my right proceeding towards his just correction." Beyond this, not merely was the bishop's action set aside, but he had to submit to such a lecture from the king's vicar-general as may have decided him to resign his office when a few months later the " Six Articles " came to be imposed by the king and it was seen that the day for Lutheranism in England had not yet dawned.

It will be sufficient here to quote the conclusion of Crumwell's letter, which dealt expressly with the matter in hand. " As for the Abbot of Reading and his monk," he writes, " if I find them as ye say they are, I will order them as I think good.[1] Ye shall do well to do your duty; if you do so ye shall have no cause to mistrust my friendship. If ye do not, I can tell that [to] you, and

---

[1] Ultimately Roger London, the reader complained of by Shaxton, found his way into the Tower. His name appears in a list of prisoners there " on the 20th day of November," 1539, as " Roger London, monk of Reading " (B. Mus. Cott. MS., Titus B. i., f. 133). His fate is uncertain.

that somewhat after the plainest sort. To take a controversy out of your hands into mine I do but mine office. You meddle further than your office will bear you, thus roughly to handle me for using of mine. If ye do so no more I let pass all that is past."

Whatever advantage the Abbot of Reading derived temporarily, at different conjunctures, from the king's partiality for him, it was by this time clear that such favour could be continued to a man of Abbot Cook's character only by the sacrifice of principles and convictions. According to the writer of the sermon already quoted, the abbot " could not abide" the preachers of the new-fangled doctrines then in vogue, and "called them heretics and knaves of the New Learning." He was also "ever a great student and setter forth of St. Benet's, St. Francis', St. Dominic's and St. Augustine's rules, and said they were rules right holy and of great perfectness." It was, moreover, recognised that discipline was well maintained at Reading and Colchester no less than at Glastonbury; "these doughty deacons," as the writer calls the abbots and their monks, "thought it both heresy and treason to God to leave Matins unsaid, to speak loud in the cloisters, and to eat eggs on the Friday." [1] It would appear probable that Abbot Cook did not refuse to take the oath of royal supremacy, although there can be little doubt that in so doing he did not intend to separate himself from the traditional teaching of the Catholic Church on the question of papal authority. "He thought to shoot at the king's supremacy," as the contemporary witness has put it, and he was apparently charged with saying "that he would pray for the pope's holiness as long as he lived and

[1] R. O State Papers, Domestic, 1539, 251.

would once a week say Mass for him, trusting that by such good prayers the pope should rise again and have the king's highness with all the whole realm in subjection as he hath had in time past. And upon a *bon voyage* would call him pope as long as he lived."

After a page of abuse, the writer continues: "I cannot tell how this prayer will be allowed among St. Benet's rules, but this I am certain and sure of, that it standeth flatly against our Master Christ's rule. . . . What other thing should the abbat pray for here (as methinketh) but even first and foremost for the high dishonouring of Almighty God, for the confusion of our most dread sovereign lord, king Henry VIII, with his royal successors, and also for the utter destruction of this most noble realm of England. Well, I say no more, but I pray God heartily that the Mass be not abused in the like sort of a great many more in England which bear as fair faces under their black cowls and bald crowns as ever did the abbat of Reading, or any of the other traitors. I wiss neither the abbat of Reading, the abbat of Glassenbury, nor the prior [*sic*] of Colchester, Dr. Holyman, nor Roger London, John Rugg, nor Bachelor Giles, blind Moore, nor Master Manchester, the warden of the friars; no, nor yet John Oynyon, the abbat's chief councillor, was able to prove with all their sophistical arguments that the Mass was ordained for any such intent or purpose as the abbat of Reading used it."

"I fear me, Hugh Cook was master cook to a great many of that black guard (I mean black monks), and taught them to dress such gross dishes as he was always wont to dress, that is to say, treason; but let them all take heed."

G

At the time of the great northern rising, the Abbey of Reading, together with those of Glastonbury and Colchester, is found on the list of contributors to the king's expenses in defeating the rebel forces. Reading itself appears to have had some communication with Robert Aske, for copies of a letter written by him, and apparently also his proclamation, were circulated in the town. Amongst others who were supposed to be privy to the intentions of the insurgent chief was John Eynon, a priest of the church of St. Giles, Reading, and a special friend of Abbot Cook. Three years later this priest was executed with the abbot; but it is clear that at the time there was not even a suggestion of any complicity in the insurrection on the part of the abbot, as he presided at the examinations held in December, 1536, as to this matter.[1]

The first sign of any serious trouble appears about the close of 1537. The king's proceedings, which were distasteful to the nation at large, naturally gave rise to much criticism and murmuring. Every overt expression of disapprobation was eagerly watched for and diligently enquired into by the royal officials. The numerous records of examinations as to words spoken in conversation or in sermons, evidence the extreme care taken by the Government to crush out the first sparks of popular discontent. Rumours as to the king's bad health, or, still more, reports as to his death, were construed into indications of a treasonable disposition. In December, 1537, a rumour of this kind that Henry was dead reached Reading, and Abbot Cook wrote to some of his neighbours to tell them what was reported. This act was laid to his charge, and Henry acquired a cheap reputation

[1] Calendar, xi, 1231.

for magnanimity and clemency by pardoning "his own abbot" for what was, at the very worst, but a trifling act of indiscretion.

The libeller thus treats the incident:—"For think ye that the Abbat of Reading deserved any less than to be hanged, what time as he wrote letters of the king's death unto divers gentlemen in Berkshire, considering in what a queasy case the realm stood in at that same season? For the insurrection that was in the north country was scarcely yet thoroughly quieted; thus began he to stir the coals *à novo* and to make a fresh roasting fire, and did enough, if God had not stretched forth His helping hand, to set the realm in as great an uproar as ever it was, and yet the king's majesty, of his royal clemency, forgave him. This had been enough to have made this traitor a true man if there had been any grace in him."

Circumstances had brought Abbot Cook into communication with both the other abbots, whose fate was subsequently linked with his own. In the triennial general chapters of the Benedictines, in Parliament, in Convocation, they had frequently met; and when the more active measures of persecution devised by Crumwell made personal intercourse impossible, a trusty agent was found in the person of a blind harper named Moore, whose affliction and musical skill had brought him under the kindly notice of the king. This staunch friend of the papal party, whose blindness rendered his mission unsuspected, travelled about from one abbey to another, encouraging the imprisoned monks, bearing letters from house to house, and, doubtless, finding a safe way of sending off to Rome the letters which they had written to the pope and cardinals.

"But now amongst them all let us talk a word or two

of William Moor, the blind harper. Who would have thought that he would have consented or concealed any treason against the king's majesty? or who could have thought that he had had any power thereto? Who can muse or marvel enough to see a blind man for lack of sight to grope after treason? Oh! Moor, Moor, hast thou so great a delight and desire to play the traitor? Is this the mark that blind men trust to hit perchance? Hast thou not heard how the blind eateth many a fly? Couldst not thou beware and have kept thy mouth close together for fear of gnats? Hath God endued thee with the excellency of harping and with other good qualities, to put unto such a vile use? Couldst thou have passed the time with none other song but with the harping upon the string of treason? Couldst thou not have considered that the king's grace called thee from the wallet and the staff to the state of a gentleman? Wast thou also learned, and couldst thou not consider that the end of treason is eternal damnation? Couldst thou not be contented truly to serve thy sovereign lord king Henry VIII, whom thou before a great many oughtest and wast most bound truly to serve? Couldst not thou at least for all the benefits received at his grace's hand, bear towards him thy good will? Hadst thou nought else to do but to become a traitorous messenger between abbat and abbat? Had not the traitorous abbats picked out a pretty mad messenger of such a blind buzzard as thou art? Could I blazon thine arms sufficiently although I would say more than I have said? Could a man paint thee out in thy colours any otherwise than traitors ought to be painted? Shall I call thee William Moor, the blind harper? Nay, verily, thou shalt be called William Moor, the blind traitor. Now, surely, in my judgment, God did a gracious deed what time He put out both thine eyes, for what a traitor by all likelihood wouldst thou have been if God had lent thee thy sight, seeing thou wast so willing to grope blindfolded after treason! When thou becamest a traitorous messenger between the traitorous abbats, and when thou tookest in hand to lead traitors in the trade of treason, then was verified the sentence of our Master Christ, which sayeth, When the blind lead the blind both shall fall into the ditch. Thou wast blind in thine eyes, and they were blind in their consciences. Wherefore ye be all fallen into the ditch, that is to say, into the high displeasure of God and the king. I wiss, Moor, thou wrestest thine harpstrings clean out of tune, and settest thine harp a note too high when thou thoughtest to set the bawdy bishop of Rome above the king's majesty." [1]

It is evident that in the Benedictine monasteries of the district, as years went on, there were many who, as they came to realise the true meaning of this new royal supremacy, made no attempt to dissemble their real opinions on the matter. The writer so frequently referred to thus expresses his conviction as to the attitude of the monks: " But like as of late by God's purveyance a great part of their religious hoods be already meetly well ripped from their crafty coats, even so I hope the residue of the like religion shall in like sort not long remain unripped; for truly so long as they be let run at

---

[1] State Papers, 1539, No. 251, p. 25. "William Moor" appears in a list of prisoners in the Tower, 20th November, 1539 (B. Mus. Cott. MS., Titus B., i, f. 133). Perhaps Moor is the same person mentioned by Stowe (ed. 1614, p. 582): "The 1 of July (1540) a Welchman, a minstrel, was hanged and quartered for singing of songs which were interpreted to be prophecying against the king."

riot thus still in religion, they think verily that they may play the traitors by authority. But now his grace seeth well enough that all was not gold that glittered, neither all his true subjects that called him lord and master, namely, of Balaam's asses with the bald crowns. But I would now heartily wish," he adds, writing after the execution of the Abbots of Glastonbury, Colchester and Reading, "that as many as be of that traitorous religion [*i.e.*, Order] that those abbots were of, at the next [assizes] may have their bald crowns as well shaven as theirs were."

On such suspicions as these the Abbot of Abingdon was called up to London and examined by Crumwell himself, whilst one of his monks was removed from the abbey to Bishop Shaxton's prison, evidently for his opinions on religious questions of the day, since he is designated by the Bishop as "the popish monk." Again one of Crumwell's spies reported his grave doubts as to Sir Thomas Eliot. It appears that Eliot had given out that he had himself told Crumwell that "the Imperator of Almayn never spoke of the Bishop of Rome but he raised his bonnet," and that he consorted in the country with "the vain-glorious Abbot of Eynesham," and with Dr. Holyman, evidently a relative of Dom John Holyman, the monk of Reading, and incumbent of "Hanborough, a mile of Eynesham," who is noted as "a base priest and privy fautor of the Bishop of Rome." Moreover, "he was marvellous familiar," so said the spy, "with the Abbot of Reading and Doctor London, Warden of New College, Oxon," a man, it is to be observed, in every way of different mind from his namesake, Dr. London, the royal Visitor.

A letter from Eliot to Crumwell, in which he expresses his willingness to give up his popish books and strives to remove from the mind of the all-powerful vicar-general of the king the suspicion that he was "an advancer of the pompous authority of the Bishop of Rome," gives some insight into the nature of his communications with the suspected abbots. There "hath happened," he says, "no little contention betwixt me and such persons as ye have thought that I especially favoured, even as ye also did,[1] for some laudable qualities which we supposed to be in them; but neither they could persuade me to approve that which both my faith and reason condemned, nor I could not dissuade them from the excusing of that which all the world abhorred. This obstinacy of both parts relented the great affection betwixt us and withdrew our familiarity."[2]

In view of the prize to be won, that is, the broad acres and other possessions of the great monastic houses, any very definite enquiry as to the opinions of the inmates was not at once pressed home. Crumwell played a waiting game. The situation at Reading Abbey is well described by Dr. London, the Visitor and royal agent in dissolving the religious houses, in a letter written to Crumwell whilst occupied in suppressing the Grey Friars' house in the town. "My lord," he writes of the abbot, "doubteth my being here very sore, yet I have not seen him since I came, nor been at his house, except yesterday to hear Mass. The last time I was here he said, as they all do, that he was at the king's command, but loathe be they to come to any free surrender."[3]

---

[1] The writer here evidently refers to the Abbot of Reading in particular.

[2] Strype, *Ecclesiastical Memorials*, ii, ii, p. 229.

[3] Gairdner, *Calendar*, xiii, ii, No. 5.

Still Crumwell evidently hesitated to try conclusions, and so matters remained for another year until he had obtained his Act of Parliament which provided for the case of a house "happening to come to the king's highness by attainder or attainders of treason." By the autumn of the year 1539 he was prepared for the final issue in the case of Reading. We have no records giving the details of Abbot Cook's arrest and his conveyance to the Tower. There is only the ominous entry in Crumwell's *Remembrances* early in September: "For proceeding against the abbots of Glaston, Reading and other in their countries." The Abbot of Reading seems to have been the first to be arrested, and there can be no doubt that they all remained for near two months in the Tower and were all subjected to the same enquiries. There is evidence to show that at Reading many arrests were made when the abbot was taken. A list of the prisoners in the Tower on November 20th, 1539, includes the following, all connected with the abbey and town: Roger London, monk of Reading, Peter Lawrence, Warden of the Grey Friars at Reading, Giles Coventry, who was a friar of the same house, George Constantine, Richard Manchester and William Moor, "the blind harper;"[1] and in one of Crumwell's *Remembrances* at this time there is noted: "Item to proceed against the Abbots of Reading, Glaston, Rugg, Bachyler, London, the Grey Friars and Heron."

Abbot Cook, like the Abbot of Glastonbury, underwent examination and practical condemnation in the Tower before being sent down to his "country to be tried and executed." What was the head and chief of

---

[1] B. Mus., Cott. MS., Titus B, i, f. 133.

his offence we may take from the testimony of the hostile witness so freely used.

"It will make many beware to put their fingers in the fire any more," he says, "either for the honour of Peter and Paul or for the right of the Roman Church. No, not for the pardon of the pope himself, though he would grant more pardon than all the popes that ever were have granted. I think, verily, our mother holy Church of Rome hath not so great a jewel of her own darling Reynold Poole as she should have had of these abbats if they could have conveyed all things cleanly. Could not our English abbats be contented with English forked caps but must look after Romish cardinal hats also? Could they not be contented with the plain fashion of England but must counterfeit the crafty cardinality of Reynold Poole? Surely they should have worn their cardinal hats with as much shame as that papistical traitor, Reynold Poole. . . . Could not our popish abbats beware of Reynold Poole, of that bottomless whirlpool, I say, which is never satiate of treason?"

Carried down to Reading for the mockery of justice, called a trial, the abbot and his companions could not swerve from their belief and their Faith, but they maintained that this was not treason against the king. "When these traitors," says the libeller, "were arraigned at the bar, although they had confessed before and written it with their own hands that they had committed high treason against the king's majesty, yet they found all the means they could to go about to try themselves true men, which was impossible to bring to pass."

The writer's object was not to state the facts, but to cover the memory of the dead men with obloquy. Taking the document, however, as a whole, and bearing in mind the interpretation placed on the word treason at that time, there is no difficulty in penetrating into his meaning.

On November 15th, the same day upon which Abbot Whiting suffered at Glastonbury, the Abbot of Reading and two priests, John Eynon and John Rugg, were brought out to suffer the death of traitors. Here the same ghastly scene was enacted as at Glastonbury; the stretching on the hurdle, the dragging through the streets of the town. Abbot Cook, standing in the space before the gateway of his abbey, spoke to the people who in great numbers had gathered to witness the strange spectacle of the execution of a lord abbot of the great and powerful monastery of Reading. He told them of the cause for which he and his companions were to die, not fearing openly to profess that which Henry's laws made it treason to hold—fidelity to the See of Rome, which he went on to point out was but the common faith of those who had the best right to declare the true teaching of the English Church. "The Abbot of Reading, at the day of his death lamenting the miserable end that he was come unto," says our authority, perverting words and deeds to the greater glory of the king, "confessed before a great sight of people, and said that he might thank these four privy traitors before named of his sore fall, as who should say that those three bishops and the vicar of Croydon had committed no less treason than he had done. Now, good Lord for his Passion, who would have thought that these four holy men would have wrought in their lifetime such detestable treason?" And later on, speaking of the three abbots: "God caused, I say, not only their treason to be disclosed and come abroad in such a wonderful sort as never was heard of, which were too long to recite at this time, but also dead men's treason that long lay hidden under the ground; that is to say, the treason of the old bishop of Canterbury [Warham], the treason of the old bishop of St. Asaph [Standish], the treason of the old vicar of Croydon, and the treason of the old bishop of London [Stokesley], which four traitors had concealed as much treason by their lives' time as any of these traitors that were put to death.[1] There was never a barrel better herring to choose [among] them all, as it right well appeared by the Abbat of Reading's confession made at the day of [execution], who I daresay accused none of them for malice nor hatred. For the abbat as heartily loved those holy fathers as ever he loved any men in his life."

Thus, from the scaffold with the rope round his neck, and on the verge of eternity, the venerable abbot gave a witness to the veneration traditional in these islands from the earliest ages for the See of Rome, "in which the Apostles daily sit, and their blood shows forth without intermission the glory of God."[2]

When the abbot had finished, John Eynon,[3] the abbot's

---

[1] This reference to Warham, Stokesley, etc., shows that what was in question throughout the proceedings was the papal *versus* the royal authority.

[2] In these terms the first council of Arles, in 314, addressed Pope St. Silvester. This is the first known official act proceeding from bishops of the British Church.

[3] The usual spelling of this name has been Onyon or Oynyon, but it really was Eynon. It is so spelt in the document already referred to (*Calendar*, xi, No. 1231), and also in the accurate entry of the conviction, to be found on the Controlment Roll, 31 Hen. VIII, m. 28 d. "Recordum attinctionis, &c., Hugonis abbatis monasterii de Redyng in dict. com. Berks. alias dicti Hugonis Cooke, nuper de Redyng in eodem com. Berks. clerici; Johannis Eynon nupe

"chief counsellor," also spoke, evidently in the same sense, and begged the prayers of the bystanders for his soul, and the king's forgiveness if in aught he had offended.[1] This over, the sentence of hanging with its barbarous accessories was carried out upon Abbot Cook and the two priests, John Eynon and John Rugg.[2]

de Redyng in com. pred. clerici; Johannis Rugge nuper de Redyng in com. Berks. clerici alias dict. Johannis Rugge nuper de Redyng capellani, pro quibusdam altis proditionibus unde eorum quilibet pro se indictus fuit, tractus et suspensus."

[1] It would seem that at the trial some attempt was made to implicate Eynon in the Pilgrimage of Grace, in connection with which his name had been mentioned in 1536; and this is doubtless the "treason" which the hostile witness declares that he not only denied, "but also stoutly and stubbornly withstood it even to the utmost, evermore finding great fault with justice, and oftentimes casting his arms abroad, said: 'Alas, is this justice to destroy a man guiltless? I take it between God and my soul that I am as clear in this matter as the child that was this night born.' Thus he prated and made a work as though he had not known what the matter had meant, thinking to have faced it out with a card of ten. And in this sort he held on even from the time of the arraignment till he came to the gallows. Marry then, when he saw none other way but one, his heart began somewhat to relent. Then both he and his companions, with their ropes about their necks, confessed before all the people that were present that they had committed high treason against the king's most noble person, but namely Oynyon, for he said that he had offended the king's grace in such sort of treason that it was not expedient to tell thereof. Wherefore he besought the people not only to pray unto God for him, but also desired them, or some of them at the least, to desire the king's grace of his merciful goodness to forgive it his soul, for else he was sure, as he said, to be damned. And yet, not an hour before, a man that had heard him speak would have thought verily that he had been guiltless of treason."

[2] Eynon was, as before stated, a priest attached to the church of St. Giles, Reading. John Rugg had formerly held a prebend at Chichester, but had apparently retired to Reading. In December

The attainder of the abbot, according to the royal interpretation of the law, placed the Abbey of Reading and its lands and possessions at Henry's disposal. In fact, as in the case of Glastonbury, on the removal of the abbot to the Tower in September, 1539, before either trial or condemnation, the pillage of the abbey had been commenced. As early as September 8th Thomas Moyle wrote from Reading that he, " master Vachell and Mr. Dean of York" (Layton) had "been through the inventory of the plate, etc., at the residence" there. " In the house," he said, "is a chamber hanged with three pieces of metely good tapestry. It will serve well for hanging a mean little chamber in the king's majesty's house." This is all they think worth keeping for the royal use. "There is also," the writer adds, "a chamber hung with six pieces of verdure with fountains, but it is old and at the ends of some of them very foul and greasy." He notes several beds with silk hangings, and in the church eight pieces of tapestry, "very goodly" but small, and concludes by saying that he and his fellows think that the sum of £200 a year "will serve for pensions for the monks."[1]

1531 (*Calendar*, v), Rugg writes for his books to be sent to Reading from Chichester. Another letter, dated Feb. 3, 1532, from "your abbey-lover Jo. Rugg" shows that the writer had obtained dispensation for non-residence at Chichester. Coates (*Reading*, p. 261), on the authority of Croke, says that John Rugg was indicted for saying "the king's highness cannot be Supreme Head of the Church of England." On being asked "What did you for saving your conscience when you were sworn to take the king for Supreme Head?" Rugg replied, "I added this condition in my mind, to take him for Supreme Head in temporal things, but not in spiritual things."

[1] R. O. *Crumwell Correspondence*, xxix, No. 76. In the "Corporation diary," quoted in Coates' *Reading*, p. 261, is the entry " before which said nineteenth of September (1539), the monastery

On September 15th another commissioner, Richard Pollard, wrote from Reading that he had dispatched certain goods according to Crumwell's direction "and part of the stuff reserved for the king's majesty's use." "The whole house and church are," he says, "still undefaced," and "as for the plate,[1] vestments, copes and hangings, which we have reserved" to the king's use, they are left in good custody and are to be at once conveyed to London. "Thanks be to God," he adds, "everything is well finished, and every man well contented, and giveth humble thanks to the king's grace."[2]

is suppressed and the abbot is deprived, and after this suppression all things remain in the king's hands."

[1] In Pollard's account of the plate of "attainted persons and places" (*Monastic Treasures, Abbotsford Club*, p. 38) Reading is credited with 19½ ounces of gold, 377 ounces of gilt plate, and 2,660 ounces of silver. It is also stated that the abbot put "to gage to Sir W. Luke three gilt bowls of 152 ounces and six silver bowls of 246 ounces."

[2] Wright, 220. Mr. Wright thinks this letter "must refer to the priory and not to the abbey." A letter from William Penison, to whom Pollard says he committed the charge "by indenture," says that on September 11th he "received possession of the Abbey of Reading and all the domains which the late abbot had in his hands at his late going away" (R. O. *Crumwell Correspondence*, vol. xxxii, No. 36). This letter shows that, to William Penison, Abbot Cook was *late* abbot—in other words, had ceased to hold the office when he was taken away to the Tower for examination early in September.

CHAPTER IX

THE LAST ABBOT OF COLCHESTER

THE Abbot of St. John's, Colchester, Thomas Marshall,[1] writes Browne Willis, " was one of the three mitred parliamentary abbots that had courage enough to maintain his conscience and run the last extremity, being neither to be prevailed upon by bribery, terror or any dishonourable motives to come into a surrender, or subscribe to the king's supremacy; on which account, being attainted of high treason, he suffered death."

Thomas Marshall succeeded Abbot Barton in June, 1533, and entered upon the cares of office at a time when religious life was becoming almost impossible. At the outset he had apparently considerable difficulty in obtaining possession of the temporalities of his abbey. " I, with the whole consent of my brethren," he writes to Crumwell, " have sealed four several obligations for the

---

[1] Thomas Marshall was also called Beche. It may be worth while here, as some confusion has existed as to the last Abbot of Colchester, to give the evidence of the Controlment Roll, 31 Hen. VIII, m. 36d, which leaves no room for doubt that Beche and Marshall are *aliases* for the same person. " Recordum attinctionis Thomæ Beche nuper de West Donylands, in com. Essex, clerici, alias dicti Thomæ Marshall nuper de eisdem villa et comit., clerici, alias Thomæ Beche nuper abbatis nuper monasterii S. Johannis Bapt. juxta Colcestr., in com. pred. jam dissolut. alias dicti Thomæ Marshall nuper abb. nuper mon. S. Johis. Colcestr. in com. pred. pro quibusdam altis proditionibus." West Donylands was a manor belonging to the abbot, and the name occurs in exchanges made by the abbot with Chancellor Audley in 1536 (see *Calendar*, xi, Nos. 385, 519).

payment of £200 to the king's use, trusting now by your especial favour to have restitution of my temporalities with all other things pertaining to the same. Unless I have your especial favour and aid in recovering such rents and dues as are withdrawn from the monastery of late, and I not able to recover them by the law, I cannot tell how I shall live in the world, saving my truth and promises." [1]

Of the earlier career of Thomas Marshall little is known except that he, like the majority of his Order in England who were selected by their superiors for a university course, was sent to Oxford, where he resided for several years, and passed through the schools with credit to himself and his Order. During this period he was probably an inmate of St. Benedict's or Gloucester Hall, the largest of the three establishments which the Benedictines possessed in Oxford, and to which the younger religious of most of the English abbeys were sent to pursue their higher studies. [2]

[1] R. O. *Crumwell Correspondence*, vi, f. 145. The temporalities were restored on Jan. 23rd, 1534, and on March 30th of this same year the new abbot took his seat in the House of Lords. It has been thought that Marshall is the same Thomas Marshall who ruled the abbey of Chester until 1530, and is counted as the twenty-sixth abbot of that house (*Monasticon*, iv). Whether, on his retirement from Chester in favour of the reinstated abbot, John Birchenshaw, he went to Colchester is uncertain. If he had been long at this latter monastery it is somewhat strange that the witnesses against him in 1539 should have professed to be unacquainted with him until his election.

[2] St. Benedict's is now represented by Worcester College; Canterbury Hall, destined for the monks of the metropolitan church, is now merged in Christ Church; and Trinity College has succeeded to St. Cuthbert's Hall, the learned home of the monks of Durham. D. Thomas Marshall, O.S.B., supplicated for B.D. January 24, 1508-9; disputed 3rd June, 1511; admitted to oppose, 19th Oct.;

Very shortly after Abbot Marshall's election his troubles commenced. At Colchester, as elsewhere in the country at this period, there were to be found some only too anxious to win favour to themselves by carrying reports of the doings and sayings of their brethren to Crumwell or the king. In April, 1534, a monk of St. John's complained of the "slanderous and presumptuous" sayings of the sub-prior, " D. John Francis." This latter monk, according to Crumwell's informer, had "declared our sovereign lord the king and his most honourable council, on the occasion of a new book of articles, to be all heretics, whereas before he said they were but schismatics." [1] These and other remarks were quite sufficient to have brought both the bold monk himself and his abbot into trouble, at a time when the gossip of the fratry or shaving-house was picked up by eavesdroppers and carried to court to regale the ears of the Lord Privy Seal. In this case, however, the report came on the eve of the administration to the monks of Colchester of what was to be henceforth considered the touchstone of loyalty, the oath of supremacy. On the 7th of July, 1534, the oath was offered to the monks in the chapter house of St. John's, and taken by Abbot Marshall and sixteen monks, including Dom John Francis, the sub-prior complained of to Crumwell.

Very little indeed is known about Colchester or the doings of the abbot from this time till his arrest in 1539. At the time of the northern rising, whilst the commissioners for gaol-delivery sat at Colchester, they were in-

received the degree of S.T.B., 10th Dec.; sued for D.D. and disputed 20th April, 1515. Boase, *Register of the University of Oxford*, p. 63.

[1] *Calendar*, 1534, Ap. viii.

vited to dine at the abbey with the Abbot of St. John's. When they were at dinner, as Crumwell's informant writes to him, one Marmaduke Nevill and others came into the hall. " I asked him," says the writer, "' How do the traitors in the north?' 'No traitors, for if ye call us traitors we will call you heretics.'" Nevill then went on to say that the king had pardoned them, or they had not been at Colchester. They were, he declared, 30,000 well-horsed, and " I am sure," he said, " my lord abbot will make me good cheer;" and asked why, said, " Marry, for all the abbeys in England be beholden to us, for we have set up all the abbeys again in our country, and though it were never so late they sang Matins the same night." He added that in the north they were "plain fellows," and southern men, though they "thought as much, durst not utter it."[1]

Another glimpse of the life led by the Abbot of Colchester during the few troubled years of his authority is afforded by a writer of a slightly subsequent period:

"Those who can call to mind the cruel deeds of Henry VIII, the confusion of things sacred and profane, and the slaughterings of which he was the author, will have no difficulty in recollecting the case of John Beche, Abbat of Colchester. Excelling many of the abbats of his day in devotion, piety and learning, the sad fate of the cardinal (Fisher) and the execution of Sir Thomas More oppressed him with grief and bitterness. For he had greatly loved them; and as he had honoured them when living, so now that they had so gladly suffered death for the Church's unity, he began to reverence and venerate them, and often and much did he utter to that

[1] *Calendar*, xi, 1319.

effect, and made his friends partakers of his grief which
the late events had caused him. And he was in the
habit of extolling the piety, meekness, and innocence of
the late martyrs to those guests whom he invited to his
table, and who came to him of their own will, some of
whom assented to his words, while others listened in
silence. There came at length a traitorous guest, a
violator of the sacred rights of hospitality, who by his
words incited the abbat to talk about the execution of
the cardinal and More, hoping to entrap him in his
speech. Thereon the abbat, who could not be silent on
such a theme, spoke indeed in their praise but with
moderation and sparingly, adding at last that he marvelled what cause of complaint the king could have
found in men so virtuous and learned, and the greatest
ornaments of Church and State, as to deem them unworthy of longer life, and to condemn them to a most
cruel death. These words did this false friend carry
away in his traitorous breast, to make them known in
due season to the advisers of the king. What need of
more? The abbat is led to the same tribunal which had
condemned both Fisher and More, and there received
the like sentence of death; yea, his punishment was the
more cruel than theirs, for in his case no part of the
sentence was remitted. Thus he was added as the third
to the company of the two former. But why should I
call him the third, and try to enumerate the English
martyrs of that time, who are past counting? The
writers of our annals mention many by name, but there
were many more whose names they could not ascertain,
whose number is known to God alone, for whose cause
they died. Yet I hope that some day God will make
known their names and the resting-places of their bodies,

LEWIS AND CLARK COLLEGE LIBRARY
PORTLAND,   OREGON   97219

which were in life the dwelling-places of His Holy Spirit."[1]

About the time of the arrest of the Abbots of Reading and Glastonbury, in September, 1539, reports were spread as to the approaching dissolution of St. John's, Colchester. Sir Thomas Audley, the Chancellor, endeavoured to avert what he thought would be an evil thing for the county. He had heard the rumours about the destruction of the two abbeys of St. John's, Colchester, and St. Osyth's, and, writing to Crumwell, he begs they may continue, "not, as they be, religious; but that the king's majesty of his goodness to translate them into colleges. For the which, as I said to you before, his grace may have of either of them £1,000, that is for both £2,000, and the gift of the deans and prebendaries at his own pleasure. The cause I move this is, first, I consider that St. John's standeth in his grace's own town at Colchester, wherein dwell many poor people who have daily relief of the house. Another cause, both these houses be in the end of the shire of Essex, where little hospitality will be kept if these be dissolved. For as for St. John's it lacketh water, and St. Osyth's standeth in the marshes, not very wholesome, so that few of reputation, as I think, will keep continual houses in any of them unless it be a congregation as there is now. There are also twenty houses, great and small, dissolved in the shire of Essex already." Audley then goes on to protest that he only asks for the common good, and can get no advantage himself by the houses being allowed to continue, and concludes by offering Crumwell £200 for himself if he can persuade the king to grant his request.[2]

[1] B. Mus. Arundel MS., 152, f. 235d.   [2] Wright, p. 246.

The circumstances attending Abbot Marshall's arrest are unknown, but by the beginning of November, 1539, he was certainly in the Tower. On the 1st of that month Edmund Crowman, who had been his servant ever since he had been abbot, was under examination. All that was apparently extracted from this witness was that a year before the abbot had given him certain plate to take care of and "£40 in a coser."[1]

The abbot's chaplain was also interrogated as to any words he had heard the abbot speak against the king at any time, but little information was elicited from him. The most important piece of evidence is a document, which, as it contains declarations as to Abbot Marshall's opinions upon several important matters, and as it is almost the only record of the examinations of witnesses against any of the three abbots, and gives a sample of the questions on which all these examinations in the Tower concerning treason must have turned, may here be given as nearly as possible in the original form.

"Interrogatories ministered unto Robert Rowse, mercer, of Colchester, 4ᵗᵒ Novembris anno regni Henrici octavi tricesimo primo (1539). Ad primam, the said Rowse sworne upon the Evangel, and sayeth that he hath known the Abbat of Colchester the space of six years at midsummer last past or thereabout, about which time the said —— was elected abbat.[2] And within a sennight after or thereabout this examinant sent unto the said abbat a dish of bass (baces) and a pottle of wine to the welcome. Upon the which present the said abbat did send for the examinant to dine with him upon a Friday, at which time they were first acquainted, and

---

[1] R. O. *Crumwell Correspondence*, xxxviii, No. 42.
[2] D. Thomas Marshall or Beche was elected June 10th, 1533.

since was divers times in his company and familiar with him unto a fortnight before the feast of All Hallows was two years past.—ROBERT ROWSE.

2. Ad secundam, he sayeth that the principal cause why that he did leave the company of the said abbat was because that abbat was divers times communing and respuing against the king's majesty's

Supremacy.

supremacy and such ordinances as were passed by the Act of Parliament concerning the extinguishment of the bishop of Rome's usurped authority,

The whole authority committed to Peter.

saying that the whole authority was given by Christ unto Peter and to his successors, bishops of Rome, to bind and to loose, and to grant pardons for sin, and to be chief and supreme head of the Church throughout all Christian realms immediate and next unto Christ, and that it was

Against the supremacy.

against God's commandment and His laws that any temporal prince should be head of the Church. And also he said that the king's highness had evil counsel that moved him to take on hand to be chief head of the Church of England and to pull down these houses of religion which were founded by his grace's progenitors and many noble men for the service and honour of God, the commonwealth, and relief of poor

Against man's law and God's law.

folk, and that the same was both against God's law and man's law; and furthermore, he said that by means of the premises the king and his council were drawn into such an inordinate covetousness that if all the water in the Thames were

Covetous.

A vengeance.

flowing gold and silver it were not able to slake their covetousness, and said a vengeance of all such councillors.—ROBERT ROWSE.

3. Ad tertiam, he sayeth that he is not well remem-

bered of the year nor of the days that the said abbat had
the foresaid communications because he spoke at divers
times, and specially at such times as he heard that any
such matters were had in use, and furthermore of this
he is well remembered of that at such time as the monks
of Syon, the Bishop of Rochester, and Sir Thomas More
were put to execution, the said abbat would say that he
marvelled greatly of such tyranny as was
used by the king and his council to put   Tyranny.
such holy men to death, and further the abbat said that
in his opinion they died holy martyrs and
in the right of Christ's Church.—ROBERT   Died martyrs.
ROWSE.

4. Ad quartam, he sayeth that the last time that ever
he heard the said abbat have any communication of
such matters was, immediately after that he heard of the
insurrection in the north parts, he sent for this examinant to come to sup with him, and in the mean time that
supper was making ready the abbat and the examinant
were walking between the hall and the garden in a little
gallery off the ground, and then and there the abbat
asked of this examinant what news he heard of the coast?
and this examinant said that he heard none. Then the
abbat said: "Dost you not hear of the insurrection in
the north?" and this examinant said "no."   Northern
"The northern lads be up and they begin   men.
to take pip in the webe (*sic*) and say plainly that they
will have no more abbeys suppressed in their country;"
and he said to this examinant that the northern men
were as true subjects unto the king as anywhere within
his realm, and that they desired nothing of the king but
that they might have delivered unto their hands the
Archbishop of Canterbury, the Lord Chancellor, and

the Lord Privy Seal; and the abbat said "would to

God that the northern men had them, for

That these lords might be delivered to the northern men. then (he said) we should have a merry world, for they were three arch-heretics," which term this examinant never heard

before; and so then they went to supper,

Arch-heretics. and since this time, which was as this examinant doth remember a fortnight or three weeks before the feast of All Saints, was two years.—ROBERT ROWSE.[1]

The evidence of Thomas Nuthake, a "physition," of Colchester, is to the like effect. He had not, he said, to his knowledge seen or known Abbot Thomas before his election, although he had divers times repaired to the abbey before that time. In reply to the third question, this doctor "sayeth that concerning the marriage of queen Anne this examinant remembers he hath heard the said abbat say that the reason why the king's highness did forsake the bishop of Rome was to the intent that his majesty might be divorced from the lady dowager and wed queen Anne, and therefore his grace refused to take the bishop of Rome for the supreme head of the Church, and made himself the supreme head."[2]

Another of the witnesses against the Lord Abbot of Colchester was a cleric, John Seyn, who deposed that when he had informed him of his neighbour, the Abbot of St. Osyth's surrender of his monastery to the king, he answered, "I will not say the king shall never have *my* house, but it will be against my will and against my

---

[1] R. O. State Papers, Dom., 1539, $\frac{v}{207}$. The marginal notes copied from the original document, indicate the chief points on which the examination turned.

[2] *Ibid.*, $\frac{v}{206}$.

heart, for I know by my learning that he cannot take it by right and law, wherefore in my conscience I cannot be content, nor he shall never have it with my heart and will." Whereunto John Seyn, clerk, answered in this wise: "Beware of such learning as ye learned at Oxenford when ye were young. Ye would be hanged and ye are worthy. I will advise you to conform yourself as a true subject, or else you shall hinder your brethren and also yourself." [1]

Nothing more is known of Abbot Marshall's last days, but the fact of his execution as a traitor on December 1st, 1539. The enamelled pectoral cross of the venerable martyr has been preserved, and is now in the possession of the Lord Clifford of Chudleigh. One one side it bears the emblems of the Five Wounds, in the centre the Sacred Heart of our Lord, surrounded by the crown of thorns, above which is the inscription, "I.N.R.I.," and below it the sacred monogram, "I.H.S." with the wounded hands and feet of our Saviour. On the back the instruments of the Passion are engraved. The following inscriptions in Latin appear in and about the cross: " May the Passion of our Lord Jesus Christ bring us out of sorrow and sadness. This sign of the cross shall be in the heavens when our Lord shall come to judgment. Behold, O man! thy Redeemer suffers for thee. He who will come after me, let him take up his cross and follow me."

It is curious to observe how frequently in this world malice defeats its own ends even when it takes the guise, to some persons apparently so attractive, of doing God a service. It is by a singular fate that the would-be

[1] R. O. *Crumwell Correspondence*, xxxviii, No. 41.

preacher, who gave himself so much trouble to defame the three Abbots of Glastonbury, Reading and Colchester and their companions, in the expectation doubtless of thereby recommending himself to the king, should have been, after three centuries and a half of oblivion, the most explicit witness of the cause for which these venerable men gave up their lives in all the terrors of as shameful and painful a death as man could devise.

The writer himself amid the periods which betoken his unhappy spirit, seems to have been haunted still with some forebodings that he was destined to make manifest a truth which it was the evident design of those in power to shroud in obscurity. He cannot help being truculent even at his best; but the form which he adopts may well be pardoned for the sake of the sense. " Is it not to be thought, trow ye," he says, "that forasmuch as these trusty traitors have so valiantly jeopardied a joint for the Bishop of Rome's sake, that his Holiness will after their hanging canvass them, canonise them, I would say, for their labours and pains. It is not to be doubted but his Holiness will look upon their pains as upon Thomas Becket's, seeing it is for like matter."

Much has since happened which the writer of these words could not have anticipated. In God's hands are times and seasons, and He alone it is Who judges rightly the acts and lives of men. The words of the wise man fittingly rise up in the mind as it recalls the story of the deaths of these holy abbots. " In the sight of the unwise they seemed to die: and their departure was taken for misery, and their going away from us for utter destruction: but they are in peace. And though in the sight of men they suffered torments, their hope is full of immortality. Afflicted in few things, in many they shall be well rewarded; because God has tried them and found them worthy of Himself. As gold in the furnace He hath proved them, and as a victim of a holocaust He hath received them, and in time there shall be respect had unto them." [1]

APPENDIX I

IN view of the want of information as to the internal arrangement of the monasteries on the eve of their suppression, caused by the wholesale destruction of documents, and especially as regards the music and church services, the following paper printed in the *Reliquary* (*New Series*, vol. vi, p. 176) seems of sufficient interest to be given here.

From the document it may be gathered that at Glastonbury there were always three organists: a chief organist and master of the singing boys, appointed for life; and two youths, who in consideration of a musical education, were bound (after two years' instruction) to serve as assistant organists for six years. It must be understood that the chief duties of these organists and of the singing boys were confined to the Masses and offices chanted in the chapel of the Blessed Virgin. These were, of course, not monastic, that is to say, they were outside of the ordinary conventual life, and were not followed necessarily by the monks. These services were evidently carried out with every accessory calculated to call forth popular devotion to the Blessed Virgin, and there can be little doubt that the sweet strains of melody heard every day in this special sanctuary of the Mother of God attracted thither high and low, rich and poor, who might find as an ordinary rule but little to call them to the more formal and simple offices daily said by the monks themselves in the high choir.

It is this music in the chapels of Our Blessed Lady in

[1] Wisd., iii, 2-6.

monasteries *apud Britannos,* which calls forth the censures of
that occasionally severe and always erratic moralist Erasmus
(*Annot. ad* 1 Cor. xiv, 26).

We have no means of saying whether on festival days the
monks of Glastonbury themselves used "that depraved kind of
chant called *faubourdon,*" though few persons at the present
day will be inclined to see in the use of what is called "har-
monised gregorians" any great enormity. It is, however, certain that on feasts and festal days the monastic offices in the
"High Choir" of Glastonbury were accompanied with such
beauty of music as the presence of the singing-school and the
playing upon the organs, under the care of the chief organist,
could give. For the rest the document will repay a careful
perusal, and for those who are interested in the subject of
ecclesiastical music in England at a time when it was assidu-
ously cultivated, the indications and suggestions which it gives
will be found to possess a high degree of interest. The spelling of the document has been modernised.

"This indenture made the tenth day of August, the 26th
year of the reign of our Sovereign Lord King Henry VIII
[*i.e.,* 1534], between the Right Reverend Father in God,
Richard Whiting, Abbot of the Monastery of Our Blessed
Lady of Glastonbury and the Convent of the same, in the
county of Somerset, of the one part, and James Renynger of
Glastonbury foresaid, in the said county, Singingman, of the
other part, witnesseth that the said James Renynger hath
covenanted and granted and agreed, and by these presents
covenants, grants, and agrees to serve the said Reverend
Father and Convent, and their successors in the Monastery of
Glastonbury foresaid, in his faculty of singing and playing
upon the organs [for the] term of his life as well in [the] daily
services of Our Lady kept in the chapel of Our Blessed Lady
in Glastonbury foresaid, as daily Matins, Masses, Evensongs,
Compline, Anthems and all other divine services as hath been
accustomably used to be sung in the said chapel of Our
Blessed Lady of Glastonbury before the time of these cove-

nants. And to do service in singing and playing upon the organs in the high choir of Glastonbury foresaid on all and all manner such feasts and festival days as hath been in times past used and accustomed there.

" And in likewise to serve the said Reverend Father and his successors with songs and playing on instruments of music as in the times of Christmas and other seasons, as hath been heretofore used and accustomed and at any other time or times when the said James Renynger shall be thereunto required by the said Reverend Father, his successor or assigns. And further the said James Renynger covenants, grants and agrees to instruct and teach six children always at the pleasure of the said Reverend Father or his successors for the chapel of Our Blessed Lady in Glastonbury, sufficiently, lawfully and melodiously with all his diligence in pricksong and descant; of the which six children, two of them yearly to be sufficiently instructed and taught by the said James Renynger in playing on the organs for the space of two years; the said children to be always chosen at the pleasure of the said Reverend Father and his successors which he or they shall think to be most apt thereto, so that the friends of the two children will be bound in sufficient bonds that the said two children and any of them shall serve the said Reverend Father and his successors in singing and playing on the organs daily in the said chapel of Our Lady and high choir of the Monastery of Glastonbury aforesaid, and other times of the year in manner and form as before rehearsed, for the space of six years next ensuing the said two years of their teaching in singing and playing. And the said Reverend Father and his successors shall find the said James Renynger clavicords to teach the said two children to play upon, for the which service well and truly done the said Reverend Father and Convent covenants and grants to the said James Renynger during his life as well in sickness as in health ten pounds of lawful money of England, as well for his stipend as for his meat and drink, at four principal times of the year in equal portions at the Right Reverend Father's chequer of receipt in Glastonbury to be taken and received, and also once in every year his livery gown or else thirteen shillings and fourpence in money for the said gown, always at the pleasure and election of the said Reverend Father and his successors: also two loads of wood brought home to the said James Renynger's house or chamber (and his house rent free, or else thirteen shillings and fourpence a year for it). Always (supposing) that if it happen the said James Renynger be taken up by virtue of any of the King's commissions, or by any authority of his, to serve his grace, that if the same James Renynger come to Glastonbury again within one year and one day the next following, and so from thenceforth do his diligent service in singing and playing on the organs, and teaching children at all times and in everything accordingly in manner and form as is before rehearsed, that then he should have his perpetuity again without any interruption or let; and also if it happen the said James Renynger does not do his diligence in teaching and instructing the said six children in singing and playing, as is before rehearsed, to the pleasure of the said Reverend Father or his successors, or else if it happen that the said James be sick or aged so that he cannot well and diligently instruct and teach the said children, then it shall be lawful to the said Reverend Father and his successors as Abbots, of the said ten pounds (to deduct) for the teaching and instructing of the said six children yearly 105s. 4d.

" In witness whereof to the one part of these present indentures remaining with the said James Renynger, the aforesaid Reverend Father, Richard Whityng, Abbot of the foresaid Monastery of Glastonbury, and Convent of the same have put their convent seal and to the other part, remaining with the said foresaid Reverend Father and Convent, the foresaid James Renynger has put his seal.

" Given at Glastonbury aforesaid the day above said."

APPENDIX II

THE following is a translation of an old paper kept with the pectoral cross of the last Abbot of Colchester. "This gold and enamelled cross belonged to Abbot John Beche, last superior of the Benedictine Abbey of St. John's, Colchester, in the county of Suffolk in England. He was elected Abbot in 1523, and refused, at the same time as the Abbots of Glastonbury and Reading, the act by which Henry VIII, King of England, was declared head of the Church, or to resign to his Majesty the property of his abbey. For this reason he was convicted of treason, and hanged in the said town of Colchester on December 1st, 1539.

"This cross was preserved in the Mannock family, whose seat was in the neighbourhood of Colchester, up to the time of the last baronet, Sir George Mannock, who gave it to the English Benedictine nuns then at Brussels, and since settled in Winchester, where two of his sisters were nuns. About the year 1788, the cross was given by the abbess of that community to the late Mr. Weld, whose aunt had long lived among them."

In this account there are certain inaccuracies which, however, do not affect the truth of the tradition as to the cross. The Mannocks' family seat was Gifford Hall, not far from Colchester and in the county of Suffolk. The Mannocks never lost the Catholic faith, and at least four members of the family were professed among the English Benedictine nuns of Brussels in the last century. One of these, Dame Etheldreda Mannock, was Abbess from 1762 to 1773. Three of the nuns were sisters to Sir George Mannock, who presented Abbot Beche's cross to the community. The Abbess, Etheldreda Mannock, was succeeded in her office by Dame Mary Ursula Pigott—a name, like that of Mannock, well known in the English Benedictine *Fasti* of the last century, and to some

persons, perhaps, through the once well-known Catholic coun-
sel, Nathaniel Pigott, of Whitton, for whose family the poet
Pope, a near neighbour, entertained a high regard. It was this
Abbess who gave the cross to Mr. Weld.

During the office of Lady Abbess Pigott, the community
were forced by the Revolution to leave Brussels, and settled at
Winchester, whence in 1857 they removed to their present
abbey at East Bergholt, near Colchester.

From the Welds the cross passed through Cardinal Weld to
his only daughter, Lady Clifford. It afterwards came into the
possession of her son, the Hon. and Right Reverend William
Clifford, third Bishop of Clifton, at whose decease it passed
into the hands of his nephew, the present Lord Clifford of
Chudleigh, to whose kindness I am indebted for these details.

AUTOGRAPH SIGNATURE OF ABBOT WHITING, FROM AN ORIGINAL
LETTER IN THE RECORD OFFICE (" RIC ABBATT THER ").

II

ENGLISH BIBLICAL CRITICISM IN THE THIRTEENTH CENTURY[1]

THE "dark ages" are often held responsible for ideas wholly foreign to the mediæval spirit. Eyes also, usually keen enough for other things, not unfrequently appear to fail strangely when they peer into the darkness which is supposed to shroud those centuries. They see there what in fact does not exist, whilst they pass over what is real without any intelligent interest. Not only are shadows and illusions allowed to do duty for realities; but creations of the essentially modern mind and temper are projected into the past and subjected to criticism as substantial objects deserving the ridicule of a more enlightened age. It is strange, but true, that of many students of past ages it may be said, " Seeing they do not see, and hearing they do not understand."

As a case in point we may take the question of the Bible. In spite of all that has been written on the subject, it is still the general belief, even among well-educated Englishmen, that the possession of the Holy Scriptures was one of the most obvious and most important practical results of the Reformation to the world at large. This notion in one form or another meets us

[1] Published in the *Dublin Review*, January, 1898.

I

at every turn. Again and again, for example, it has
been pointed out and proved to be a fact from written
records, that the very literature and language of the
Middle Ages is moulded and formed upon the Scriptures. Still the result is the same; and the fundamental
article of popular belief is that it certainly was Pro-
testantism which in the sixteenth century gave to the
world any real knowledge of the Bible. It is this pre-
possession which prevents many from seeing the plain
evidence of its use and its study in the earlier centuries.
Few, however, even of those who do not allow themselves to be blinded by prejudice, really understand how
seriously and thoroughly the Scriptures were studied in
the so-called dark ages. How many are there, for
example, who realise the sound work in textual criticism which characterised the scriptural studies of the
thirteenth century? Abroad, it is true, more attention
has been paid to the matter, and the eminent French
scholar, M. Samuel Berger, and others, have written on
this special subject. In England, however, this aspect of
their work has apparently failed to attract the notice it
deserves. This is all the more strange, since England,
or at least Englishmen and English scholarship, had a
very large share in the attempts made in that century
to secure a purer text of the Latin Vulgate version of
the Bible. My purpose in the following pages is to give
a slight sketch of the history of this important movement, and specially in regard to the influence of Englishmen in it.

Our knowledge in this, as in so many other matters
connected with the history of mediæval thought and
work at this period, is mainly derived from the works
of Roger Bacon. In fact this illustrious Franciscan

philosopher had himself much to do with the subse-quent correction of the Latin Bible on what may be described as thoroughly sound principles of criticism. Hody, long ago in his work, *De Bibliorum textibus*, at great length quoted the words of Bacon on the state of the then received text, as giving the best, if not the only reliable, account of the matter. He did not, however, apparently, fully realise the extent of Bacon's personal influence in the work of correction, nor how the lines of sound critical investigation laid down by him were in reality those upon which the subsequent rectification of the sacred text was actually accomplished. Had Clement IV, the Pope to whom Bacon addressed his remarks in 1267, lived, he might in the thirteenth cen-tury, with the assistance of the English Franciscan, have anticipated the work of the Council of Trent in regard to the Latin Vulgate.

In view of the part played by Bacon in so important a matter as the determination of the text of the Bible, it may be of interest to understand something of the influences under which he received his early training. It is not very difficult to see where he first derived his ideas as to the paramount importance of biblical know-ledge, which he holds must form the foundation of all ecclesiastical studies. In fact, so strongly does he main-tain this, that it is hardly too much to say that even his scientific researches, for which he is so justly celebrated are, in his mind, subordinated to their usefulness in clearing up difficulties and more exactly determining the sacred text.

Roger Bacon, according to his own account of him-self written in A.D. 1267, commenced his studies about forty years previously, or some time about A.D. 1227.

He names as his chief masters at Oxford, Bishop Grosseteste, Friar Adam Marsh, and Thomas Wallensis, afterwards Bishop of St. David's. These three illustrious men had all taught in the Franciscan school at the University; and it was most probably owing to the influence of that great churchman and scholar Grosseteste, for whom Bacon so frequently expresses unbounded admiration, and possibly also the example of Adam Marsh, who late in life had given up a distinguished career as professor in the universities of Paris and Oxford, that he himself joined the English Franciscans. Of Adam Marsh and Bishop Grosseteste, their illustrious pupil speaks in terms of the highest praise. He considers them, he says, "perfect in all knowledge," and "the greatest clerics in the whole world, excelling in all wisdom human and divine."[1] The Bishop of St. David's he especially names as distinguished for his great knowledge of foreign languages. These three had themselves all been pupils of St. Edmund Rich, afterwards Archbishop of Canterbury, and they had evidently taken to heart their master's favourite maxim for himself and his disciples: "Study as if you were to live for ever; live as if you were to die to-morrow."

Shortly after the first establishment of the Franciscan friars at Oxford, Eccleston tells us that their first Provincial in England, Friar Agnellus, "persuaded Master Robert Grosseteste, of holy memory, to read lectures to the brethren there." Owing chiefly to the reputation of this great master, in a brief time the fame of the Franciscan school at Oxford had spread even beyond the limits of this country, and through the influence of the

---

[1] Bacon, *Opera inedita* (Rolls series), pp. 70, 74.
[2] *Mon. Franciscana*, i, p. 37.

bishop, other professors of learning and repute were induced to come and lecture to the Oxford friars. The
foundation of a school of European reputation was the
result. The first of the Franciscans to read public
lectures at Oxford was Adam Marsh, who had joined
the friars in their first fervour, and became the eminent
instrument in the formation of that school from which
came a succession of celebrated Franciscan teachers
such as Richard of Coventry, John Wallis, Thomas
Docking, Thomas Bungay, associated in popular tradition with Roger Bacon, John Peccham, the Franciscan
Archbishop of Canterbury, Richard Middleton, Duns
Scotus, Occham, and Burley. The friars at Oxford
attained a world-wide renown. Lyons, Paris, and
Bologna had their first professors from the ranks of the
English Franciscans, whilst repeated requests were
made for English friars from Ireland, Denmark, France,
and Germany, and foreigners crossed the seas to study
in this English school, established by the learned and
devout Bishop Grosseteste. " The three schoolmen of
the most profound and original genius, Roger Bacon,
Duns Scotus, and Occham, were trained at Oxford. No
other nation can show anything like the results which
sprang from the English Franciscans of Oxford. Italy
produced its St. Thomas of Aquin and St. Bonaventure;
Germany could boast its Albertus Magnus, and Spain
its Raymond Lully; but the Oxford friary was the
fruitful mother of almost every Franciscan schoolman
St. Bonaventure and Lully excepted." [1]

Grosseteste, the founder of this renowned body of
teachers, cannot have failed to impress upon the mind
of Roger Bacon his own veneration and love of Holy

[1] Cf. Brewer, *Mon. Franciscana*, i, pp. lxxx, li.

Scripture. Frequently, says Eccleston, the Bishop of
Lincoln urged the friars to study and sedulously to
occupy themselves in working at the Holy Bible.[1] Nor
were his exhortations confined to the circle of his immediate pupils among the Franciscans. As Chancellor of
the University he addressed his letters to the teachers in
the theological schools of Oxford, urging them to make
the Bible the foundation of all their lectures. " The
skilful builder," he says, " sees carefully that all the
stones put into a foundation are really proper for the
purpose; namely, that they are such as by their solidity
are fit and useful to support the building to be raised
upon them. You are the builders of the house of God,
raising it upon the foundation of the *Apostles and
Prophets*, etc.; and the foundation-stones of the building
of which you are the architects—and no one can find
others or set others in the foundation—are the books of
the Prophets, amongst whom we must count Moses, the
law-giver, and the books of the Apostles and Evange-
lists. These foundation-stones you place and set in the
foundation of your building, when by the gift of dis-
cerning spirits you expound these books to your hearers
according to the mind of the writers. Take heed therefore with all diligence not to put among the foundation-
stones, nor to use as foundation-stones what are not
such, lest the strength of your building, made to rest
upon what is no true foundation, is first shaken and
then falls to ruin. The most proper time, moreover, for
placing and setting the said stones in the foundation
(for there is a fitting time for laying the foundation and
one for raising the building) is the morning hour when
you commonly read your lectures. It is proper, there-

[1] Cf. Brewer, *Mon. Franciscana*, i, p. 64.

fore, that all your lectures be taken especially at that time, from the books of the Old or New Testament, lest otherwise what are not really foundation-stones be laid as if they were." [1]

Roger Bacon, at a later time, bitterly complains that this supremacy of Holy Scripture in theological studies, so strongly urged by the illustrious Grosseteste in the foregoing letter, was not acknowledged in practice in the University of Paris. Writing in A.D. 1267 to Pope Clement IV, he points out that *de facto* the work, called the *Book of the Sentences*, was preferred to the Bible itself in the system of education pursued. The lector of the Scripture lesson, he said, had even to beg the hour of his lecture from the teacher of the *Sentences*. The latter was regarded as *par excellence* the "Doctor of Theology," whilst the former suffered from obvious University disabilities. Whilst every other faculty, moreover, took its *text* as the basis of the lectures delivered, the text of the Bible, although all the ancient teachers had made it the subject of their readings, was, when he wrote in 1267, relegated to a secondary place in the teaching of theology.

The *Book of the Sentences*, Bacon declares, was never used by his old masters, Bishop Grosseteste, Brother Adam Marsh, "and other of the greatest men" he had seen. Alexander of Hales it was, he says, "who first read the work," and even he merely used it sometimes, just as the "*Book of the Histories* used to be, and still is, read," that is, only very rarely. The work of Peter Comestor on the *Histories*, the Franciscan philosopher holds to be much more useful and necessary for theology than the Lombard's work on the *Sentences*, because the

[1] *Roberti Grosseteste Epistolae* (Rolls series), p. 346.

first follows and explains the *text* of Holy Writ from the beginning to the end, whereas the other does not do so. For this reason, as he tells the Pope, he is strongly of the opinion that if any theological *summa* is required, it should be modelled upon the work of Peter Comestor rather than upon that of Peter the Lombard. The use, or rather, as he considers, the abuse, of the *Book of the Sentences*, must, in his opinion, tend to make people ignorant of the actual *text* of the Bible, or at best give them but a very superficial and secondary knowledge of it.[1]

As preparatory to the study of the Bible, or, at any rate, as necessary for any revision of its text, Bacon insists upon the absolute need of a fair knowledge of Hebrew and Greek, and a thorough knowledge of Latin grammatical construction.[2] Here again we can without difficulty recognise the influence of his Oxford training in the school of Marsh and Grosseteste. The former, as appears in a letter to the Minister-General of the Friars Minor in England, when giving advice to a student destined for Paris, strongly urged the need of investigating the original works of the Fathers in any exposition of Holy Scripture.[3] The latter was well known as the patron of those devoted to the study of Greek, Hebrew, and other foreign languages. In fact, England had taken the initiative in these studies, and even before the beginning of the thirteenth century Englishmen had realised the importance of helping forward a movement for the revival of letters. More than one of our countrymen was at work in foreign countries studying Eastern languages and collecting precious manuscripts. Thus,

[1] *Opera inedita*, pp. 329-330.   [2] *Ibid.*, p. 92.
[3] *Mon. Franciscana*, i.

to take an example, before the year 1200, Daniel de
Morlai had come back from Spain to England learned
in the languages and science acquired in the schools of
Toledo, and had brought with him to this island "a
precious number of books." It had grieved him, he says,
to find that even Aristotle and Plato had been so entirely forgotten in the Western world, and until he received encouragement from his friend and patron John
of Oxford, Bishop of Norwich,[1] he even hesitated to
return for fear that he should be the only one among
those he calls the "Romans" to cultivate Greek studies.
In 1224 Pope Honorius III, and three years later Pope
Gregory IX, wrote to Cardinal Langton, Archbishop of
Canterbury, in behalf of another celebrated Englishman,
Michael Scot. He had studied at Oxford, Paris, and
Toledo, and proved himself to be well versed "not only
in Latin, but also in Hebrew and Arabic," by the translations he had made of Aristotle and other philosophers
for the use of students in the Universities of the Western
world.[2] Of Grosseteste, the master he so much revered,
Bacon says that, though so learned as to be able "to
master anything he undertook, he still only knew languages well enough to understand the fathers, philosophers, and wise men of the ancients, but that he did
not know them sufficiently well to translate properly
till towards the end of his life, when he sent for Greeks
and caused them to bring books of Greek grammar to
England from Greece and elsewhere."[3] The zeal of the
bishop, however, was well known where studies of this
kind were in question. He gave preferment to two

---

[1] Arundel MS. 377, f. 88.
[2] Denifle, *Chartularium Universit. Parisiensis*, i, Nos. 48 and 54.
[3] *Opera inedita*, p. 91.

ecclesiastics who were recognised as learned men: John
of Basing, Archdeacon of St. Alban's, who some time
about 1240 returned from Athens laden with Greek
manuscripts; and Nicholas, chaplain to the Abbot of
St. Alban's, surnamed the " Greek," who is said to have
assisted the bishop in some of his translations from the
Greek.

As regards biblical translations in particular, a certain
amount of evidence exists to show that even in this
there was real work done here in England. M. Samuel
Berger has pointed to manuscripts, all or nearly all in
English libraries, and chiefly at Oxford, which contain
portions of the sacred Scripture translated from Hebrew
into Latin in the thirteenth century. The eight manuscripts to which the writer refers contain, in all, the
translation of about one-half the entire Bible from the
original. Although the translator evidently was familiarly
acquainted with French, there is nothing in the circumstances inconsistent with his being of English nationality.
The French language was at the time as much the language of the educated in this country as in France, and
the manuscripts are written in the characteristic English
writing of the period. M. Berger, after pointing this out,
adds: "It must not be forgotten that the school of
Oxford was one of the few Universities in the Middle
Ages where Hebrew was taught. Nor was there any
other seat of learning which could boast of such ability." [1]

Roger Bacon was thus prepared by his early associa-
tion with Grosseteste, Adam Marsh, and the Oxford
Franciscans generally, to face the many difficult questions which lay in the path of any one undertaking to

[1] S. Berger, *Quam Notitiam Linguae Hebraicae habuerunt Chris-
tiani medii aevi temporibus in Gallia*, p. 49.

correct the then received text of the Latin Bible. To understand what these difficulties were, it is necessary very briefly to outline the history of the Vulgate. We may conveniently take our sketch from the account of the early translations given by the learned Barnabite, Padre Vercellone. The Latin version made by St. Jerome in the fifth century was in reality hardly used by the Church until the influence of St. Gregory the Great in the beginning of the seventh century caused it to be very generally adopted. Before this, St. Jerome's version was read and studied only by the learned few, or was occasionally used to illustrate certain obscure passages in the ancient Latin version, known as the "Itala," as may be seen in the works of St. Augustine, Cassiodorus, etc. From the age of St. Gregory, however, St. Jerome's version displaced the "Itala" almost entirely. The new translation was used, cited, and read in the churches in the public liturgy, and in time so completely took the place of the ancient translation that no complete copy of the latter is known to have survived. It is possible, and indeed probable, that there had been some authoritative direction as to the adoption of St. Jerome's version; and it is certain that by the beginning of the eighth century, and still more in the ninth, scribes multiplied this translation exclusively.

Inevitably, with the multiplication of manuscripts by the pens of not always too-careful copyists, errors crept, or rather flowed, into the sacred text in an almost continuous stream. Scribes who were used to the ancient version seem not unfrequently to have unconsciously introduced words and phrases from the ancient "Itala" into the more recent translation. The result was confusion. Before the close of the eighth century Charle-

magne had recognised the need for a careful revision,
and the illustrious Englishman, Alcuin, was employed
upon the correction of the corrupted text. This he did
from an examination of the oldest manuscripts, and not,
as was at one time supposed, by any comparison with
the original Hebrew and Greek. From this period—the
beginning of the ninth century—whether from the great
reputation of Alcuin, from the authority of Charlemagne,
from the intrinsic merit of the revision, or from all three,
the revised text of Alcuin became the accepted text of
the Latin Church. The evil, however, was not put an
end to. Errors began immediately once again to find
their way into the version, and even grew to greater
proportions than before, by the admixture of the old
and new texts, according to the whim and fancy of individual copyists.

Lanfranc, in the eleventh century, before becoming
Archbishop of Canterbury, did something to remedy the
ever-increasing confusion and again purify the text which
then, as a contemporary says, " was by the carelessness
of the scribes greatly corrupted." But this, as a matter
of course, did not stay the evil for long, and by the
middle of the next century we have the testimony of
Nicholas, the Deacon-librarian of the Holy Roman
Church, that the words of St. Jerome about the state
of things in his day were again applicable, and " there
were almost as many versions as there were manuscripts."

Nor is this the verdict of an individual: the unreliable
character of the text was at this time fully recognised in
the University of Paris, and many efforts were made to
correct it. Our chief information about these essays in
correction comes from Roger Bacon, whom Vercellone

in this regard styles "Uomo di maraviglioso ingenio e di erudizione incredibile." Hody quotes at great length Bacon's remarks on the unsatisfactory nature not only of the text itself, but of the attempts made to correct it. Writing, as I have said, in 1267 to Pope Clement IV, the Franciscan says that the Paris edition of the Vulgate was published about forty years previously. He is not far wrong, for M. Berger tells us that the most ancient known copy of this edition is dated in A.D. 1231. This manuscript, it is not uninteresting to note, was written at Canterbury, where Cardinal Langton had for some years been archbishop.[1] Langton's connection with biblical studies is well known: as Chancellor of the University of Paris he had been eminent as an earnest student of the sacred Scriptures, and it was to him that the present division of the Bible into chapters, etc., is to be attributed.

It is impossible to describe here all that was undertaken by the University of Paris during the reign of St. Louis in regard to biblical scholarship, and in particular to remedy the unsatisfactory state to which the text of the Vulgate had been reduced by ill-considered corrections, as much as by the almost unavoidable errors of copyists. "The study of the Bible," says M. Berger, speaking of this period, "was taken up with an enthusiasm which we can hardly conceive." Foremost amongst those who strove to improve the text of the sacred writings must be named the Paris Dominicans, who, in A.D. 1236 and in A.D. 1248 produced two corrected editions of the entire Bible. No sooner was the first put into circulation than it was found to be faulty, and a second was undertaken, under the direction of Friar Hugh de

[1] S. Berger, *ob. cit.*, p. 26.

Saint-Cher, who, before its completion, was made Cardinal in 1248. In A.D. 1256 the General Chapter of the Dominicans forbade the use of the "Bible of Sens," or, as we now know it to be, the first Dominican correction of the text. The second, or Great Bible of Hugh de Saint-Cher, which took its place, became that commonly used by the professors in the Dominican schools of Paris, and was that quoted by St. Thomas of Aquin in his works.[1]

But there were others at work: the University of Paris established—or rather, perhaps, approved—a revision of the text to which Bacon chiefly refers, and which he calls the "*Exemplum vulgatum, hoc est Parisiense?*" This, we are told, did not much differ from the Dominican text, and there is evidence to show that the very copy used by Cardinal de Saint-Cher for his corrections was a copy of the University text.[2] This version itself was due in part at least, if not wholly, to the labours of an English Franciscan friar named William Briton.[3]

What, it may be asked, was the substantial effect of these attempts to improve the biblical text in the thirteenth century? In the event, did they make it more reliable? It is in answer to this question that the opinion of Roger Bacon becomes of such value and interest. In 1267 he declares that the text of the Paris copy was most seriously corrupted; and, where not corrupt, was very doubtful. At this date, it may be remarked, most of the attempts at correction had been made, and the

---

[1] S. Berger, *Des essais qui ont été faits à Paris au 13me siècle pour corriger le texte de la Vulgate*, pp. 48-49.

[2] S. Berger, p. 51.

[3] Berger, *Quam notitiam*, etc., *ut sup.*, p. 26.

Franciscan philosopher had them distinctly before his mind when he wrote. The corruption of the text, he says, had mainly come from the disputes of the various correctors, " for there were as many correctors, or rather corrupters, as there were readers. Every one presumes to change anything he does not understand: a thing he would not dare to do for the books of the classical poets." [1] The evil is, he considers, most grave, for the false text is very extensive, and the necessary corrections consequently immense. For forty years previously many theologians, and an almost infinite number of copyists in Paris, have taken this edition as the model to follow, and the scribes, by making many changes of their own, have added greatly to the corruption of the true text. Then modern theologians, not being able to examine the copies in the first instance, trusted to the scribes; but subsequently they came to understand the errors, defects, and numerous additions. They consequently proposed again to make their own corrections, and the two Orders of Dominicans and Franciscans had already commenced their work of changing the received text. Inasmuch, however, as there was no head to direct them, each one had up to that time made what alterations he deemed best. The consequence is obvious: since they have had a variety of opinions as to the true meaning to be expressed, the variations of text which have resulted are endless.[2]

Once commenced, the mania—for we can hardly describe it in any other way—for correcting the Latin text constantly grew. Every professor, as Bacon in another place informs us, made changes at his own sweet will. Amongst the Friars Minor and the Dominicans this was

---

[1] *Opera inedita*, p. 330.   [2] *Ibid.*, p. 333.

so, whilst secular teachers were not behind-hand. When any one did not understand something, he changed the text to accord with what he thought it should be. "The Dominicans, in particular," he says, "have busied themselves in thus correcting. Twenty years and more ago they presumed to make an entire corrected copy of the Scriptures and had it multiplied, but subsequently they made another and forbade the first." [1] The changes in this second revision were so extensive that in quantity they were more than the whole New Testament, and even by reason of their very quantity they contained more errors than the first correction. [2] In this way the Dominicans, more than others, changed about the sacred text, not knowing exactly what they were at. Consequently, in Bacon's opinion, their correction was really the most pernicious corruption, and even the manifest destruction of the Word of God. For his part, he thinks it much less hurtful—and, indeed, without comparison much better—to use the uncorrected Paris version, bad as it is, than the Dominican version, or, indeed, any other.

Whilst making allowances for the best intentions, the Franciscan blames his own Order as well as that of St. Dominic, and this not only as a body, but individual members of it. Those, he says, who have in all truthfulness attempted to correct the text of the Bible as far as they can, are the two Orders of Preachers and Minors. Already they have prepared corrections which in point of size would be more than the whole Bible. They contend, he adds, one with another in numberless ways, and not merely the Orders one against the other, but the

---

[1] *Opera inedita*, p. 333.
[2] *Obus Maius*, ed. Bridges, i, p. 78.

brethren of both Orders contradict the opinions of other brethren even more than do the two Orders themselves. Indeed, every master may be said to contradict every other master; and correctors, following one after the other, strike out or alter previous corrections to the infinite scandal and confusion of all.

As the fertile causes of errors in the text, Bacon notes negligence in following the readings of the ancient Bibles, and the prevailing ignorance of Greek and Hebrew. The text, he says, has come to us from the Hebrew and Greek, and has in it a vast number of words derived from those languages; and beyond this, modern theologians and correctors, who do not know the Latin language as St. Jerome did, do not, in their ignorance, hesitate to change the ancient grammatical construction.

But what perhaps, more than anything, had led to the grave corruption of the sacred text was, that people did not realise what the translation was which the Latin Church used, or to which it lent the weight of its authority. For, finding the text changed according to the mind of any individual, the common run of theologians did not stop to consider whether the translation was or was not that of St. Jerome at all; but concluded that it was some other version made up and compiled from various other versions. Under this idea they used their own words to supersede the received text as they liked. The idea that this received text was not that of St. Jerome's translation was most false. The Latin Church, Bacon points out, makes use only of this translation, except for the Psalter, which is a translation of the Septuagint, and remained in use, because this version of the Psalms was so common in the Church of God before St. Jerome translated them, that it was found practically

K

impossible to supersede it. The only version of the
Bible, however, used by the Church is certainly that
made by St. Jerome, though, unfortunately, it has been
seriously changed for the worse by a succession of scribes
and correctors into the Paris edition.

Bacon then goes on to describe at considerable length
the origin of the various translations before that of
St. Jerome, and to explain the correct meaning of the
word Vulgate as applied to the Latin version authorised
by the Church. In following his lengthy argument the
reader cannot fail to be impressed by the range of reading in the history of the early translations which the
learned Franciscan displays, and by his extensive ac-
quaintance with the works of the Fathers. Josephus,
Origen, Eusebius, and other ancients are freely quoted,
evidently with full knowledge of their writings. Bacon
points out, too, that people in ignorance have taken
various quotations from Holy Scripture which they have
read in the works of the ancient Fathers, and, on the
supposition that they represented the approved Vulgate
version, have without hesitation substituted them for the
ordinary text. Some even have adopted the words of
Josephus as true Scripture, whilst others again have corrected their versions to accord with the various quotations from the Bible read in the liturgy of the Church in
which, as is well known, the actual wording had frequently been changed to facilitate public reading, and
even to assist devotion. In brief, the general belief, when
Bacon wrote, was that the Latin version then in use did
not in any way represent the approved Vulgate of
St. Jerome, and that even individuals were fully at liberty
"to put into it what they liked, to alter and change anything they did not understand." Bacon pleads that this

state of things should be put an end to at once; that they should be told by authority that the only recognised text was that translated by St. Jerome, and that the only attempt at revision must be an authorised endeavour to recover that text in its early purity.

It is for this that he appeals to the Pope. He states that in his opinion nothing can be suggested for remedy to the Holy See of greater importance than the then corrupted state of the sacred text.[1] For without any possibility of doubt, he says, I prove by a demonstration, overwhelming in its force, that the whole text of the copies in common use is false and doubtful; and doubt ever has the same effect upon a wise man as fear has upon a brave one.[2]

"Roger Bacon," writes M. Berger, impassioned but clear-sighted in his criticisms, considered that "the would-be correctors of the thirteenth century had by their work rendered the corruption of the text incurable. Seeing correction follow upon correction, the reader knew not whom to believe. . . . The most learned men of the age of St. Louis lacked something which not all the teaching of the Paris University was able to give them, namely, the scientific spirit. It is much that in the thirteenth century they knew the need of applying Hebrew and Greek to the correction of the Vulgate, but it must be remembered that it was not a question of Hebrew but of the text of St. Jerome, and that to establish the text of a version, the study of the original is dangerous when not directed with prudence and sobriety. Hugh de Saint-Cher and his disciples with their methods could only succeed in making the text of the Bible still

---

[1] *Opus Majus*, ed. Bridges, i, p. 77.
[2] Vatican Preface (*Eng. Hist. Review*), July, 1897, p. 514.

worse, and Roger Bacon was not wrong in proving this to them."[1]

It was precisely in "the scientific spirit" that Bacon desired that the question of correcting the text of the Bible should be approached. He demanded that the most scientific method should be applied to the restoration of St. Jerome's version of the Vulgate. Put briefly, the principles upon which in his opinion the necessary corrections should be based were—(1) unity of action under authority; (2) a thorough consultation of the most ancient manuscripts; (3) the study of Hebrew and Greek to help where the best Latin manuscripts left room for doubt; (4) a thorough knowledge of Latin grammar and construction; and (5) great care in distinguishing between St. Jerome's readings and those of the more ancient version. Upon the consultation of the older manuscripts Bacon laid great stress, and reminded the Pope of the advice given by St. Augustine: "If variations are found in Latin codices, recourse must be had to ancient manuscripts and to several copies. For ancient copies are to be considered before newer ones, and a reading found in many before that of a few. And [he adds] all the old Bibles which lie in the monasteries which are not yet glossed or touched, have the true translation which the Holy Roman Church received from the beginning and ordered to be spread in all the churches." These, he says, on examination would be found to be quite different from the Paris copies, which then passed as the current version.[2] This latter is one manuscript against the almost infinite number to be found in the various provinces, and must therefore give way to their reading, both as

---

[1] S. Berger, *De l'Histoire de la Vulgate en France*, p. 13.
[2] *Opus Majus*, ed. Bridges, i, p. 78.

being more recent, and as contradicted by the multitude of these ancient manuscripts.[1]

Roger Bacon's works are sufficient proof that he was fully entitled to speak with authority on the question of the revision of the Latin Vulgate. The passages dealing with the matter in the *Opus Majus*, and even more so the long treatment of the question in the *Opus Minus*, prove that he had prepared himself most carefully by a thorough study of the matter. In fact, it would almost appear as if, when writing to Clement IV in 1267, he had already drawn up a special tract dealing directly with the proposed correction, or, at any rate, that he was ready to furnish the Pope with a text fully amended in accordance with the principles he had set down, and an accurate justification of the needful corrections. "This example of the errors," he says in the *Opus Minus*, "together with what I state in the third and fourth parts of my *Opus* (*Majus*), may suffice until such time as your Holiness require the correction of the whole text, with the certain proofs (of the truth) of the correction."[2]

And that something of this was really ready would seem to be implied by the words of the preface to the *Opus Majus*, published for the first time in the *English Historical Review*. "This particular and special proof can be presented to your Wisdom when you shall order.[3]

In this laborious undertaking, however, Bacon expressly says that he had been aided and had associated with himself a student who had toiled at scriptural work during many years. In the *Opus Minus* he thus speaks to the Pope of this biblical scholar: "In the Church you have subjects who are fully able (to make the much-needed

---

[1] *Opera inedita*, p. 330.   [2] *Ibid.*, p. 333.
[3] *Eng. Hist. Review*, July, 1897, p. 516.

corrections in the Latin text of the Bible and to justify their work), though the errors are most grave, both by reason of their number and the serious nature of their falsity." [1]

In the *Opus Tertium*, he speaks somewhat more clearly about the learned man who could do so much in this matter. " It is necessary," he writes, "that to be able to correct properly, a man should know Greek and Hebrew sufficiently well, and his Latin grammar really well according to the works of Priscian, and that he shall have considered the principles and method of correcting, as well as the way to justify his corrections, so as to correct with knowledge. This no one ever has done except the wise man I have spoken about. Nor is this to be wondered at, for he has spent nearly forty years in the correction of the text and in explaining its literal sense. All others are but idiots in comparison with him, and know nothing about the subject." [2]

In another place the Franciscan speaks of the great knowledge of foreign languages possessed by this un-named biblical scholar, whom in this respect he thinks worthy to be compared with Grosseteste, Bishop Thomas Wallensis, and Friar Adam Marsh. " Some old men are still living," he writes in 1267, "who know a great deal, like him who is so wise in the study of Holy Scripture, who has never had an equal since the time of the Fathers in correcting the text and explaining its literal sense."

Still more clearly again does he speak about this wonderful man in the Vatican Preface just named, when he offers to send to the Pope the special and particular proofs of his suggested corrections. " But not by me alone," he says, "but much more by another who has

[1] *Opera inedita*, p. 333.   [2] *Ibid.*, p. 93.

worked at this matter for thirty years and has sketched out the whole mode of correcting, what is required for it, and what can be accomplished, provided that assistance be given in the matter of books in other languages. For already this man would have given certain specimens [of his corrections] had he possessed a Greek and Hebrew Bible and a book of etymologies in those languages such as are as common with them as Isidore and Papias are with us, and of which copies are to be found even in England, in France, and in many places in the hands of Christians. With these books this man would give the true text and a reliable exposition of the literal sense so that any one could then understand God's Word without difficulty and labour. . . . And, as all philosophy is understood by the exposition of the wisdom of God, what in this regard is wanting in this man can by your help and command be sufficiently supplied by others."[1]

Unfortunately, as in so many other instances where we would gladly have some information as to the names of people mentioned by Bacon, he fails us. It would certainly be interesting to know who this man was, so learned in the Holy Scripture as to call forth the unreserved praises of the illustrious Roger Bacon. So diligent a student of biblical texts during thirty or forty years, and one who, even when Bacon wrote in 1267, had apparently already prepared a critical and scientific correction of the Bible, can hardly have passed away without leaving some trace of his long and laborious investigations, and without in some way or other inscribing his name on the page of history. It may be taken for granted that the principles upon which the correction of the Bible would have been undertaken by this un-

[1] *Eng. Hist. Review*, p. 516.

named scholar were entirely in accord with those laid down by Bacon. In fact, we may almost suppose from the words already quoted from the Vatican manuscript, that they had collaborated in the work, at least to some extent. Is there any evidence of such a work ever having existed?

To answer this question it is necessary to make a few preliminary observations. In several libraries of Europe there are extant certain manuals made during the course of the thirteenth century, with the object of furnishing copyists with the means of correcting the Bibles they were engaged to copy. These manuals are called *Correctoria*, and one such volume is now in the British Museum,[1] whilst the actual manual from which the great Dominican Bible of Saint-Cher was corrected is in the National Library at Paris. Many other *Correctoria* more or less founded upon this latter, are known to students of the subject. Vercellone has furnished us with an account of three manuscripts of this kind now in the Vatican. The three have some connection one with the other, and they all not only correct the errors of transcription and the still more serious errors of rash critics, but point to the existence of much larger works of the same kind. The author of the third has certainly known of the existence of the work upon which the second and to a less extent the first is founded, although it is not, like them, founded upon it. This third is in all ways the most important: not only is it much more extensive, but it is a characteristic of the writer that he rarely cites the authority of any ancient author, and he says expressly that he underlines all words which do not fully agree with the Hebrew, Greek, or ancient Latin. This *Correc-*

[1] MS. Reg. 1 A. viii.

torium is also markedly more scientific than the other
two, and it is based precisely upon those principles
which, as we have seen, Bacon laid down as the only
proper principles to ensure any proper correction of the
text. Vercellone has no hesitation in classing these three
Vatican *Correctoria* as follows: Nos. 1 and 2 are drawn
up for the purposes of a correction of the text similar to
that undertaken by the Dominicans, and No. 3 for some
such rectification of the Bible as that suggested by Roger
Bacon. In fact, the learned Barnabite suggests, somewhat tentatively and timidly it is true, that the real
author may have been Bacon himself.

M. Berger, in more than one work, has written a good
deal about this, to him, most interesting and important
manuscript, known as the *Correctorium Vaticanum*. If
other *Correctoria*, he says, are necessarily the work of
learned men, the author of this must have been a real
scholar. The others are the works of bibliographers, this
of a critic who knew what the true science of criticism
was. He was acquainted with Hebrew and Greek, knew
the value of manuscripts and how to make the best use
of them. He has made researches too, has looked everywhere for the oldest, because the best, codices ; has
worked in the library of Sainte Genevieve, has examined
the Bible of Charlemagne at Metz, and has studied the
Codex Amiatinus in Italy. He is wise and learned and
patient. Vercellone says that he shows himself to be of
" vast learning and of right judgment." The object of
all his criticism is the restoration of the true text of
St. Jerome and the removal of every trace of the " Itala,"
of the Greek, and of the Latin translation of the Septuagint from the then accepted version. In any doubt
he consults the originals, he distinguishes between manu-

scripts of France and of Spain, and he has read St. Matthew in the Hebrew. It is quite remarkable what stress he lays upon the examination of ancient manuscripts, such as the Bible of Charlemagne, of the more ancient manuscripts written before the time of Alcuin, and he cites what he calls the Bible of St. Gregory the Great.

When the manuscripts disagree the author of the *Correctorium Vaticanum* adopts St. Jerome's principle and has recourse to the Hebrew, but he warns students not to be unfaithful to the Latin text on the strength of a single Hebrew or Greek version. His work is aimed directly against correctors of the type of Cardinal Hugh de Saint-Cher, and he strongly objects to those who would cut out of the Latin every word not found in the Greek and Hebrew, words which had been introduced into the Vulgate text for the sake of clearness of expression. This, says M. Berger, after an examination of the principles which guided the author in the composition of his *Correctorium*, is "true criticism, and we could do no better to-day." And this, he adds, was a criticism two centuries and a half before the coming of Erasmus.[1]

The same eminent writer says that for himself he does not much care what may be the actual name of this anonymous critic of the thirteenth century, for with Vercellone he thinks one may safely recognise in him the biblical scholar referred to by Roger Bacon and in evident relation to him, but whose name, alas! the Franciscan philosopher does not give.

"This much," says M. Berger, "is certain, that we must look for this scholar, who was born out of due time, among the disciples of that precursor of modern science, Roger Bacon. Either he had the *Opus Majus*

[1] *De l'Histoire de la Vulgate en France*, p. 15.

under his eyes or he received the counsels of its author: the spirit is the same, and the style, though less virulent and personal, is the same. Thus we are brought back to the school of the *doctor mirabilis* [Roger Bacon], to the school of that mysterious savant who had such astounding lights on all the sciences, but for whom no study possessed greater fascination than the correction of the biblical text." [1]

In another work the same writer suggests from internal evidence that the author of the *Correctorium Vaticanum*, which manifests the same critical spirit in every part as that of the illustrious Franciscan philosopher, Bacon, was in all probability a Frenchman. He, however, confesses that the slight indications are hardly sufficient to warrant any certain conclusion, particularly as Roger Bacon was a man of all countries. [2] Later on, however, owing to a discovery of a manuscript at Einsiedeln, made by the Dominican, Father Denifle, M. Berger was enabled to give the actual name of the great biblical critic named by Bacon in his works, who was almost certainly the author of the *Correctorium Vaticanum*. To us it can hardly fail to be a matter of great interest to know that he was another Englishman, himself also a member of the Order of St. Francis. His name is Friar William de Mara or de la Mare, [3] and he is another of the illustrious pupils in the school established by Bishop Grosseteste for the sons of St. Francis at Oxford. De la Mare has indeed long been known for his attack upon the teaching of St. Thomas of Aquin, called *Correctorium Operum fratris Thomae*, and some have even

---

[1] *De l'Histoire de la Vulgate en France*, p. 15.
[2] *Ibid.*, p. 65.
[3] S. Berger, *Quam notitiam*, etc., *ut supra*, p. 35.

considered that "the serious part of the work was directly inspired by Bacon,"[1] but, until the discovery above referred to, he was not recognised as the author of a work which before all others laid down sound principles of true scientific criticism upon which to base a correction of the Vulgate text. It is not uninteresting too, to recognise in the biblical scholar referred to by Bacon, and so greatly praised for his wisdom, learning, and industry, another English Franciscan, and to add his name to the many of our countrymen who were in the Middle Ages renowned for their work of textual criticism. Whatever may have been the immediate result of his labours, in the end the principles he enunciated were those upon which the Vulgate text was corrected, and we may say with M. Berger that the result of the labours of this critic and others in the thirteenth century was certainly to "render the Bible more reverenced, was to make it better known and without doubt better loved."

[1] Little, *The Grey Friars in Oxford*, p. 215.

III

ENGLISH SCHOLARSHIP IN THE THIRTEENTH CENTURY[1]

THE most trustworthy account that we possess of the condition of learning at the eve of the thirteenth century comes from the pen of an Englishman—John of Salisbury. This great man, who died in A.D. 1180 finished his twelve years' study in Paris and elsewhere probably about the middle of the twelfth century. What he says in the *Metalogicus*, as to his training, though it may seem somewhat remote from the present subject, is worth quoting:

"When I was a very young man," he says, " I went to study in France, the second year after the death of that lion in the cause of justice, Henry, King of England [*i.e.*, 1136]. There I sought out that famous teacher and Palatine peripatetic philosopher [Abelard] who then presided at Mount St. Geneviève, and was the subject of admiration to all men. At his feet I received the rudiments of this art (*i.e.*, rhetoric), and manifested the utmost avidity to pick up and store away in my mind all that fell from his lips. When, however, much to my regret, Abelard left us, I attended Master Alberic, a most obstinate dialectician and unflinching assailant of the nominalist sect.

[1] Published in *Dublin Review*, October, 1898.

"Two years I stayed at Mount St. Geneviève under the tuition of Alberic and Master Robert de Melun, if I may so term him, not from the place of his birth, for he was an Englishman, but by the surname which he gained by the successful conduct of his schools. One of these teachers was scrupulous even to minutiae, and everywhere found some subject to raise a dispute, for the smoothest surface presented inequalities to him, and there was no rod so smooth that he could not find in it some knot and show how it might be removed. The second (that is the Englishman who afterwards became Bishop of Hereford), was prompt to reply, and never for the sake of subterfuge avoided any question that was proposed; but he would choose the contradictory side, or by many words would show that a simple answer could not be given. In all questions, therefore, he was subtle and profuse, whilst the other in his answers was perspicuous, brief, and to the point. If two such characters could ever have been united in the same person, he would be the best hand at disputation that our times have produced. Both of them possessed acute wit and indomitable perseverance, and I believe they would have turned out great and distinguished men in physical studies if they had supported themselves on the great base of literature and more closely followed in the tracks of the ancients."

From this account it is clear that academic education in the early days of the Paris schools was chiefly confined to dialectics and such kindred subjects as were considered best fitted to sharpen wits for keen disputation. The genius of John of Salisbury, himself a child of scholasticism, enabled him to put his finger upon the danger to true education inherent in the system. In common with the two masters he names, the scholastics very generally lacked " the great base of literature " and neglected to follow " in the tracks of the ancients," and in their minute and strictly scientific examination of the form often neglected the substantial reality behind it. This was the defect of the system against which a century later another English scholar, Roger Bacon, protested loudly, and his condemnation could hardly be better summarised than in the words used a hundred years before by John of Salisbury.

In this sketch of the education given in the schools of Paris in the twelfth century, we have distinct evidence, however, of a stirring of the waters, and of a striving to increase the narrow limits of general knowledge. Already there were some who were looking even to the East and to Greece for the " great base of literature, and seeking to find again there the tracks of the ancients." Adelard the Englishman, a monk of Bath, and a teacher of renown in Paris, had travelled in Egypt, Greece, Asia Minor, and in Moorish Spain, to seek for science unknown to the nations of the West. His works contain evidence of his proficiency in the liberal arts, even in astronomy, but with what seems to us in these days some curious limitations. Of Aristotle, for example, he he knew little or nothing, and, like John of Salisbury, regarded this light of ancient learning merely as an authority on logic, then the all important branch of education. If the latter, John of Salisbury, was acquainted with Greek as a language at all, there is nothing to show it in his voluminous writings, nor, indeed, in those of Adelard of Bath. Hardly later, however, we catch the first impressions of a change. In 1167 there is some evidence of a desire to procure Greek manuscripts from the East, for in that year a certain William, a doctor of medicine and monk of St. Denis, returned to Paris from Constantinople, bringing with him many precious Greek codices, to seek for which he had been sent to the East by his abbot.

But this, after all, can only be regarded as an isolated instance, and, as it were, an indication of a real renaissance at hand. It was not till the thirteenth century had begun that a closer connection between West and East brought about a greater knowledge of Greek writers and of Eastern literature generally. Just as in the fifteenth century it was the capture of Constantinople by the Turks, which immediately secured the triumph of the new learning, so it was the taking of the same imperial city by the Crusaders, and the establishment of the Latin Empire of the East in 1204, that brought the peculiar genius of Greek thought and the subtle power of Greek models to bear upon the thought of the Western world. It is difficult to-day to realise all that Constantinople was in the thirteenth century. As a city it was the storehouse of the accumulated wealth of ages, and it displayed untouched monuments of the Roman Empire and of ancient Greek art. Its population, estimated by some at over a million, was greater, ten, twenty times greater, if not more, than that of the then existing cities of London and Paris; in fact, it more than outnumbered the inhabitants of the chief cities of the Western world taken collectively. " In magnificence," says Hallam, " she excelled them more than in numbers; instead of the thatched roofs, the mud walls, the narrow streets, the pitiful buildings of those cities, she had marble and gilded palaces, churches and monasteries, the works of skilful architects; whilst in the libraries of Constantinople were collected the remains of Greek learning."

This was the city, rich alike in its monuments of ancient art and its evidences of ancient learning which, hitherto closed against the nations of Europe, was thrown open to the Western world by the Latin conquest of 1204. Already there were signs of a wish to profit by such an event on the part of those more immediately concerned in the fields of learning. There were indications of an awakening, of a yearning, after the knowledge of the ancients, and of a desire to know something of the languages of the peoples with which the three great crusades had brought the Christian nations into contact. Perhaps it is not too much to say that the best result of the crusading efforts—certainly one of the most obvious and lasting—was the effect they had upon the education of Christendom by bringing the nations of Europe into relation with Greeks and Arabs, and with the many-tongued peoples of Asia and Africa. The influence of the East can be traced almost immediately in all branches of knowledge and modes of thought: in the languages and literature, and in the sciences and arts of Western nations. Inspired probably by the tales of returned crusaders, travellers and scholars had, by the beginning of the century, penetrated into regions long unexplored, and by their strange travellers' tales, and even more by the literary spoils they brought back with them, they helped to turn men's thoughts in the same direction. Thus, to take one example of such enterprise: we find that just at this time one Englishman, Daniel de Morlai, had returned to England, and encouraged by his friend, John of Oxford, Bishop of Norwich, had brought back to his native country a number

L

of precious manuscripts and a practical knowledge of the Greek language, acquired apparently in the Arabic schools of Toledo. He appears almost as the first herald of the coming spring, and the statement of his fear lest he should be the only one among his countrymen—whom he calls " the Romans "—to cultivate the Greek tongue is at least sufficient evidence of how completely this learning had died out in England, as indeed in Europe generally. For this reason alone the name of Daniel de Morlai deserves to be remembered with honour, and his own brief account of his search after learning is not uninteresting.

" When some time since," he writes, " I departed from England to study, and remained for a while in Paris, I there saw certain animals [*bestiales*] teaching in the schools with great authority. They had before them two or three desks on which were placed large codices illuminated with golden letters representing the traditional teachings. Holding leaden styles in their hands, they reverentially marked their books with asterisks and stops. These men were like statues in their ignorance, and their silence alone they desired to be taken for wisdom. When they attempted to open their mouths I found they were childish, and when I saw this to be their case, for fear that I might fall into the same evil way, that is, be content with the art of illustrating or epitomising works not worth even a passing consideration, I took serious counsel with myself. And inasmuch as the teaching of the Arabs at Toledo (which is almost entirely imparted in the Quadrivium) is in these days highly praised, I hastened thither to listen to the wisest philosophers in the world. At length, invited and pressed by my friends to return from Spain, I came back to

England with a number of precious manuscripts. When, however, I heard that there was in these parts no liberal education, and that to make way for Titius and Seius, Aristotle and Plato were forgotten, I was greatly grieved; and, for fear lest I should be the only Greek among the Romans, I remained where I understood these studies flourished. On my journey, however, I met my lord and spiritual father, John, Bishop of Norwich, who, receiving me with honour, was pleased to congratulate himself upon my arrival."[1]

To make a long story short, the bishop questioned De Morlai about the Toledo teaching, and especially about astronomy, in which he was greatly interested. The result of De Morlai's information is given in the tract, to which the foregoing forms the preface.

Travellers proverbially tell strange tales, and this Englishman's declaration as to the general ignorance of Aristotle then prevailing in the Western world may seem somewhat exaggerated. In reality, however, it is not far from the truth. No works, of course, had such a paramount and lasting influence upon the scholastics generally as those of Aristotle. The philosophy of the Middle Ages may be described as Aristotelian philosophy in Christian clothes; and yet, until the thirteenth century, it is in regard to logic only that the influence of Aristotle can be traced in contemporary thought, or that his authority was ever invoked. The early Christian Fathers, as Roger Bacon so clearly points out, were for many reasons attracted rather to the works of Plato than to those of Aristotle, and, since the time when St. Gregory of Nazianzum had attributed the apostasy of Julian to his studying the works of the philosophers,

[1] Ar. MS. 377, ff. 88-104.

there had been a disposition among Christians generally
to avoid the influence of pagan writers. Whatever be
the cause, the result is certain: Aristotle's philosophy
was practically unknown to Western nations until the
Crusaders returned from the East with a knowledge of
the use that had been made of his works by the Arabian
writers. A few facts will illustrate the previous ignorance of a philosophy, which subsequently obtained, and
for generations maintained, a supremacy over the minds
of Christian scholars. In the great work of Peter the
Lombard, the *Book of the Sentences*—a work that became
the text-book of scholastic theology and philosophy—
the name of Aristotle does not appear at all. John of
Salisbury, it is true, says that he was acquainted with
Aristotle, but it is clear he knew him only in his *Logic*,
as a master of the art of reasoning, and that, we have no
reason to doubt, merely in a translation of Boëthius or
Victorinus, or in the abridgment which bore the name
of St. Augustine.

Within a few years of 1204—the date of the taking
of Constantinople—the change was already manifest.
William the Breton tells us that up to 1209 no version
of the *Metaphysics* was known in the Western schools,
but that in this year a Latin translation was made from
a Greek manuscript brought from one of the libraries of
Constantinople. Paris, then the acknowledged capital
of the intellectual world, was directly in touch with the
East, for one of the first acts of Baldwin of Flanders, on
being chosen to rule over the Latin Empire of the East,
was to establish a Greek, or, as it was called, a Con-
stantinopolitan college in connection with the Paris University. Even then, however, the works of the great
Greek philosopher, whose influence over the minds of

the greatest lights of the schools—Albert the Great, St. Thomas and the rest—seems to have been supreme, were known only in translations, many of which had been taken from Arabic versions, and all of which—if we are to believe that rather severe critic, Roger Bacon—were ill made. Moreover, many of the recognised teachers were still suspicious of the growing influence of a pagan philosopher, and an outcry was raised against allowing theology to rest, even for form and manner of proof, on his authority. The highest powers were invoked, and the University of Paris prohibited the teaching of Aristotle's physics and metaphysics in the schools. This, however, was caused not so much by any fear of the works themselves as by a dread of the influence of the Arabian philosophers, Averroes and Avicenna, who had made so much of these works in their writings. These Arabians were suspected of pantheistic tendencies, and for many years every means was taken to stop the circulation of their commentaries upon Aristotle, with what success may be best seen in the works of St. Thomas.

"In these days," writes Bacon in 1267, "whatever Averroes says has won favour with the learned. For a long time he was neglected, and his authority repudiated and condemned by the most celebrated teachers in their lectures, but little by little his wisdom appeared sufficiently worthy of attention, though in some matters he may have spoken incorrectly. We know also," he adds, "that in our own days for a long period of time Aristotle's natural philosophy and metaphysics, as expounded by Avicenna and Averroes, were forbidden, and through crass ignorance their works were excommunicated, as well as those using them."

Whilst touching on the rise of Aristotle's influence in the Schools of the West, one point must not escape notice—the extent to which the knowledge of his works in the early thirteenth century was due to Latin translations of Arabic versions. These versions were mainly brought to the schools of Europe by students who had frequented the great centre of Arabian learning at Toledo. It has been noticed how Daniel de Morlai, at the end of the previous century, had returned thence to England with a knowledge of Aristotle, and it was from the same Arab source that many of the early Latin translations reached the Universities of Europe. Frequently they appear to have been rather transliterations than translations, made by people alike ignorant of the matter and the language. Speaking of those early translations, Renan says that such editions " only furnish a Latin translation of a Hebrew translation of a commentary made upon an Arabic translation of a Syriac version of the Greek text." Under these circumstances it is hardly a matter for wonder that Aristotle should have been so often misinterpreted, or that Roger Bacon should, by condemning the translations in use, have expressed, it may be somewhat harshly, his disgust at the ignorance of Greek displayed by professors, who would not learn the language to discover their master's real meaning.

Among the influence which in the thirteenth century brought about a renaissance of letters must be placed first the authority ot the Popes. Innocent III, for example, who in his youth had studied in Paris, exerted his supreme power in favour of that school of learning which was just then awakening to the possibilities within its reach. He urged the clergy to turn themselves seriously to studious occupations, and in the council of the Lateran in 1215 passed a universal law that a school of grammar should be a necessary adjunct of every cathedral church. So, too, Popes like Honorius III (1224) and Clement IV (1267) are found commending the work of those engaged in learned pursuits and endeavouring to obtain some temporal recognition of their services.

Without doubt, however, what probably did more than anything else to assist the Western world to understand that the night was past and the day was at hand, and to wake it up to the opportunities offered it by the reopening of communication with the East in the fall of Constantinople, was the rise of the mendicant Orders in the early part of the century. Most people on reflection will be inclined to agree with the late Mr. Symonds in his opinion that of all the names in this century, which produced so many illustrious men, those of St. Francis and St. Dominic stand out above all others. With the latter, this utilisation of the power of letters and culture in the service of the Church was no mere accident; but with St. Francis, Providence seemed to have overruled his wish that none of his sons should aspire to the learning of the schools. According to his original design the qualification best suited to the needs of the Order, as he conceived it, was to be found in a capacity to attend the leper hospitals and to wait upon the poor and sick generally. "But in thus qualifying themselves for working among the large populations of the towns," writes Mr. Brewer, "the friars were forced upon other studies secondary only in importance to their main concern." In this way they came to give themselves generally to physical studies and pursuits, and to medicine and natural philosophy specially. Their knowledge quickly became more than theoretical, for they tested their theories by observation and actual experiment. Shakespeare, in his portrait of Friar Lawrence, has made us familiar with this characteristic of Franciscan learning. At first—at least with these friars—the study of languages was necessitated by a missionary activity which sought for a wider scope than could be found in the Western world, and brought them into immediate contact with forms of thought and languages to which they were strangers. To do good at all, they were obliged to master the tongues of the peoples of whom they would be Apostles. This was the impulse—the service of God and His Church—and in their enthusiasm in this sacred cause they swept the world on with them and helped to convince the learned of the need of mastering the languages and learning of the East. Up to this period the Christian and the follower of the prophet had met only to exchange blows on the field of battle. The idea that good of any kind could possibly come from an attempt to master the languages of the enemies of the Cross, or from an endeavour to understand their modes of thought, does not appear to have suggested itself to the minds of the Crusaders. They were warriors for the truth—men who would compel adhesion to the Faith at the point of the sword—they asked for nothing more, and expected nothing less. It was left to the friars to conceive other ideals of Christian missionary enterprise, and in their endeavours to realise them, they were destined to assist materially in reawakening the Western mind. The chronicle of Friar Eccleston, the letters of Adam Marsh, and, above all, the works of Roger Bacon manifest the constant activity of the friars in the early days of their existence. Before the middle of the century we find them in Russia, and rigorously keeping their Lenten observances in the regions of Crim Tartary. As missioners, they noted whatever might be useful to the future preachers of the Gospel in the countries through which they passed, and, as travellers, they carefully recorded their observations upon the natural features ot hitherto unexplored regions, and set down peculiarities of animal life, of vegetation, and the rest. The travels of the Franciscan, William de Rubruquis, in Inner Asia for example—travels so much appreciated by Roger Bacon—" still," writes Mr. Brewer, " hold their place in that species of literature which has done more than any other for the promotion of science."

As somewhat allied to this subject, the following passage from Roger Bacon may be here noted:

" There is more trouble and labour in the work of wisdom," he writes to the Pope in 1267, " than one unused to such work might think. Nothing can be properly completed without instruments of astronomy, geometry, perspective, and many other sciences. Wherefore without such instruments nothing of any high order can be known, and they must be obtained, since few of them are made among Latin nations. Copies also of books on all the various sciences are needed, the works of learned men, both ancient and modern, and these, neither I nor any of my acquaintances have, and they must be searched for in the libraries of the wise through many different countries. Further, as authors contradict one another in a great many things, and have written much from report, it is needful to examine into the truth by actual experience. . . . Hence I have frequently sent beyond the sea and into foreign countries and to celebrated fairs and markets in order to have ocular testimony about things of nature, and prove the truth of something by sight, touch, smell, and sometimes by hearing, and thus by the certainty of experiment [get to know] what I could not get from books."

Before the close of the century, a Franciscan friar of the third Order, Raymund Lully—the *doctor illuminatus*, as he was called—had eclipsed even De Rubruquis in the magnitude of his travels. These had extended, indeed, over three-quarters of the globe, and yet his journeying and missionary labours were by no means the full measure of his gigantic activity and industry. He, too, was interested deeply in the study of Greek and various other languages, and his letters on this subject to the Pope and to the authorities of the Paris University are worthy of a passing notice. His desire was to see the establishment of a college where men might be taught the tongues and even the idioms of the infidels:

"I can vouch from experience," he says, "that there are many of the Arabian philosophers who strive to pervert Christians to the errors of Mahometanism;" and, in his opinion, the establishment of such a place in Paris, where Greek, Arabic, and the languages of the Tartar races could be taught, would do more than anything else to assist those who were willing to carry the Gospel to the Eastern peoples. It would enable them at least to know the tongues of those they had to deal with.

So far, the reader has been asked to take a general survey of the revival of letters in the early thirteenth century. Attention may now be restricted to England somewhat more closely, and the names of some of those Englishmen at this time illustrious by their conspicuous learning recalled to the memory. Where the material is so abundant it is difficult to select, and all that it is here possible to do is to make choice of some few who may be taken as types of the men whose energy and ability materially assisted in this general awakening of minds.

In the first years of the thirteenth century a student named Michael Scot, born probably in the Lowlands of Scotland, and educated in his early years at Oxford and Paris, was working at Toledo. After having visited Bologna and Palermo in his search after learning, he had come to Spain, attracted thither by the high reputation of the Arabian philosophers. Here he learnt Arabic sufficiently well to be able to translate the works of Aristotle. Roger Bacon rather disparages his learning, but there is little doubt that he really did much to spread the knowledge of the philosophy which subsequently bore so great a part in the mediaeval revival. In his work of translating he was assisted by a Jew named André, and Bacon not only charges him with having allowed himself to be deceived by this assistant, but with being really ignorant of the sciences he was introducing to the Western world. Leaving Toledo sometime after 1217, Michael Scot became attached to the Court of Frederick II, a great patron of learning, with whose name many of the translations are associated. In 1224 Pope Honorius III wrote to Cardinal Langton to beg that the English Archbishop would assist Michael Scot, " who, even among men of learning, was singularly pre-eminent," to some worthy ecclesiastical benefice in reward for his services in " giving us for the use of the learned of these days many translations of Aristotle and other works from the Hebrew and Arabic." A few months later the same Pope wrote again more fully as to the claims and merits of this illustrious student, who was well versed both in Hebrew and Arabic, besides Latin. "From childhood," he says, "he was ardent in his pursuit of literature, and without consideration for anything else he has wooed it with constant study, raising up on the foundation of the arts a splendid structure of learning."

Later on, in the same year, Honorius III appointed Scot to the See of Cashel, and on his refusal of the honour gave him leave to hold a benefice in Italy. In 1230, according to Bacon, Michael Scot came to Oxford, bringing his works upon Aristotle to introduce them to the teachers there. Probably this was the mission sent by Frederick II to all the schools of Europe to interest them in these translations which had been made under his patronage.

The reputation of this great student long survived him, and, as was common in the times in which he lived, his very learning caused him to be looked upon with suspicion by those who were unable to appreciate such ardour in the cause of letters. Boccaccio uses his name as that of a well-known "great master in necromancy" to introduce one of his tales. Dante speaks of "his magical deceits," and his memory still lives in many legends of the border country: any work of great labour or difficulty or antiquity being usually ascribed to the agency of "auld Michael," Sir William Wallace, or the Devil. Readers of *The Lay of the Last Minstrel* will remember that the second canto tells of the visit of "bold Deloraine" to Melrose "to win the treasure of the tomb," the "Mighty Book" of Michael Scot, which, according to legend, had been buried with him.

Probably no English name deserves to be better

known in relation to the revival of letters in the thirteenth century than that of Bishop Grosseteste. He was,
it is true, neither the first nor the greatest of English
scholars at the time, but his influence and example can
be traced in the work of those who followed him. He
was the pupil, together with Thomas Wallensis and
Adam Marsh, of St. Edmund of Canterbury in the
schools of Paris. Probably, also, he had listened there
to the lessons of Stephen Langton, who, according to
Pope Honorius III, "shone even among those most
celebrated throughout the world for eminent literary
knowledge and profound theoretical learning." Grosseteste was already a brilliant scholar when, becoming
greatly interested in the new institute of Franciscan
friars then recently come to Oxford, he undertook to
direct their studies. He not only kept his promise, but
persuaded other teachers of eminence to come and lecture
in the friars' school. Amongst others were Adam Marsh
and Thomas Wallensis, both Grosseteste's fellow-pupils
in Paris, and the former of whom, after a brilliant career
as a professor in that University, had joined the Franciscans in their early days.

Grosseteste and Adam Marsh undoubtedly laid the
foundation in the Friary at Oxford of a school of European reputation. Out of it came a series of brilliant
scholars and teachers, the like of which is unknown in
the history of letters. No three schoolmen have shown
such profound and original learning as Bacon, Scotus,
Occham, and no other nation can show such results.
Roger Bacon, the stern critic of others, has nothing but
praise for his old masters, Grosseteste and Adam Marsh.
" These," he says, " were perfect in all wisdom." [1] Of all

[1] *Opera inedita*, p. 70.

the learned men of his day, "one only, that is the Bishop of Lincoln, knew all science as Boëthius knew all languages." [1]

"A translator," he says in another place, "should know the science and the two languages from which and into which he wishes to translate. But no one knew languages except Boëthius, the famous translator, no one science except Robert, Bishop of Lincoln, both by reason of the length of his life, his experience, study, and diligence, and because he knew mathematics and perspective he could master anything; at the same time, he only knew languages well enough to understand the fathers, philosophers, and wise men of the ancients. But he did not know them sufficiently well to translate properly till towards the end of his life, when he sent for Greeks and caused them to bring books of Greek grammar to England from Greece and elsewhere." [2]

This reference to those who assisted Bishop Grosseteste in his linguistic studies recalls the name of John de Basing, or Basingstoke. This eminent scholar had passed some time in Athens perfecting himself in the Greek language where, as he told Matthew Paris himself, he was taught by a young girl not twenty years of age named Constantia, the daughter of the Archbishop of Athens. She had mastered every difficulty of the trivium and quadrivium, and John de Basingstoke used to call her "another St. Catherine." "She," says Matthew Paris in the *Chronica Majora*, "was his instructress in everything he knew, as he often asserted though he had long studied and read in Paris." [3]

On his return to England, John de Basingstoke brought

---

[1] *Opera inedita*, p. 33.   [2] *Ibid.*, p. 91.
[3] *Chronica Majora*, v, p. 286.

with him many Greek manuscripts, and among others the original Greek text of the pseudo Denys the Areopagite. He had told Bishop Grosseteste, who became acquainted with him at St. Alban's, that at Athens there existed much learning of which the Latins were wholly ignorant. Amongst other things, says Matthew Paris, he pointed out that there was a work called: " The Testament of the twelve Patriarchs, the sons of Jacob, which was of the substance of the Bible; but which, through the hatred of the Jews had been long concealed, since in them the prophecies about Christ were most clear.[1] But the Greeks, the most diligent seekers after manuscripts, coming to the knowledge of the document, translated it from Hebrew to Greek and have preserved it to our own times.[2]

At this period in the thirteenth century there was much talk as to the possibility of bringing about the conversion of the Jews. In 1231, the king built in London, somewhere about the site now occupied by the Public Record Office, what was called the *Domus Conversorum* for the support of those who should embrace the Christian Faith. The great controversy as to whether the Old Law was to be considered abrogated or merely enforced, expanded and explained by the promulgation of the New Testament, induced Grosseteste to write his *De cessatione legalium*. On being told by John de Basingstoke of the existence of the *Patriarcharum Testamenta*, the Bishop sent special messengers to Athens to obtain a copy of what then appeared to be a most important work. " This," says the antiquary, Samuel Pegge, " was a noble effort, equally noble if not superior, considering the difference of the times, to the spirit of the Scaligers,

[1] *Chronica Majora*, v, p. 285.   [2] *Ibid.*, iv. 233.

the Lauds, the Ushers, and other learned men of later ages." [1]

On the return of his messengers to England Grosseteste, says Matthew Paris, " translated the tract fully and completely word for word into Latin with the assistance of Master Nicholas 'the Greek' clerk of the Abbot of St. Alban's," [2] and here I may note that the original manuscript brought back to Grosseteste and used by him in his work of translating is probably that now in the University Library, Cambridge (Ff. 1, 24). Of course, it is now known that the *Testamenta* had not the importance attached to it by Bishop Grosseteste and others in the thirteenth century; but all the same, few on reflection would be disposed to echo the words of the late Dr. Luard, where he says: " It is lamentable to think that the Greek books which chiefly occupied Grosseteste's attention were the wretched forgeries of the *Testamenta duodecim Patriarcharum* and the Pseudo Dionysius Areopagita."

This learned editor of Grosseteste's letters thinks that the bishop and others of his time " completely received this as genuine Scripture; " but the very contrary would seem to appear from what Roger Bacon says about the work. " Though not in the canon of Scripture," he writes, " wise and holy men, both Greek and Latin, have made use of these books from the earliest ages of the Church." [4]

To Bishop Grosseteste, moreover, we in the first place owe our knowledge of a very important early Christian document—certainly not a " wretched forgery." In 1644,

[1] *Life of Grosseteste*, p. 15.   [2] *Chron. Mai.*, iv. 233.
[3] *Grosseteste's Letters*, pref. xxvi.
[4] *Ob. Maj.*, p. 58.

Archbishop Usher published a Latin version of what Bishop Lightfoot calls the *middle* form of the letters of St. Ignatius, which he considers the most important of the three recensions. The Archbishop had observed that the quotations from St. Ignatius' writings found in the works of Bishop Grosseteste, John Tyssington (*c.* 1381) and William Wodeford (*c.* 1396) although different from the text of the Epistles (the longer form) then received, yet agreed exactly with quotations to be found in the works of Eusebius and Theodoret. He concluded therefore that there must have existed in England from the time of Bishop Grosseteste, a version corresponding to the older text of St. Ignatius. His examination of the English libraries was rewarded by the discovery of two manuscripts of this version the translation of which he suspected was due to Bishop Grosseteste himself, especially as some notes upon the margin of one of the MSS. proved that the translator was an Englishman. Subsequent writers pointed out, as confirming Usher's opinion, that Tyssington and Wodeford, who had used the same version, both belonged to the Franciscan convent in Oxford to which Grosseteste had bequeathed his books. Before the publication of Bishop Lightfoot's second edition of his monumental work upon the Epistles of St. Ignatius, Usher's theory of the authorship of the version was confirmed in an unexpected way. A friend pointed out to him that among the MSS. in the library of Tours was one professing to contain the translated Epistles and assigning the work to Bishop Grosseteste. Upon examination this was found to be the case, and we have now the authority of a fourteenth-century MS. for holding that the Bishop did translate these letters, "de Graeco in Latinum." It must be borne in mind that when Usher

M

found this Latin version of the Epistles, the Greek version subsequently discovered in the Medicean library at Florence was unknown, and thus the earliest knowledge of the most correct version of the Ignatian Epistles was due to Bishop Grosseteste's work of translation in the thirteenth century.

In regard to John de Basingstoke, who so greatly assisted Bishop Grosseteste as we have said, Matthew Paris notes that he first introduced to the English the meaning and use of the figure numerals of the Greeks, where one figure represents each number "which is not the case with the Latins." In his *Chronica Majora*, Paris sets down a table of the Greek method of notation, which he obtained evidently from John de Basingstoke himself.[1]

The same Greek scholar was the author, or perhaps translator, of a work on Greek grammar which he called the Greek Donatus, of a book called *Templum Domini*, which Paris says is "very useful," and of another on the order of the Gospels—a sort of harmony probably— which he named *Athenae*.

Amongst those who assisted Bishop Grosseteste in his Greek studies was one, already named, Nicholas, "natione et conversatione," a Greek. He had come over to England, at least so Pegge considers, at the invitation of John de Hertford, Abbot of St. Alban's. This much is certain, that he found a home at that abbey and was made clerk to the Abbot. It was here that Bishop Grosseteste apparently found him and obtained his assistance in the work of translating the *Testamenta Duodecim Patriarcharum*. He was still living late in the century and had been rewarded by Grosseteste with a

[1] *Chron. Maj.*, v, 234.

prebend at Lincoln. And here it may be worth noting that St. Alban's, then in the height of its greatest glory, with Matthew Paris working as our national archivist in its scriptorium and training others in historical methods, was apparently the focus from which Greek learning and a love of letters spread to other parts of England. It had been long known for its encouragement of literary efforts, and at the beginning of the century we have the distinct testimony of that illustrious Englishman, Alexander Neckham, as to the good work done in this way by the great Benedictine monastery. He ought to have known, for he was born beneath its shadow, received his early training and passed what he calls "happy years and days of peaceful joy" within its walls. Not only were the two great scholars just named, John de Basingstoke and Nicholas the Greek, connected with the abbey, but one of the most celebrated early English Dominicans, John of St. Giles, was born at, and received his early education at St. Alban's. He subsequently studied in Paris and at Montpellier, becoming a doctor of eminence before he entered religion. In 1223, at Paris, during a sermon, he received a call to renounce the world and declared his intention of joining the Dominicans. He became the first teacher in their schools at Oxford.

It is impossible, here, to speak fully of the great light of this century, so far as England at least is concerned, Roger Bacon. The authors of the volume of the *Histoire Littéraire de la France*, dealing with this period, declare that "his works neither in his own age nor even in our present time have received the recognition they deserve. No writer, in that dark age, could have thrown such a vivid light upon physical sciences and upon any point in the whole range of human knowledge if he had been allowed to propagate his discoveries."[1]

Perhaps the highest praise that can be accorded to him is that it is to his works that we must have recourse to obtain information about the trend of human thought during this period. In them we see him as a deep student of natural science far in advance of his age: as an accomplished and enthusiastic linguist, as an exact mathematician, as a biblical scholar and as a scientific, if perhaps somewhat a too severe, critic. His principles of textual criticism are sound, and recently M. Samuel Berger, the French biblical scholar, has declared that in his opinion we could not do better at the present day. Even by the side of Albert the Great, St. Bonaventure, and St. Thomas, Bacon is worthy to hold his place, and the more his works are known and studied the greater will be the position accorded to him.

And here I would recall a passage from John of Salisbury already recorded. Of course every age has its own particular tendencies, and men can only act effectually by taking full account of them and by working in the prevalent spirit of the day. Now, without any doubt at all, the spirit of the thirteenth century was essentially *scientific*. That wonderful creation of the human mind, certainly one of the most marvellous creations of any age—the *Summa* of St. Thomas, is what it is precisely because it is scientific in its system and construction. But this great characteristic of the thirteenth century was purchased at a price. Looking back to the previous age, and comparing the twelfth and thirteenth centuries, we can hardly fail to see that the price paid was the sacrifice of literature in its highest and truest sense; a

[1] Tom. 16, p. 25.

great price indeed, for after all it must be remembered that literature is the supreme and fullest expression of all the highest powers of man. We have only to look, for example, at the writings of John of Salisbury and Peter of Blois, and set them by the side of those—say of Albert the Great, or Alexander of Hales—to see that the former are really classical in thought and expression as compared with the later.

Grosseteste and Bacon were essentially men of their own age, and they show themselves possessed to the full of the true scientific spirit. But they, more than others, are also in reality the heirs of the twelfth century, for in them, more fully than in others, we find what John of Salisbury desired, that " they supported themselves on the great base of literature and endeavoured to walk in the tracks of the ancients." I fully believe that the more this question is examined the more it will be found to be a matter of regret that the lines initiated by Grosseteste and Bacon were not those which ultimately prevailed.

TWO DINNERS AT WELLS IN THE FIFTEENTH CENTURY

OUR antiquaries have not as yet devoted much attention to the meals of our mediaeval forefathers. Descriptions of pageants, religious ceremonies, battles and tournaments are plentiful enough; but as to how the people fed and what they were fed upon, as to how the viands were cooked and how they were served up, our masters in the history of social manners and customs have so far told us very little. There is, however, no lack of material out of which to construct the picture of the mediaeval state banquet or the humble mid-day meal. Here and there in the transactions of some Archaeological Society, or in some antiquarian note-book, we have, it is true, indications of the matter, but these are, alas! now again too deeply buried in the mass of more ephemeral literature, and hidden away on the shelves of our larger libraries, to have much chance of being disinterred by any ordinary reader. Of late, it is true, more special attention has been devoted to the question of cookery and cooks' recipes in the Middle Ages, and several collections of such recipes have been printed by some of our learned societies, but as yet not much use has been made of them in order to reconstruct the scenes enacted in the great dining-halls, or in the

more common meal chambers, of by-gone generations
of Englishmen. The one fixed idea, apparently, which
most people have of our mediaeval parents at feeding
time is that they were altogether a very coarse and
boorish set, who devoured their ill-made dishes after the
manner of their ill-bred dogs, which, among the rushes
that covered the floor, fought over the bits and bones
their masters cast to them from their platters. Few, who
have not examined the question for themselves, probably
dream of the height to which during the fourteenth and
fifteenth centuries gastronomic art had reached, or of the
courtesy and good manners expected from all at the
festive board in spite of that absence of some of the
things which to us in this century seem to make decent
eating possible. The poet Chaucer's Squire, for instance,
is the very beau ideal of the chivalrous English gentleman. He tells us that " Curteys he was, lowly and
servysable, and karf beforn his fadur at the table." Of
course, some of the things our ancestors were constrained
to do at food time do not seem very nice to us to-day.
Fancy, for example, how we should get through a dinner
now without *one*, or for that matter perhaps, a multitude
of forks! To our forefathers the fact that " fingers were
made before forks " was patent, and I have no doubt
that they thought very little of helping themselves from
their dishes with thumb and forefinger. Here, as in so
many similar cases, we are so apt to import our modern
ideas into by-gone ages when such things as silver
forks, and for that matter forks of any kind, were not.
The fact is that our ancestors provided as well as they
could against the unpleasantness, and I fear we must
say filthiness, occasioned by the habit of eating with
their fingers, by constantly washing their hands both

before and after their meals. In every large establishment a special officer, called the *Ewerer*—the bearer of
the jug and basin—was told off to provide the necessary
water and towel. Spoons too were in more frequent use
than now, and served their purpose well in days when,
as the recipes show, the food in great measure partook
of the nature of hashes, stews, soups, and other made
dishes easily eaten with the spoon. The antiquary Pegge
believed that large pieces of meat and great joints were
not in common use till well into the reign of Queen
Elizabeth. It was the server's place to see, as the ancient
Book of Kerving tells us, "that every person had a
napkin and a spoon," and most minute directions exist
as to the manner in which the carver was to dismember
birds, to free the fish from its bones, and to slice the meat
into "gobbetts" which could be managed by the guests
with a spoon. Sometimes, however, the diners apparently helped themselves from the dishes before them
without waiting for the carver to do his office. This
must have been far from pleasant, at least as Barklay
describes the custom:

> If the dishe be pleasaunt, eyther flesh or fyshe,
> Ten handes at once swarme in the dishe;
> And if it be fleshe ten knives shalt thou see,
> Mangling the flesh in the platter, flee.
> To put there thy handes is perill without fayle
> Without a gauntlet, or els a glove of mayle." [1]

Then the platters—to mention but one other accessory
of the table in which we have decidedly the advantage
over our mediaeval ancestors—must have been, at least
to our modern notions, an objectionable feature of a

[1] Alexander Barklay (quoted by Warner, *Antiquitates Culin-
ariae*, p. 95).

mediaeval banquet. Till late in the sixteenth century wooden trenchers, and, for that matter, bowls were the rule in the most highly respectable houses of the land.

But while the accessories of the table were somewhat defective according to our way of thinking, there was a well-recognised method of preparing and serving the meal, especially when circumstances required a grander display than usual. I remember once, in turning over the leaves of an old account-book in the Record Office, that I came upon a statement of the preparations made by a distinguished ecclesiastic for a dinner he gave to King Edward III. The royal arrival was apparently unexpected; but sufficient notice had been given to set the whole place in a ferment of excitement. People were despatched here, there and everywhere to procure provisions and other necessaries for the feast, to which the king was coming with all his household (cum tota familia sua). Here are some of the items required as I find them set down on a page of an old note-book that I was using at the time. I fear they will appear rather miscellaneous, and some may seem not to have very much to do with a dinner. First there were sacks of fine flour for pasties and table bread (payndemayn); then came ells of linen to make towels, tablecloths, "saven-apes," and cloths to wipe out the cups and cleanse the platters. Next came a long list of spices, such as cloves, mace, ginger and galingale, which in those days were so constantly used to flavour sauces and disguise the taste of meat otherwise unpalatable. With these were rice-flour and dates, prunes, pines, and "Reys corens," that is, Corinth raisins, now better known to us as "currants." Of meats there was the usual profusion found in the Middle Ages. Besides the beef, mutton, veal and pork,

for this particular banquet we find provided for the royal
guest " 77 capons, 156 pullets, 188 pigeons, 2 pheasants,
5 herons, 6 egretts, and 6 brews." [1]   All these were purchased in London, apparently alive, because "the carriage
and keep of them " to the place where they were to be
cooked is charged at 43 shillings and 6 pence. The same
messenger brought along with him 5 lb. of salt and 6
gallons of cream.

As the day approached—it was August 8th, 1373—
the hurry and scurry became more apparent. Men were
at work unremittingly setting up trestles for tables, side-
boards and forms in the dining-hall, and dressers, chop-
ping-boards and baking-boards for the cooks, for whom
also a canvas tent was erected, apparently to serve as a
larder. Women, too, were kept hard at work making up
linen and canvas into aprons for cooks, strainers for use
in the kitchen, and cloths for tables and dressers. Bakers
were busy for three days before the king's arrival making
the bread for the company and preparing "horse loaves"
for their animals. Lastly we find set down the wages
for the cook who came to supervise the preparations
for the banquet. Perchance this same professor of the
culinary art may have been the king's own cook, for
some of the old royal accounts show that our kings, then
as now, provided themselves when on a journey, like the
Canterbury pilgrims described by Chaucer at this very
time:

> A coke they hadden with hem for the hones
> To boil the chickenes and the marie bones
> And poudre marchant, tart and galingale.
> Wel coud he knowe a draught of London ale,

---

[1] This was probably the whimbrel, or half-curlew, to be eaten
" with watere of the rivere "—sugar and salt.—*Prologue.*

He couthé roste, and sethe, and boyl, and frye,
Makyn Mortrews, and bakyn well a pye.

There were, however, other professional cooks, not distinctly attached to this or that great family or house,
who went about to furnish forth a banquet wherever
their services might be required. Like Gunter, Bertram
and Roberts, and the rest, of our days, there were apparently mediaeval refreshment contractors, or at any rate
high-class artists in cookery ready to undertake the
preparation of the feast with which some great national
event was celebrated, or to cater for the supply of refresh-
ments to clerics brought together by some ecclesiastical
function. The cookery books of more than one of these
artists are still in existence, and not only do they reveal
the secrets of their triumphs in the gastronomic art, but
in several cases they record the times and places of their
most successful efforts, and even the *menu* of the banquets themselves.

One such note-book, written by a fifteenth-century
Gunter, may be seen among the MSS. treasures in the
British Museum,[1] and has within the last few years been
printed by the Early English Text Society. It is a
beautifully written collection of recipes for making tasty
dishes arranged under various headings, so that any one
of them might be easily found by the index prefixed to
the collection. In addition to this collection, moreover,
there is a most interesting set of *menus*, each distinguished
by a brief account of the occasion upon which the banquet described was served up. They are *menus* of dinners
given on various occasions in the first half of the fifteenth
century. Two of them describe the dishes of two great

---

[1] *Harl. MS.*, 279.

dinners given in the Bishop's palace at Wells. The *chef* must have been, I fancy, a distinguished man in his own profession in those days, for his list of triumphs includes: the feast at the coronation of King Henry IV at Westminster in 1399; royal dinners at Winchester and elsewhere; a great fish banquet given by Lord de la Grey, and another by Bishop Flemming, of Lincoln, in 1420; the installation feast of Bishop John Chaundler of Sarum, in 1417, etc., etc.

Besides these, as I have said, our unknown master in the art of cookery superintended two great dinners at Wells. The first occasion was in December, 1424. In the month of September there died Bishop Nicholas Bubwith, whose chantry chapel was built by himself on the north side, in the nave arcade of Wells Cathedral, opposite the perhaps better known chapel of Treasurer Sugar. A great concourse of people, distinguished ecclesiastics, laymen and the religious of the diocese would have come to Wells for the funeral. The deceased prelate had been a man of considerable importance to the country in general and to the city of Wells in particular. He had been Bishop of London and Treasurer of England. He had, as Bishop of Bath and Wells, attended the Council of Constance, and had been one of the thirty who had, by command of the Council, taken part in the election of Martin V. Traces of the care and love he had bestowed upon his Church can still be seen. The eastern alley of the cloister with the lavatory and upper library owed much to his zeal. The interesting chapel in the vicar's close is of Bubwith's time, and the upper portion of the north-west tower is probably his work. He was buried, a considerable time after his death, on the 4th of December, 1424, where his body now lies, in his little chantry in the nave of his Cathedral. After the funeral, the ecclesiastics repaired to the great hall of the palace where the dinner described in the two menus here printed was served. Some of the dishes will, no doubt, appear to be very strange to most of us. I have tried to set down over against the name by which the dish was called in the fifteenth century, where the meaning is not obvious, some indication at least of what it might now be called. In some instances I have failed to identify the description even with the help of the recipe book. If the courses may appear to us unnecessarily lengthy, we must bear in mind that the various dishes were probably not served up one after another; but, like the very sensible modern Russian plan, various meats and birds were dished up together that everyone might make his choice.

It will be noticed that a special dinner was provided for the religious who at this time had to abstain from meat, since the funeral had been appointed for Monday in the first week of Advent. This provision for the meals of those who were bound by special ecclesiastical laws is a very noticeable feature in mediaeval accounts. It was reciprocal in its operation, and monastic account-books show how meat repasts were provided for workmen and strangers on days when in the community refectory only fish was allowed; just as this menu shows how a meagre dinner was got ready for all who had to abstain on this Advent day. Nothing is said about vegetables in the courses of these dinners, and it is at least very remarkable, not only in these mediaeval menus, but in the great variety of recipes for making dishes which exist, that there is hardly any mention of "green meat" beyond the herbs used for flavouring. The truth is that in the matter of vegetables mediaeval banquets were perforce very deficient, for the best of all reasons, that there were very few known to the art of even the fifteenth-century gardener. With this brief introduction I now give the menu for the funeral dinner. It is so plentifully supplied with meat that the lines

> Thrift, thrift, Horatio: the funeral baked meats
> Did coldly furnish forth the marriage feast,

would hardly apply here.

CONVIVIUM DNI. NICHOLAI BUBBEWYTH NUPER EPISCOPI BATHON. ET WELL. AD FUNERALIA; VIDELICET QUARTO DIE DECEMBRIS ANNO DOMINI 1424.

IN CARNIBUS.

LE I COURS.

NOMBLYD DE ROO	(Loin of Roe deer).
BLAMANGERE . . . . . . ·	(Meat beaten up with rice into a cream).
BRAUN CUM MUSTARD	(Brawn).
CHYNES DE PORKE	(Chine of pork).
CAPONA ROSTE DE HAUT GRECE	(Stuffed capon).
SWAN ROSTE.	
HEROUN ROSTYD	(Heron roasted).
ALOES DE ROO	(Ribs of venison).
PUDDYING DE SWAN NECKE.	
UN LECHEMETE	(Sliced or minced meat).
UN BAKE VIZ CRUSTADE . . .	(A pie, probably sweet).

LE II COURS

RO STYUYD	(Stewed venison).
MAMMENYE	(Minced).
CONNYNG ROSTYD	(Roast rabbit).
CURLEW.	
FESAUNT ROSTYD.	
WODECOKKE ROST.	
PERTRYCHE ROSTE.	
PLOVER ROSTE.	
SNYPYS ROSTE	(Snipe roasted).
GRETE BYRDYS ROSTED.	

LARKYS ROSTYD.
VENYSOUN DE RO ROSTYD.
IRCHOUNS . . . . (Pork prepared, with spikes made of almonds, to look like a hedgehog).
UN LECHE . . . . (Sliced meat or bread with spices).
PAYN PUFFE . . . . (A pastry puff with yolk of eggs, etc., inside).
COLDE BAKEMETE . . . . . (Cold fruit pie).
 Convivium de Piscibus pro viris Religiosis ad funeral. predict.

LE I COURS

ELYS IN SORRY . . . . . . (Eels, with a sauce made of fried onions, wine, and spices).
BLAMANGER . . . . (Fish beaten up with rice into a cream).
BAKOUN HERYNG. . . . . . (Baked herring).
MULWYL, TAYLYS . . . . . (Cod).
LENGE, TAYLYS . . . . . (Ling).
JOLLYS OF SAMOUN . . . . (Salmon jowls).
MERLYNG SOTHE . . . . . (Whiting boiled).
PYKE.
GRETE PLAYS.
LECHE BARRY . . . . . . (A sliced cake with bars of gold and silver as ornament).
CRUSTADE RYAL . . . . . (A pie with currants, dates, eggs, etc.).

LE II COURS

MAMMENYE . . . . (A mince of fish).
CREM OF ALMAUNDYS . . . . (Almond cream).
CODELING . . . . (Codling).
HADDOK . . . . (Haddock).
FREYSSE HAKE . . . . . . (Fresh hake).
SOLYS Y SOTHE . . . . . (Boiled sole).
GURNYD BROYLID WITH A SY-
 RYPPE . . . . (Gurnard).
BREM DE MERE . . . . . . (Sea bream).
ROCHE . . . . (Roach).
PERCHE . . . . (Perch).

MENUSE FRYED	. . . . . .	(Fried minnows).
IRCHOUNS	. . . .	(Pork prepared with spikes made of almonds, to look like a hedgehog).
ELYS Y SOSTYD	. . . . . .	(Eels boiled).
LECHE LUMBARD	. . . . . .	(A sweet made of dates, etc.)
GRETE CRABBYS	. . . . . .	(Crabs).
A COLD BAKEMETE	. . . . .	(Cold fruit pie).

It may be of interest to give the recipe for one or two of these dishes as they are found in the old cookery book used in the preparation of this banquet. They may seem somewhat strange nowadays, but it must be remembered that our forefathers liked, and the materials for their meals probably needed, good strong-smelling and tasting sauces. One of these dinners much affected by those who lived in the Middle Ages is described by Alexander Barklay in the lines:

> What fishe is of savour swete and delicious
> Rosted or sodden in swete herbes or wine;
> Or fried in oyle, most saporous and fine—
>   The pasties of a hart.
> The crane, the fesaunt, the peacocke and the curlew,
> The partriche, plover, bittorn and heronsewe:
> Seasoned so well in licour redolent,
> That the hall is full of pleasant smell and sent.[1]

We may take a sample of the dishes at haphazard. For example, this is how *Blamangere* was prepared by our professional cook. I take the liberty of somewhat modernising the spelling and expressions.

"Take rice, pick it clean, and wash it well in warm water. Then soak it in water and afterwards in almond milk. Add to it brawn made of capons and then put the whole into more almond milk. Beat it small with a (rolling) pin and when it sticks to it, stir it well

[1] Quoted by Warner, *ut sup.*, lv.

up. Take sugar and add to it, and then thicken it. Then take white almonds, fry them and put them on it when you serve it up. If you please you may serve it up with *Cawdelle Ferry* described above."

This *Cawdelle Ferry*, is a sauce made in this way:

"Take raw yolks of eggs separated from the whites. Then take good wine, warm it in a pot over a good fire and casting in the yolks, stir well, but do not let it boil till it thickens. Add sugar, saffron, salt, mace, gilli-flowers, and galingale ground small and flour of cinnamon. When serving it up put *blank powder*—a powder made of ginger, cinnamon and nutmeg—on it."

Irchons—or as we call them, urchins or hedgehogs—hardly perhaps sound a very inviting course. This is how the dish is made:

"Take pig's stomach and scald it well. Take minced pork and mix with spices, powdered ginger, salt and sugar and put into the stomach, but not too full. Then sew it up with strong thread and put on a spit like we do pigs. Then take white almonds and cut them long, small and sharp and fry them in grease and sugar. Take a small skewer and prick the irchons and put almonds into the holes. Put it then to the fire and when roasted, cover it with flour and milk of almonds, some green, some black with blood. Let it not brown too much and then serve it up."

The above will be sufficient to give the reader some notion of the elaborate care taken in the fifteenth century in the preparation of the various dishes. Of course, great banquets were in those days as rare probably as in our own, but even in the case of the simpler meals the like care appears to have been taken over the cooking of the dishes. Chaucer's Frankeleyn was probably not

N

a very much overdrawn picture of a well-to-do man in the fourteenth century so far as the table pleasures were concerned:

> His bread, his ale, was alway afternoon
> A bettre envyned man was nowher noon
> Withoute bake mete was never his hous
> Of fleissch and fissch, and that so plentyuous
> It snewed in his house of mete and drynk
> Of alle deyntees that men cowde thynke
> Aftur the sondry sesouns of the yeer,
> He chaunged hem at mete and at soper,
> Ful many a fat patrich had he in mewe
> And many a brem and many a luce in stewe.
> Woo was his cook, but if his sauce were
> Poynant and scharp, and redyal his gere.
> His table dormant in his halle alway
> Stood redy covered all the large day.

If there was plenty there was also thrift. It is impossible to read the accounts of monastic houses and noble families without being struck with the exceeding care with which those whose duty it was, regulated household expenses and zealously guarded against waste. It was doubtless in this way that in the great halls of the higher nobility so vast a number of retainers and guests could have been entertained almost continually, and in the monastic refectories such boundless hospitality was able to be dispensed. As an example of the way in which a royal home was regulated in the fifteenth century, at the risk of wearying the reader I will give a long extract from the rules for the household of the mother of King Edward IV.

" A compendious recytation compiled of the order, rules and constructione of the house of the righte excellent princesse Cicile, late mother unto the right noble prince King Edward IV.

" We semeth yt is requisyte to understand the order of her own person concerning God and the Worlde.

" She useth to arrise at seven of the clocke and hath readye her chapleyne to saye with her mattins of the daye and mattins of our ladye; and when she is fully readye, she hath a lowe masse in her chamber, and after masse she taketh somethinge to re-create nature; and soe goeth to the chappell hearinge the divine service, and two lowe masses; from thence to dynner; duringe the time whereof she hath a lecture of holy matter, either Hilton of contemplative and active life, Bona-venture de infantia, Salvatores legenda aurea, St. Maude, St. Katherine of Sonys, or the Revelacyons of St. Bridgett.

"After dynner she giveth audyence to all such as hath any matter to shewe unto her by the space of one hower, and then sleepeth one quarter of an hower, and after she hathe slepte she contynueth in prayer unto the first peale of evensong; then she drinketh wyne or ale at her pleasure. Forthwith her chapleyne is readye to saye with her both evensongs; and after the last peale, she goeth to the chappell and heareth evensonge by note; from thence to supper, and in the tyme of supper, she recyteth the lecture that was had at dynner to those that be in her presence.

" After supper she disposeth herself to be famyliare with her gentlewomen; and one hower before her going to bed, she taketh a cuppe of wyne, and after that goeth to her priyvie closette and taketh her leave of God for alle nighte, making end of her prayers for that daye; and by eighte of the clocke is in bedde. I trust to our lordes mercy, that this noble princesse thus divideth the howers to his highe pleasure."

" The rules of the house.

" Upon eatyng dayes at dynner by eleven of the clocke, a first dynner in the tyme of highe masse, for carvers, cupbearers, sewars, and offycers.

" Upon fastinge dayes, by twelve of the clocke and a later dynner for carvers and for wayters.

" A supper upon eatynge dayes for carvers and offycers at four of the clocke; my ladye and the householde at fyve of the clocke, at supper . . .

" Uppon Sundaye, Tuesdaye, and Thursdaye the householde at dynner is served with beefe and mutton and one roste; at supper, leyched beefe and mutton roste.

" Uppon Mondaye and Wensdaye at dynner, one boyled beefe and mutton; at supper, ut supra.

" Uppon fastinge dayes salt fyshe and two dishes of fresh fishe; if there come a principal feaste, it is served like unto the feaste honorably.

" If Mondaye or Wensdaye be hollidaye then is the household served with one roste, as in other days.

" Upon Satterdaye at dynner, salt fyshe, one fresh fyshe and butter; at supper salt fishe and egges.

" Wyne daylie for the heade offycers when they be presente, to the ladyes and gentlewomen, to the dean of the chappell, to the almoner, to the gentlemen ushers, to the cofferer, to the clerke of the kytchin, and to the marshall. . . . Breakfastes be there none, saving onely the head offycers when they be present; to the ladyes and gentlewomen; to the deane of the chappell, to the almoner, to the gentlemen ushers, &c., &c. . . .

" To all sicke men is given a lybertye to have all such thinges as may be to theire ease; if he be a gentleman and will be at his own dyett, he hath for his boarde weekely 16*d*. and 9*d*. for his servante and nothin out of the house.

" If any man fall impotente, he hath styll the same wages that he had when he might doe best service during my ladyes life."

But to pursue the subject with which we are more immediately concerned: The second Wells banquet, the *menu* of which has come down to us, was given also in the great hall of the Bishop's Palace on the installation of Bishop Bubwith's successor. John Stafford was consecrated at the Dominican Church in London, and on the 16th of September, 1425, he took possession of his See. On that occasion the dinner was furnished apparently by the same professional cook that arranged the repast at the funeral of Bishop Stafford's predecessor. It will be seen that there was now no need of making preparation of a fish dinner for those who were bound to abstain; but two dinners were, however, prepared, one for the more exalted guests and the other for those who had seats in "the lower part of the hall and elsewhere." The two *menus* are as follows:

Convivium Johannis Stafforde Episcopi Wellensis in inductum Episcopatus sui. Videlicet 16 die Septembris Anno Domini Millessimo cccc^mo vicessimo quinto.

Le I Cours

Furmenty with Venysoun .	(Venison with wheat "husked and boiled").
Mammenye	(Mince).
Brawne.	
Rede roste	(Eggs treated with violet flowers).
Capoun de haut grece . . .	(Stuffed capon).
Swan.	
Heyroun	(Heron).

CRANE.
A LECHE . . . . (Sliced meat or bread spiced).
CRUSTADE RYAL . . . . . . (A pie with currants, dates, eggs,
&c.).
FRUTOURE, SAMATA . . . . . (Fritter or pancake).
A SOTELTE . A doctor of law.

LE II COURS

BLAMCHE MORTREWYS . . . . (Forced meat of fowl or pork).
VYAND RYAL . . . . (Almond rice mould).
PECOKE.
CONYNG . . . . (Young rabbit).
FESAUNTE.
TELE.
CHYKONYS DORYD . . . . . (Chicken glazed with almond
milk).
PYJONS.
VENYSONN ROSTYD.
GULLYS . . . . (Gulls).
CURLEW.
COKYNTRYCHE . . . . (Capon and pig roasted to-
gether).
A LECHE . . . . (Sliced meat or bread spiced).
PYSTELADE CHAUD . . . . . (Hot pasty?)
PYSTELADE FRYID . . . . . (Pasty cooked in a frying pan).
FRYTOURE DAMASKE . . . . (Fritter with Damascus dates).
A SOTELTE . Eagle.

LE III COURS

GELY.
CREME MOUNDY.
PETY CURLEWE . . . . . . (Small Curlew).
EGRET . . . . (Young Heron).
PERTRYCHE.
VENYSON ROST.
PLOVERE.
OXYN KYN.
QUAYLYS.
SNYPYS . . . . (Snipe).
HERTE DE ALOUSE.
SMALL BYRDYS.

DOWCET RYAL . . . . (A kind of cheesecake).
PETELADE FRYID . . . . . . (Pasty cooked in a frying pan).
HYRCHOUNS . . . . (Fish prepared as above).
EGGS RYAL . . . . (Eggs royal).
POMYS . . . . (A kind of forced-meat ball with spices).
BRAWN FRYID.

A SOTELTE . Sent Andrewe.

FRUTE.
WAFFRYS.
VYN DOWCE.

Pro inferiori parte Aule et in aliis locis.

LE I COURS

FURMENTY WITH VENYSOUN . (Venison with wheat "husked and boiled").
MAMMENYE . . . . (Mince).
BRAWN.
REDE ROSTE . . . . (Eggs treated with violet flowers).
CAPOUN.
LECHE . . . . (Sliced meat or bread with spices).
A BAKEMETE . . . . (A fruit pie).

LE II COURS

MORTREWS . . . . (Forced meat of fowl or pork).
PYGGE.
CONYNGE.
CHYKONS.
VENYSOUN ROSTED.
LECHE . . . . (Sliced meat or bread spiced).
FRUTOURE.
BAKEMETE CHAUD . . . . . (Fruit pie hot).
BAKEMETE FRYID.

To these last *menus* it may be useful to add a few words upon the use of what was called in the upper banquet the *sotelte*, with which each course was concluded. These were designs, more or less ambitious, in sugar and paste, which generally pointed some allusion to the circumstances of the feast. They were often preceded by what were called *warners* or dishes meant to prepare the guests for the great *tour de force* of the chef in the *sotelte* proper. Probably the great designs which ornamented our dinner tables some years ago may be considered as the more civilised descendants of the mediaeval subtlety. Sometimes these artistic erections on the tables were meant to be eaten, like modern ornamented wedding cakes; and frequently they were of considerable size. Hunting scenes were depicted with trees, hounds and stags, and in one case the whole interior of an abbey church with its various altars. The two subtleties at the second and third course of the installation banquet of the same John Stafford, the *menu* of whose feast at Wells has just been given, when in 1443 he was translated to the Archiepiscopal throne of Canterbury, may be here given as samples. " A sotelte: The Trinity sitting in a sun of gold, with a crucyfix in his hand, Saint Thomas on the one side, Saint Austin on the other, my lord (John Stafford) kneeling *in pontificalibus* before him, his crosier (bearer) coped, with the arms of Rochester: Behind him on the one side, a black monk, Prior of Christchurch, on the other side, the Abbot of Saint Austin's."

The subtlety at the third course was the following: " A Godhead in a sun of gold glorified above; in the sun the Holy Ghost as a dove: St. Thomas kneeling before him with the point of a sword in his head and a mitre thereupon crowning St. Thomas: on the right hand Mary holding a mitre, on the left John the Baptist and in the four corners four angels with incense."

The allusions in these two great dishes do not require

any explanation. At the installation at Wells the subtleties were as we see of a simpler character, namely: " A
doctor of law " for the first course, with apparent reference to the state of the bishop before consecration :
(2) " An eagle," the emblem of St. John; and (3) " St.
Andrew," the patron saint of the Cathedral Church at
Wells. This last formed the first subtlety exhibited at
the installation at Canterbury as having reference to the
previous position occupied by the new Archbishop. At
this latter feast it is more fully described as " Saint
Andrew, sitting on his high altar in state, with beams of
gold, (*i.e.*, the rays of a nimbus). Before him kneeling
the Bishop *in pontificalibus*; his crosier (bearer) kneeling behind him coped."

V

SOME TROUBLES OF A CATHOLIC
FAMILY IN PENAL TIMES

WE who live in these days of religious liberty can
with difficulty realise all the "troubles of our
Catholic forefathers" in penal times. The late Father
Morris and others have done much to illustrate the sufferings of those who were called upon—and were indeed
happy in being called upon—to bear witness to their
Faith by laying down their lives for religion in the sixteenth and seventeenth centuries. The names and the
glorious "passions" of these strong soldiers of Christ are,
thanks to Bishop Challoner and subsequent writers, well
known and held in benediction by us who are heirs to
the Faith for which they suffered and died. But beyond
those specially "signed" with the seal of martyrdom
there is "a great multitude which no man could number"
of men and women, of every rank and degree, who clung
to the Catholic Faith and worship of their ancestors in
spite of every form of refined persecution which the ingenuity of those "men of the New Learning" could
invent to force them to adopt the State religion. The
names of these noble confessors for conscience' sake are
for the most part unknown, but the statute book would
of itself be sufficient evidence of the rigour with which
they were treated by those in power for their "recu-

sancy " or refusal to accept the " Elizabethan settlement
of religion " and against their consciences be present at
the Protestant service which the authority of the law
substituted for the ancient sacrifice of the Mass in every
parish church in England. So terrible, indeed, and so
shocking to our modern ideas are these penal laws, designed to bring our Catholic forefathers into conformity
with the State religion, that many even of ourselves have
come to regard them as having been, in fact, from the
first a dead letter on the page of the statute book, never
intended to have been enforced by those in authority, and
most generally disregarded and ignored by those against
whom they were directed. Non-Catholic writers have
gone to the point of trying to wipe from this page of
English history even the memory of this religious coer-
cion, or of trying to represent "recusancy" as an obstinate
determination on the part of some bigoted Catholics not
to recognise the title of Elizabeth to the Crown, and to
refuse the oath of fidelity to her. The truth is that a
" recusant Catholic " was one who simply refused to be
present at the new service of the Protestant religion in
the parish church, and in the vast majority of cases there
was no question about any oath of fealty, or even of any
declaration of belief in the supremacy of the Queen over
the Church; although of course a Catholic would have
equally refused to acknowledge her ecclesiastical title.
There can be no manner of mistake in this matter, as
there is a definition of "recusancy" upon almost every
Crown record at this period. Thus in the Royal Receipt
Books, during the last twenty years of Elizabeth's reign,
there are entered the fines levied on recusants to the
amount of £120,305 19s. 7½d.; or something like a million
and a quarter of our money; a very considerable por-

tion of the revenue of the country. In each case the receipt is entered as: *Fines de recusantibus accedere ad ecclesiam ubi communis oratio utitur.* That is, " fines from those refusing to come to church where the Common Prayer is made use of."

Now the principle of " forgetting " what it is unpleasant to remember may be carried too far, till we are in danger of ignoring the plain facts of history which we owe it to our Catholic ancestors to keep with gratitude before our memory. The truth is certain; they were treated with a rigour it is difficult now to credit; they were imprisoned, taxed and fined because they would not, as it was called, conform and attend the Protestant service; their lands were seized and granted out for long terms to royal officials and favourites to pay two-thirds of their annual value into the royal purse; their goods and chattels were taken possession of and sold to pay at least a portion of the " debt owing to the Crown " by reason of recusancy. As we turn over the records of these days we are forced to wonder not that so few were found faithful to their consciences, but that any Catholic family could possibly have survived the long and relentless persecution by which it was sought to force all into the State established church, and to take the form of religion from the Crown.

Nor are we to suppose that it was only the rich landlords, and those who possessed special power of any kind, that were treated in this way as enemies to the State. The strong arm of the law was stretched out to crush also the poor but staunch adherent of the religion of his Catholic ancestors. The Recusant Rolls, and other documents innumerable, prove that there were none too lowly for the royal officials to persecute. The poorest in

the smallest village were not exempt from fines imposed
for recusancy, and from distress levied upon their goods
upon conviction. Not that for the most part the Catholics
could pay the sums demanded of them. Still the fact
that they were indebted to the Crown to the amount of
£20 a month or £260 a year, and in consequence were
constantly subject to the demand, "Pay what thou
owest," was quite sufficient to render their lot a pitiable
one. We have only to look at the long lists of *recusants*
as they constantly appear on the parchments of the
official rolls to find the names of people of all sorts and
conditions. To pass over the gentry and those able even
partially to pay; we find millers, tailors, shoemakers,
husbandmen, yeomen, labourers, blacksmiths, even mil-
liners. Praise be to the women folk! They seem to have
clung with heroic courage to the ancient Faith in spite
of the special pressure put upon the husbands of many
to drive their wives to attend the Protestant service.

It is impossible to examine the Recusant records
without feeling a desire that somehow or other the
names of these true confessors for the Catholic Faith
were better known—or I might say known at all. Gladly
would I see in every church in England a memorial
tablet, such as has been set up in the church of St. Lawrence, Petersfield. It records the names of those who in
that part of Hampshire had the happiness of being "convicted recusants," and who by their staunch and loyal
adherence to the Catholic Faith, in spite of every form
of persecution, have contributed to hand down to us of
these days that most precious of gifts.

My present purpose, however, is not to write about
the recusant laws generally, nor to illustrate the way in
which they were executed in any special district. It is

simply to relate the special troubles of one Catholic family in Wiltshire. The incidents may perhaps be all the more interesting to some, inasmuch as the chief people concerned in this sad history are the father and mother of the first abbess of the Benedictine convent at Cambrai, now established at Stanbrook. The story itself illustrates the great difficulty which Catholics in those days experienced in obtaining permission to lay their dead in any churchyard; and we may preface it by giving an old account of what happened in Winchester on the death of a Catholic gentleman in prison, where he had long lain because he was unable to pay the amount of the fines claimed by the Crown for his recusancy, his little property having previously been seized by the royal officials and sold. This account, which I owe to the kindness of Mr. F. J. Baigent, is as follows:

"In the year of our Lord 1589, Nicholas Tychborne, a gentleman of rank, died in the gaol of Winchester. This gentleman, after having suffered multiplied and grievous injuries, together with the spoliation of all his goods, was at length captured by the fraud of his enemies, brought to Winchester and cast into prison. Where, having been detained therein for the profession of the Catholic religion during the space of nine years, he fell ill, seized with a grievous malady, and he sent for a priest who might administer the rites of the Church to him, now approaching the end of his existence.

"The priest did the duties of his office, after which the only wish of the sick man was, that, as he must pay the debt of nature, he might be permitted to survive until the festival of St. James, for he ardently desired to depart this life on the feast of that saint, under whose guardianship and protection he had lived seventy years.

Nor was the wish in vain; for beyond all hope and expectation of both the physicians and his friends, he was preserved for the space of fifteen days—that is, until the feast of St. James, in which, towards night, in the presence of many of his Catholic fellow prisoners, he began more ardently to implore the saint's assistance. He then commended himself to God, to the Virgin Mother of God, and to all the other princes of heaven, addressing them in the most moving language; and having crossed his hands, with his eyes devoutly lifted up to heaven, he laid in that posture about two hours, sometimes breaking forth into the praises of his Maker, but for the most part quietly meditating within himself, till at length, without any agony or symptom of pain, he most sweetly expired.

"After his death no small contention arose between Cooper, the superintendent of Winchester (*i.e.*, the Protestant bishop) and the Catholics and his other friends, for he would not grant them a place of interment in any church or cemetery; declaring that his conscience would not permit him to allow a Papist to be buried in any of his churches or cemeteries. To this the Catholics answered that the churches had been built, not by them [the Protestants] but by men of their [the Catholic] religion, and by these the cemeteries were consecrated, and that therefore it was very unjust to deny them the right of sepulture in those places which Catholics had formerly erected at their own expense for this very purpose. But this argument, though indeed most powerful, availed nothing with him. They therefore, knowing his power and authority, which was very great in the city, and struck, at the same time, with the novelty of the affair, continued for a long time in painful suspense, uncertain how to proceed.

"At length an old man came forth and said the following: 'The affair is, indeed, one of the very greatest difficulty, but if you follow my advice, we shall do what seems easier than was first intended to be done, and of which the Protestants have not the slightest suspicion. You know that upon a hill, about a mile distant from this city, is a place on which there was formerly a chapel dedicated to St. James, the vestiges of which still remain, and from which the hill itself has borrowed its name. I remember as a boy seeing several persons there buried; even there let us take this good man, especially as in the very agony of his death we beheld him particularly recommending himself to that saint as to his holy patron, to whom also, during his whole life, he was singularly devout, and actually died on his festival day, all of which seems to demand this for him as of right, and necessity itself compels.'

" The advice of the old man was adopted and put into execution, and the bones of the good gentleman now rest on the summit of that high and most beautiful hill, in the very place where formerly existed a celebrated chapel dedicated to St. James, but which, not many years ago, the heretics, as is their custom, pulled down and completely demolished."

I need only add that from that date, 1589, to the present, the Catholics have always retained possession of the ancient cemetery of St. James. It is the Catholic cemetery of Winchester, and in its holy ground repose the bodies of many confessors for the Faith in that neighbourhood.

But to return to my main point. The Gawen family— for it is about them I write—were among the most respectable and respected gentry of Wiltshire. Aubrey says they were settled on the land at Norrington for 450 years, and Chaucer puts the name of "Gawain" into his tales of Arthur. Hoare, in his account of the Hundred of Chalk, gives two views of the family house at Norrington, and he describes it—his description being borne out by the pictures—as a handsome Gothic edifice, probably built by John Gawen, who bought the estate in the first year of the reign of Richard II. " It would," he writes, "be unpardonable in the impartial topographer to pass over such an one [as the Gawen family] without doing justice to their memory," and "hand down to posterity [whilst he recounts the high and dignified offices they held in the county] the unmerited sufferings they endured for their attachment to the religion they professed, and for their loyalty to the House of Stuart, previous to and in the time of the Commonwealth."

So far as the Wiltshire estates are concerned they had practically passed out of the possession of the Gawens before the advent of the Stuarts; having been seized by Queen Elizabeth in payment of fines due for the obstinate refusal of Thomas Gawen to attend his parish church for the Protestant service. By an inquisition held in the last year of that queen he was fined £1,380 for this legal offence, and was further fined £120 for not having subsequently made his submission according as the Act of Parliament required. It is also stated in the same inquisition that he was a *popish recusant*, and that consequently two-thirds of his annual estate, valued at £389 7s. 4d., was seized to the Queen's use.

This Thomas Gawen had married into a staunch Catholic family, his wife being Katherine, daughter to Sir Edward Waldegrave, K.G., who in the first years of Elizabeth's reign had refused to be bound by the royal

O

settlement of religion, and who, together with his wife and seven others, was sent to the Tower for having Mass said in his house. There in 1561 he died, a confessor for the Faith. By his marriage Thomas Gawen had two children: a son Thomas, who succeeded to the remnant of the family estates which had not been seized to pay the recusancy fines, and a daughter Frances, who became the first abbess of the Benedictine convent at Cambrai.

By the last year of the sixteenth century the ruin of the Gawen family was almost complete. In a letter written from England on July 22nd, 1599, the writer takes their case as typical of many others in England at the time, and as the description given in it is not only of interest in itself, but directly introduces us to the family at a time about which I shall have something to say, I quote some portions of it.

" Felton " (the great official discoverer and persecutor of Catholics) "brings Papists to great misery," writes our informant. "When the statute was made that those who did not pay £20 a month should forfeit all their goods and two-thirds of their lands, the guard and others about the court procured the Lord Treasurer's warrant that any who indicted and convicted such a Papist should have a commission to find his land and have a lease of two-thirds of it at the rent found for her majesty. This obtained, they would offer composition to the recusant, and when this was agreed upon and paid, would find it under the rate and pass the lease to some friend ; for they might not by covenant grant it to the owner nor any recusant. Yet were all these leases during pleasure, so that first the recusant was compelled to a grievous fine, and yet had yearly to pay the Queen a rent for his own living, and besides had to make away with all his goods.

"Then when this course was taken all England over, Felton informed the Queen that it would be very profitable to grant a commission for further inquiry into recusants' livings. He got many base fellows in different shires, who seized on all recusants' goods, surveyed their lands, examined their tenants on oath, found their livings [to be] at higher rates, and so frustrating the first leases took new ones, dispossessed the recusants and lived there, or placed there some bankrupts like themselves, so that the recusant had to maintain himself and family only on a third part of his estate. . . .

"If a gentleman, reconciled [to the Church of Rome] during his parents' life, when he was unable to pay the statute, should afterwards come and offer arrears and the £20 a month in future—which is what the law exacts—that is not allowed; but the Queen may take the fairest, and for £260 she has some £400 a year, and yet must Felton and his companions choose their fairest house and domains, and assign them what they list for their third. Thus have Caruell, Thimbleby, *Gawen*, and many others been dealt with."

The writer goes on to describe the ruin which everywhere falls on estates, and concludes: "Some, seeing that Felton must get all, have broken their windows, turned up their gardens, destroyed their dovecots and warrens, and would have burnt their corn; but the law prohibits this." [1]

I may now introduce the reader to the two documents which afford special information about the troubles of the Gawen family for religion and conscience. They are

[1] State Papers, Dom. Eliz., vol. 271.

contained in some Star Chamber proceedings of the
reign of James the First which have lately been privately printed.[1] To understand the first it is necessary
to remember that when Queen Elizabeth died, the
Catholics, rightly or wrongly, expected that under her
successor—the son of Mary Queen of Scots—they
would be treated with greater mildness, if not with
toleration.

On Friday, 9th May, 1606, in the Star Chamber, before
seven counsellors and judges, the suit of one Richard
Kennelle against Gawen and others came on for hearing. The plaintiff was the tenant in possession of Mr.
Thomas Gawen's house at Norrington, and the defendants were Mr. Gawen, his wife Katherine, his son Thomas,
Sir Edmund Ludlowe, a Justice of the Peace, and one
Nicholas Tooman, the "tithing man." At this date, when
the case came before the court, Mr. Thomas Gawen was
already dead; but as the others were held to be the
principal "rioters," it was allowed to proceed.

The counsel for the plaintiff Kennelle, in opening the
pleadings, stated that Thomas Gawen being a recusant,
Queen Elizabeth had granted his lands to one Fortescue,
who had leased them for a term of years to Kennelle.
This latter, "having servants in the kitchen and the
barn, and corn growing on the land," was in possession,
when on 7th August, in the first year of James I, Katherine Gawen, "with two servants, on the Sabbath day,
in the time of divine service, entered into the house and
barred the doors." The following day she "assembled
more servants and friends with weapons, and kept possession by force, and took the goods and spoilt them
and spent them." She then sent for Tooman the tithing

[1] Haywarde, *Les Reportes del Cases in Camera Stellata.*

man, and Sir Edmund Ludlowe, a Justice of the Peace,
to uphold her in possession of her husband's house.

The tithing man—the representative of our modern
constable—"assembled more people and encouraged the
rioters, and assisted them in the king's name to keep
possession." Upon this he was admitted into the be-
sieged house, and when Sir Edmund Ludlowe came,
" Katherine Gawen said he was welcome and her friend,
and he walked into the garden and so into the house."
It was part of the case of the plaintiff that this Justice
was wholly on the side of the Catholic mistress of the
house, and adverse to the tenant, who by means of the
laws against recusants had dispossessed the family and
taken up his abode in the mansion. There is little doubt
that both his sympathy and that of the people round
about were on the side of the persecuted owners. Sir
Edmund Ludlowe, it was contended, "would see but
three rioters in the house and no weapons, whereas it
was proved that there were fourteen, and all with
weapons."

Sir Edmund, however, made at least a show of partiality, and bound both parties over to keep the peace.
But, said Mr. Counsellor Pine, in pleading the plaintiff's
case, "he apprehended a servant,—thinking him to be
one of Kennelle's men; but on Mrs. Gawen telling him
he was her servant, he allowed him to go." He further
ordered Kennelle to find " sureties," and seizing him " by
the collar struck him, declaring that he would drag him
off to gaol, tied to his horse's tail."

This action did not tend to settle the matter quietly;
but for "many days together there was shooting of guns
and bows out of the windows at some of the servants ";
and strangely enough, as it seems to us now, at a sessions

held a few days afterwards, the plaintiff was condemned by the Justices of the county to pay £300 as a fine for the riot. The present application to the Star Chamber was to set this verdict aside, and to punish the defendants as well as to reinstate Kennelle in possession of Norrington.

In reply the counsel for the Gawens showed that Mrs. Gawen "conceived by the king's general pardon" on his coming to the throne that they should have their property free again, and get rid of the objectionable tenant who had been quartered in their house by the royal officials. The property was mostly "her jointure," and great waste was being done on the lands by the plaintiff.

In the course of the case it was proved that Mrs. Gawen was a recusant, and "did report, upon the king's coming," that times would be changed for Catholics "now that the bloody queen was dead, under whom the Lord Chief Justice did rule the roste and Sir John Fortescue and that bloodsucker, Sir W. Rawlie."

Of course, the result was a foregone conclusion. The plaintiff obtained an injunction against the Gawens, and an order for the sheriff to put him in possession of Norrington again. The defendants were not unprepared for this, and seem to have taken the result as philosophically as possible. Mrs. Gawen said that "a dogge Kennelle were a fytter place for" the plaintiff than her house, and Sir Edmund Ludlowe, finding that the actual words of the judgment were that the sheriff "should establish those in possession," cheerfully said, "That is all right. Mrs. Gawen is in possession, is she not?" But the matter did not end here, and in the result Mrs. Gawen was fined £500; Sir Edmund Ludlowe £300 and was deprived of his office; the tithing man £100 and discharged from his post; five other male defendants £50 a-piece; and three women £10 each. Of course, all were to be imprisoned till the money was paid, and as most of them were servants, the mistress was ordered to pay if they could not do so.

Then, continues Haywarde, the writer of these notes on the Star Chamber cases, "The lords much insisted upon the vile words about Queen Elizabeth, and wished they could give Mrs. Gawen exemplary punishment. And the Lord of Northampton took occasion to say that it being reported that King James had sent privately to Rome to promise good treatment to Catholics when he should come to England, he had informed the king of the report, and received from him assurance that he would execute justice." Further, that on the king's way down from Scotland "the Catholics of Berwick proffered a petition for better treatment," but the king re-established the laws against them, and after a report being traced "to one Watson, a priest condemned to death, the said Watson acknowledged that the king had never given him any such hope."

So ended this case; but the following day, 30th May, 1606, the Star Chamber was occupied in hearing a case in which Mrs. Gawen was plaintiff against two Protestant ministers named Willoughby and Tines, the constable and tithing man and two coroners of the county of Wiltshire. As a preliminary it is noted that Mr. Gawen was a "stiffe and roughe recusant," and for this reason his lands had been granted for his life to Fortescue (no doubt Sir John, about whom Mrs. Gawen had expressed her opinion so forcibly), and by him leased to Kennelle.

It appears that on 1st August, 1603 (the first year of James I), Mr. Gawen died, either on the Sunday night or Monday morning; "and being a fat and corpulent man, his wife made all haste to bury him." In one church, however, Mr. Willoughby refused to allow him to be buried in church or churchyard, because he was "excommunicate." The family pleaded that there was a king's pardon, but Mr. Willoughby, repairing to his ordinary, the Bishop of Salisbury, "was advised that he could not be buried in consecrated ground." Upon this going to another parish of which the defendant Tines was minister they got into the church at night—ten or twelve in number—and buried the body in the chancel, without "minister, clerk, or sexton." They locked themselves into the church, and others having obtained an entrance into the other parish church they tolled the bells all next day in both churches. Finally the constable and posse got in at a side door, and in ejecting them from the chancel "a woman spat in his face, upon which he had her to the stocks."

Now Kennelle, having an estate for Mr. Gawen's life, suspected or pretended to suspect, that he was not dead at all, and getting into the church at night with his man dug up the grave. He found a coffin, however, and thereupon leaving it uncovered suggested that the coroner of the district should hold a quest. A jury was summoned, but for fear of the plague, which was much dreaded, one of the jury got it adjourned for fourteen days, leaving the body as it was. At the expiration of the fortnight the coroner ordered the tithing man to dig up the body, which, however, he absolutely declined to do, and upon this Kennelle hired some one to do the job.

This man, continues the record, "was enforced by reason of the waighte of the corps to dragge him at the lightest ende, whereby his feet being upward, the whole

waighte of his corps swayed to his heade and necke
(which [by] Kennelle himself he was charged to do), and
so draged him into a meadowe farre off, [for] the jury
desyred that the body, having long lyen in the earthe
and of very strong savoure, the churchyard small and
the assembly of people great—almoste a hundred—
might be broughte into a meadowe close adjoining,
where there would be more and better ayre." None of
the jury would even then come near to examine the
body; so Kennelle "caused the shroud to be ripped
up," and gave evidence that there was a suspicious looking circle round about the neck, and suggested that Mr.
Gawen had been strangled and made away with. The
jury, however, found that he had died a natural death,
probably from "an impostume in the stomache."

The quest being finished, the coroner gave an order
to the church officials to bury the corpse again, which
they absolutely refused to do. On this, Kennelle caused
it to be drawn into the church porch, hid the key of the
church door, and there left it to lie several days, "whereby all the parish were so annoyed that they durst not
come to the church." Finally Kennelle, after some time,
gave directions to have the body buried, but as "moste
parte are buried east and west," he had it laid north and
south, saying "as he was an overthwart neighbour while
he lived, so he shall be buried overthwartely; and if you
mislike it, I will have him dragged at a horse's tail and
laid upon the downs."

In the result the Star Chamber judges blamed Kennelle
for proceeding "with such malice" against the dead.
"His principal offence whereon the court grounded their
sentence was his inhuman usage in the burial of the
corps overthwarte, and his malicious words of him, for

de mortuis nil nisi bonum; and our usual manner of burying is very ancient, as Basil noteth and used by the apostles in the primitive church "; and for this reason, too, we pray to the east. Consequently they sentenced Kennelle to pay a fine of £100 and to be imprisoned.

At the end "The archbishop delivered a secret practice of the Papists, that of late days they used to wrap their dead bodies in two sheets, and in one of them strew earth that they themselves had hallowed, and so bury them they care not where, for they say they are thus buried in consecrated earth."

It is impossible here to follow the fortunes of the Gawens further. I will only say there are many records of recusancy fines levied upon Mrs. Gawen, and in 1607 all benefit that could be got from her refusal to attend the Protestant service was granted by King James I to a certain John Price. History does not relate what profit Mr. Price made out of this staunch Catholic lady.

Thomas Gawen, the son, went to live at Horsington, in Somerset, and his son William, born in 1608, sold his remaining interest in Norrington to the Wyndhams in 1657, the year after his father's death. Thus the ancient and Catholic family of Gawen lost their possessions in Wiltshire.

VI

ABBOT FECKENHAM AND BATH [1]

B ATH, perhaps more than most other cities, has always been pleased to recognise and do honour to its worthies. To me, the very streets of the city appear to be peopled by the ghosts of bygone generations. If I shut my eyes upon electric tramways and such like evidences of what is called "modern civilisation," the beaux and belles of ancient days seem to come trooping from their hiding places and appear tripping along the streets as of old; the footways are at once all alive with the gentry of the cocked hat and full-bottomed wig period, with their knee breeches and small clothes to match. Ladies, too, are there, with their hooped and tucked dresses, their high-heeled shoes, and those wonderful creations of the wigmaker's art upon their heads; whilst sedan chairs of all sorts and kinds are borne quickly along the roadways, now desecrated by every kind of modern conveyance.

It was in the eighteenth and early nineteenth centuries, of course, that the city rose to the zenith of its renown, and the crowd of notabilities who then came to seek for rest, health and pleasure in this queen of watering-places, has served to make Bath almost a synonym for a city of gaiety,

[1] A paper read before the members of the Literary and Scientific Institution, Bath, December 14, 1906.

diversion and life. Indeed the memories of that period of prosperity and glory almost seem to have obliterated the thought of persons and of incidents of earlier days. It is one such person that I would recall to your memory to-night. When honoured, by the request of your President to read a paper before this learned Society, my thoughts almost immediately turned to Abbot Feckenham, of Westminster, who is one of the personages my imagination has often conjured up whilst passing along the streets of this city. Most of those who listen to me probably know very little of this grave and kindly ecclesiastic, but the name. But in the sixteenth century he was a generous and true benefactor to the poor of this place, and that at a time when he was himself suffering grievous trials for conscience' sake. At the outset I should like to disclaim any pretence of originality in my presentment of the facts of Abbot Feckenham's life. I have merely taken what I find set down by others, and chiefly by the Rev. E. Taunton in his history of the English *Black Monks*. He has been at great pains to collect every scrap of information in regard to the last Abbot of Westminster, and I borrow freely from the result of his labours.

Feckenham's real name was Howman, his father and mother being Humphrey and Florence Howman of the village of Feckenham, in the county of Worcester. They appear to have been of the yeoman class, and to have been endowed with a certain amount of worldly wealth; at any rate they seem to have sent their son John, who was born somewhere about the first decade of the sixteenth century, to be trained in the monastery of Evesham, which was near their home. Here the boy, who had probably received an elementary education from the

parish priest of his native village, would have been taught
in the claustral school of the great abbey. In time he
joined the community as a novice, and in accordance
with the very general custom of those days, became
afterwards known by the name of his birthplace, as John
Feckenham.

From Evesham the young monk proceeded to Oxford
to study at " Monk's College," or Gloucester Hall, now
known as Worcester College. It is not important here
to determine the actual date when he commenced his
studies at Oxford; probably he went to college about
1530, when we are told definitely that he was eighteen
years of age. His Prior at the house at Oxford was a
monk of his own abbey of Evesham, named Robert
Joseph, and an accidental survival of a manuscript letter-
book gives us not only the information that it was this
religious who taught the classics, but shows in some way
at least how a professor lectured to his students in those
bygone days. The MS. in question is a collection of
Latin letters and addresses, made by this Prior Robert
Joseph. It was, as you are all aware, the fashion in
those times for scholars to send Latin epistles to their
friends, and then to collect them into a volume. We
have many printed books of Latin epistles of this kind.
Prior Joseph, though his elegant letters were never
destined to see the light in all the glory of a printed
dress, still made his collection, which somehow or other
got bound up with a Welsh MS.,—one of the Peniarth
MSS.—and so was preserved to tell us something more
than we knew before about the work of a professor at
Gloucester Hall, when the monks were students there.
Amongst other interesting items of information afforded
in this MS., we have Prior Robert Joseph's inaugural

lecture on a play of Terence; and, by the way, very practical and good it is. There is also another lecture of a different character, which was carefully prepared for delivery to the young Benedictine students at Gloucester Hall. It seems that one of the monks had been " pulling his old professor's leg," as we should say, by telling him that many of them thought that as a teacher he was getting a little past his prime, and that it might perhaps be a good thing if he were to give place to a younger man more in touch with modern scholarship. Prior Robert was deeply wounded, and his carefully prepared address upbraids his pupils for their ingratitude, and practically calls upon those amongst them who considered that he ought to retire, to come forward boldly and say so: an invitation which it is hardly likely was accepted. At any rate, the old professor certainly continued to occupy his chair for some time longer.

In special regard to the young monk, John Feckenham, this same collection of letters is of some interest, since it contains a Latin epistle addressed to him on the occasion of his ordination to the priesthood. " It is a dignity," the writer says in the course of a long letter, " which in our days can never be despised or held in little regard. . . . From this time forth your very carriage and countenance must be changed; from this time forth you are to live after a fashion different to what you did before.

" Now have to be given up the things of youth and the ways of a child, for now you take up the sword of the Spirit, which is the Word of God." This would have been written probably about the year 1536, and in the following year Feckenham was certainly at Oxford. " I find him," writes Anthony à Wood, " there in 1537, in

which year he subscribed, by the name of John Feckenham, to a certain composition then made between Robert
Joseph, prior of the said college (the writer of the Latin
letters), and twenty-nine students thereof on one part (of
which number Feckenham was one of the senior) and
three of the senior beadles of the university on the other."

In 1538 Feckenham supplicated for his degree as
Bachelor of Divinity and took it on June 11th, 1539.
Previously he had, in all probability, been for some time
teaching in the abbey school at Evesham, as he had
himself been taught, and he was there on January 27th,
1540, when the monastery was surrendered to Henry
VIII. In the pension list his name appears as receiving
15 marks (£10) in place of the usual pension (10 marks)
for the younger monks; probably because of his university degree. After the dissolution of his religious
home, John Feckenham at first gravitated back to his
old college at Oxford to continue his studies; he was
soon, however, induced to become chaplain to Bishop
Bell of Worcester. This office he held until the resignation of that prelate in 1543, when he joined Bishop
Edmund Bonner in London, remaining with him until
that prelate was committed as a prisoner to the Tower
of London in 1549, for his opposition to many religious
changes during the reign of Edward VI. At this time
Feckenham, whilst still in London, received the living
of Solihull in Warwickshire. During the time of his
rectorship his parents—Humphrey and Florence Howman—left a bequest of 40s. to the poor, and among the
records of the parish is said to be an old vellum book
"containing the charitable alms given by way of love
to the parishioners of Solihull, with the order of distri-
bution thereof, begun by Master John Howman *alias*

Fecknam, priest and doctor of divinity—in the year of our Lord 1548."

Though moderate and gentle in his disposition, and ever considerate in his dealings with the convictions of others, Feckenham was strong in his own religious views and uncompromising in his attitude to religious change. He consequently quickly found himself involved in an atmosphere of controversy, and at this time probably developed those oratorical powers for which he afterwards became really famous. It was not long, however, before he found himself a prisoner in the Tower, out of which he was, to use his own expression, "borrowed" frequently, for the purpose of sustaining the "ancient side" in the semi-public religious controversies which were then in much favour with all parties. The first of these disputes was held at the Savoy, in the house of the Earl of Bedford; the second was at Sir William Cecil's at Westminster, and the third in the house of Sir John Cheke, the great Greek scholar and King Edward VI's tutor.

Although held all this time as a prisoner, Feckenham was somehow or other still possessed of his benefice at Solihull, of which, for some reason or other, he had not been deprived. He was consequently taken down from London and opposed to the bishop of his own diocese, Bishop Hooper, in four several disputations; the first was arranged at Pershore whilst the bishop was on his visitation tour, and the last in Worcester Cathedral, where amongst others who spoke against him was John Jewel, afterwards Bishop of Salisbury.

With Mary Tudor's advent to the throne Feckenham of course obtained his liberty. On Tuesday, September 5th, 1553, he left the Tower, and according to Machyn's

Diary, on Sunday the 24th of the same month "master doctor Fecknam did preach at Paul's Cross, the Sunday afore the Queen's coronation." He again became chaplain to Bishop Bonner, now also set at liberty, and was nominated a prebendary of St. Paul's in 1554. Other preferment came to him very rapidly: Queen Mary made him one of her chaplains and her confessor, and before November 25th, 1554, he was appointed Dean of St. Paul's. Fuller, the historian, says of him at this time: " He was very gracious with the Queen and effectually laid out all his interest with her (sometimes even to offend her, but never to injure her) to procure pardon of the faults, or mitigation of the punishment of poor Protestants. The Earls of Bedford and Leicester received great kindness from him; and his old friend, Sir John Cheke, owed his life to Fecknam's personal interest with the Queen. He took up the cause of the unfortunate Lady Jane Dudley, and remonstrated with the Queen and Gardiner upon the policy of putting her to death. He visited the poor girl in prison; and though unsuccessful in removing the prejudices of her early education, he was able to help her to accept with resignation the fate that awaited her. Neither did he forsake the hapless lady until she paid by death the penalty of her father-in-law's treason and her own share therein. When the Princess Elizabeth was sent to the Tower in March, 1554, for her supposed part in Wyat's rebellion, Fecknam, just then elected dean, interceded so earnestly for her release that Mary, who was convinced of her sister's guilt, or at any rate of her insincerity, showed for some time her displeasure with him. But Elizabeth's life was spared; and she was released, mainly by his importunity, after two months' imprisonment."

P

On 19th March, 1556, Giovanni Michiel, the Venetian ambassador, wrote from London to the Doge about the restoration of the Benedictines. He says: "Sixteen monks have also resumed the habit and returned to the Order spontaneously, although they were able to live and had lived out of it much at ease and liberty, there being included among them the Dean of St. Paul's (Feckenham) who has a wealthy revenue of well nigh 2000 (£); notwithstanding which they have renounced all their temporal possessions and conveniences and press for readmission into one of their monasteries." There were obvious difficulties in the way of any large scheme of monastic restoration: the property of the old abbeys had long since been granted away mostly to laymen, and at some of the greater houses, like Westminster and Gloucester, chapters of secular priests had been established in place of the dispossessed monks. At Westminster, however, arrangements were quickly made with the view of restoring the Benedictines to their old home: promotion was given to the dean and the interests of the other secular canons were secured, and on 7th September, 1556, the Queen appointed Feckenham abbot of restored Westminster. The Venetian ambassador says that the monks with their new abbot were to make their entry at the close of September, but this they did not do: there was evidently much more preparation necessary than had been calculated upon. Dean Stanley, in his *Historical Memorials of Westminster Abbey*, says "the great refectory was pulled down" and "the smaller dormitory was cleared away," and other conventual buildings had either been destroyed or adapted to other uses. So there was obviously much to be done before the new community could take up the old life again, and it was not until 21st November that the monks were able to begin once again the regular round of conventual duties in the cloisters and choir of Westminster.

I cannot resist quoting here the account given by the contemporary writer Machyn, in his quaint style, of this restoration. "The same day (21st November) was the new abbot of Westminster put in, Doctor Fecknam, late dean of Paul's, and xiv. more monks sworn in. And the morrow after, the lord abbot with his convent went a procession after the old fashion, in their monk's weeds, in cowls of black saye, with his vergers carrying his silver-rod in their hands; at Evensong time the vergers went through the cloisters to the abbot and so went into the church afore the high altar and there my lord kneeled down and his convent; and after his prayer was made he was brought into the choir with the vergers and so into his place, and presently he began Evensong xxii. day of the same month that was St. Clement's Even last." "On the 29th day was the abbot stalled and did wear a mitre. The Lord Cardinal was there and many bishops and the Lord Treasurer and a great company. The Lord Chancellor (Archbishop Heath) sang Mass and the abbot made the sermon."

Feckenham lost no time in setting his house in order and in gathering round him other monks and novices. Giovanni Michiel, the ambassador before referred to, tells us that on St. Thomas' Eve (20th December) the Queen "chose to see the Benedictine monks in their habits at Westminster," and so going for Vespers was received by the abbot and twenty-eight other monks all men of mature age, the youngest being upwards of forty and all endowed with learning and piety proved by their renunciation of the many conveniences of life."

The restoration of Benedictine life at Westminster was not destined by Providence to continue for very long. Queen Mary died 17th November, 1558, and her funeral rites were solemnised at Westminster. Feckenham preached one sermon at the obsequies, and White, Bishop of Winchester, the other. Both gave umbrage to the new Queen, and the bishop's led to his confinement in his own house. As for Feckenham, it is said that Elizabeth greatly desired to win over to her side one whom she respected, and who was universally popular. One story has it that she offered him the Archbishopric of Canterbury if he would assist in the settlement of the national religion on the lines she desired. The abbot, however, remained staunch to his conscientious convictions, and in Parliament strenuously opposed all the measures by which the religious settlement was finally effected. During the time of the debates in the Parliament, Feckenham was quietly awaiting at Westminster the approaching ruin of his house, which to him at least could hardly be doubtful. He went on in all things as if no storm clouds were gathering, leading his monastic life with his brethren. The story goes that he was engaged in planting some elms in his garden at Westminster when a message was brought to him that a majority of the House of Commons had voted the destruction of all religious houses, and the messenger remarked that as he and his monks would soon have to go, he was planting his trees in vain. " Not in vain," replied the abbot. " Those that come after me may perhaps be scholars and lovers of retirement, and whilst walking under the shade of these trees they may sometimes think of the olden religion of England and of the last abbot of this place," and so he went on planting.

The end of monastic Westminster came on the 12th July, 1559. On that date, for refusing the Oath of Supremacy, Feckenham and his monks were turned out of their house. What immediately became of them we do not know, and probably never shall, but judging from the case of the bishops we may suppose that they were probably assigned places of abode. It was, however, soon considered injurious to the new order, that the bishops of the old order and Abbot Feckenham should be allowed even the semblance of liberty comprised in the order for a fixed place of abode, from which they could not depart without permission. So on May 20th, 1560, it was agreed in the Queen's Council that Feckenham and some of the bishops should be confined straightway in prison, and so by order of Archbishop Parker "at night about 8 of the clock was sent to the Fleet doctor Scory, and Master Feckenham to the Tower."

In this confinement the abbot remained until 1563. In the March of that year Parliament had given authority to the new bishops to administer the Oath of Supremacy, with the new penalty of death for those who refused it. The plague was at that time raging in the city of London, and the prisoners petitioned " to be removed to some other convenient place for their better safeguard from the present infection." This was so far granted that they were committed to the charge of the bishops. Stowe, the careful historian, thus relates the fact: " anno 1563 in September the old bishops and divers doctors, (were sent to the bishop's houses) there to remain prisoners under their custody (the plague being then in the city was thought the cause ").

Feckenham was brought, first of all, back to his old home at Westminster to the care of the new dean, Goodman. But before the winter, at the suggestion of Bishop Grindal, he was removed to the house of Bishop Horne, of Winchester. In spite of all he could do and say and notwithstanding all his arguments, the Bishop of Winchester was unable to shake the resolution of the abbot and prevail on him to take the Oath of Supremacy. Horne indeed complains that Feckenham, at the end of all discussion, used to declare that it was with him a mere matter of conscience; and, pointing to his heart, would say: " The matter itself is founded here, and shall never go out." And so in the end, Horne gave up the task of trying to change his prisoner's opinion; and by January, 1565, Feckenham was back once more in the Tower. From that time until 17th of July, 1574, he remained either there or in the Marshalsea, under more or less strict restraint.

After fourteen years' confinement he was permitted to go out on conditions. He was bound not to try and gain others to his way of thinking; he was to dwell in a specified place, " was not to depart from thence at any time, without the licence of the lords of the Council," and he was not to receive any visitors. As a prisoner on parole, then, Feckenham went in July, 1574, to live in Holborn; whereabout, it is not exactly known. No sooner had he gained his liberty, even with restrictions, than the abbot's old passion of doing good to others reasserted itself, and he at once became engaged in works of true charity and general useful- ness. " Benevolence was so marked a feature in his character that," as Fuller says, " he relieved the poor wheresoever he came ; so that flies flock not thicker about spilt honey than the beggars constantly crowded about him."

We have unfortunately no information about the source of the money, which he evidently had at his disposal. But clearly considerable sums must have been given to him for charitable purposes, as, no doubt, the donors were assured that they would be well and faithfully expended by him. Whilst dwelling in Holborn, Feckenham consequently was able to build an aqueduct for the use of the people generally. Every day he is said to have distributed the milk of twelve cows among the sick and poor of the district, and took under his special charge the widows and orphans. He encouraged the youth of the neighbourhood in many sports, by giving prizes and by arranging Sunday games, such as all English lads love.

And now comes the connection of Abbot Feckenham with this city of Bath. Whilst labouring for the good of others in London, his constitution, naturally enfeebled by his long imprisonment, gave way, and he became seriously ill. On July 18th, 1575, the Council in reply to his petition, ordered "the Master of the Rolls, or in his absence the Recorder of London, to take bondes of Doctor Feckenham for his good behaviour and that at Michaelmas next he shall return to the place where he presently is, and in the meantime he may repair to the Baths." "*The* baths," of course—at any rate in those days—meant this city, which had been pre-eminently the health resort of Englishmen for centuries.

Hither then, some time in the summer of 1575, came Abbot Feckenham, with leave to remain until the feast of Michaelmas. He, however, certainly remained longer than that, as we shall see, as it was the common practice at this time to extend such permissions. Whilst here the abbot was the guest of a then well-known physician of the city, Dr. Ruben Sherwood, who, although a recognised "popish recusant," had probably, like so many other doctors, been allowed to remain unmolested because of his skill, and the paucity of such men of talent in medicine in the sixteenth century. I may perhaps, here, be allowed a brief digression to point out to you, from an interesting article in *The Downside Review* called "A seventeenth century West Country Jaunt," by Father N. Birt, that this Dr. Ruben Sherwood died in 1599, and that in the seventeenth century there was certainly a Sherwood tomb and brass in the Abbey, with the arms of the family and a Latin inscription; this has, however, since disappeared.

It is not improbable that Dr. Ruben Sherwood, at the time of Abbot Feckenham's visit, occupied a long building, parallel to the west end of the abbey church on the south side, which existed till 1755. This had probably been the Prior's quarters and was subsequently known as Abbey House. Collinson says that the house was again rendered habitable some time after the dissolution, and that parts of it, "obsolete offices and obscure rooms and lofts," were left in their former state and had never been occupied after their desertion by the monks. The historian of Somerset also speaks of a find of old vestments and other ecclesiastical garments in a walled-up apartment in this old house in 1755; but unfortunately the things fell to dust, and we have no description of them. It strikes me, however, as more than possible that they were vestments for the use of priests, who were compelled to hide away during penal times. Be that as it may, it would appear more than likely that Dr. Ruben

Sherwood lived in these old quarters, and that it was here that he received Abbot Feckenham when he came to take the waters in 1575. Certainly his son, John Sherwood, also a physician and a "recusant," had a lease of the house and premises till his death in 1620, and used to receive patients who came for the Bath waters.

During his stay at this renowned watering-place, Abbot Feckenham was not wholly occupied with the cure of his own ills. It seemed impossible for him not to think of others, and here in this city he felt himself moved with compassion to see how the poor, deprived of their charitable foundations during the religious upheaval, were excluded from the use and benefit of the medicinal waters. He therefore built for them, with his own means, a small bath and hospital. In his *Description of Bath*, written nearly two centuries after, a writer thus speaks of it: " The lepers' hospital is a building of 8 ft. 6 in. in front towards the East on the ground floor, 14 ft. in front above and 13 ft. in depth, but yet it is furnished with seven beds for the most miserable of objects, who fly to Bath for relief from the hot waters. This hovel stands at the corner of Nowhere Lane, and is so near the lepers' bath that the poor are under little or no difficulty in stepping from one place to the other."

A slight record of the abbot's work in this matter is found in the accounts of the City Chamberlain for 1576: " Delyvered to Mr. Fekewand, late abbot of Westminster, three tonnes of Tymber and x foote to builde the howse for the poore by the whote bath, xxxiiis. iiiid. To hym more iiiic of lathes at xd the c, iiis. 4d." Feckenham placed his little foundation under the direction of the hospital of St. Mary Magdalene, and it seems that in 1804, when the Corporation pulled down "the hovel," £200 was paid to the hospital in Holloway in compensation. The old bath itself was utilised by Wood as an underground tank when he built the Royal Baths.

Besides this practical act of charity to the poor of Bath, Abbot Feckenham drew up a book of recipes and directions to help those who could not afford a physician to recover their health. This MS. is now in the British Museum, and at the beginning of the volume the reader is told that, "This book of Sovereign medicines against the most common and known diseases both of men and women was by good proofe and long experience collected of Mr. Doctor Fecknam, late Abbot of Westminster, and that chiefly for the poore, which hathe not at alle tymes the learned phisitions at hand."

In these days a collection of simple remedies such as those here brought together, is, of course, of small value or interest. Many of these remedies are old family recipes and are said to be taken "from my cosen's D. H.'s book "—or from " Mistress H's "—no doubt one of the family of Howman. But what is of interest in this regard, is a set of rules drawn up by the Abbot for those who would profit by taking or bathing in the Bath waters.

"Prescriptions and Rules to be observed at the Bathe

"When you com to Bathe after your joyrnneing rest and quiet your bodie for the space of a daie or two and se the faccion of the Bathe how and after what sort others that are there do use the same.

" If it be not a faire cleare daie to, go not into the open bathe, but rather use the water in a bathing vessel in yor own chamber as many men doe.

" The best time in the daie to go into the bathes is in the morning an houre or half an houre after the sunne riseing, or there about, in the most quiet time. And when you shall feel your stomache well and quiet and that your meet is well digested and have rested well the night before. But before you goe into this bath you must walke an houre at the leaste in your chamber or else where.

" You must go into your Bath with an emptie stomake and so to remayne as long as you are in it except great necessitie require the contrarie. And then to take some little supping is not hurtefull. Let your tarrying be in the Bathe accordinge as you may well abide it, but tarry not so long in any wyse at the fyrst allthough you may well abyde it that yor strength att no tyme may fayl you.

" You may tarry in the crosse bathe an houre and a halfe att a tyme after the firste bathinge. And in the Kynges Bathe you may tarry after the first batheinges at one time half an houre or 3 quarters of an houre. But in any wyse tarry at no time untyll you be faynt, or that yor strength fayld you.

" And yf at any time you be faynt in the bath then you may drynke some ale warmed with a taste or any other suppinge, or green ginger, or yf need be aqua composita metheridate the bignes of a nut kernell at a time either by itself or mixed with ale or other liquor.

" As longe as you are in any of the Bathes you must cover your head very well that you take no colde thereof, for it is very perilious to take any cold one your head in the bathe or in any other place during your bathinge tyme.

" When you forth of any of the Bathes se that you cover your head very well and dry of the water of your bodie with warme clothes and then put on a warm shert and a mantle or some warm gowns for taking of cold and so go straight way to warmed bed and sweat ther yf you can and wype off the sweat diligently and after that you may sleepe a whyle, but you must not drynke anything until dinner tyme, except you be very faint and then you may take a little sugar candie or a few rasons or a little thin broath but small quantitie to slake your thirste onlie, because it is not good to eat or drynke by or by after the bathe untill you have slept a little yf you can.

" After that you have sweat and slept enough and be clearly delivered fro the heat that you had in the bathe and in your bedd then you may ryse and walk a lytle and so go to your dynner, for by mesureable walking the evill vapers and wyndines of the stomache that are take in the Bathe be driven away and utterlie voyded.

" After all this then go to your dynner and eate ot good meat but not very much that you may ryse fro the table with some appetite so that you could eat more yf you wolde and yet you must not eat too little for de- caying of your strength.

" Let your bread bee of good sweet wheate and of one dayes bakeinge or ii at the most and your meat well boylled or rosted. And specially let these be your meates, mutton, veale, chicken, rabbet, capon, fesaunt, Patrich or the like.

" You may eat also fresh water fish, so it be not muddie as eles and the like, refraining all salt fish as lyng, haberdyne, &c. Avoyd all frutes and rare herbs, salletts and the lyke.

"Apparell your bodie accordinge to the coldness of the wether and the temperature of the eyre, but in any wyse take no cold.

"And yf you bathe agayne in the after noune or att after Dinner then take a very lyght dinner as a cople of potched eggs, a caudell or some thine broath with a chicken and then 4 or 5 hours after your dynner so taken you may bathe agayne and in any wyse tarrie not so longe in the bathe as you did in the fore noone."

It is apparently impossible to determine certainly how long Abbot Feckenham remained at Bath—probably it was until the spring of 1576. In the middle of 1577 he was certainly back in London, for Aylmer, Bishop of London, in June of that year, had complained of the influence of those he called "active popish dignitaries," amongst whom he names the abbot, and begs that they may be again placed in the custody of some of the bishops. In consequence of this representation, Walsingham wrote to some of their lordships to ask their advice as to "what is meetest to be done with Watson, Feckenham, Harpefield and others of that ring that are thought to be leaders and pillars of the consciences of great numbers of such as be carried with the errors."

As a result of the episcopal advice, Cox, the bishop of Ely, in July, 1577, was directed to receive Abbot Feckenham into his house, and a stringent code of regulations was drawn up for the treatment of the aged abbot. Dr. Cox did his best to convert his prisoner to his own religious views, but without success, and in August, 1578, was fain to write to Burghley that his efforts had failed and that Feckenham "was a gentle person, but in

popish religion too, too obdurate." Nothing was done at
that time, and the abbot remained on until 1580, when
in June Bishop Cox wrote to say that he could put up
with him no longer; so in July, 1580, the late abbot of
Westminster was once more moved, this time to Wisbeach
Castle, the disused and indeed partly ruinous dwelling
place of the bishops of Ely.

Wisbeach was not a cheerful abode. It has been well
described in the following words: "During the winter
the sea mists drifting landwards almost always hung over
and hid the castle walls. Broad pools and patches of
stagnant waters, green with rank weeds, and wide
marshes and sterile flats lay outspread all around for
miles. The muddy river was constantly overflowing its
broken-down banks, so that the moat of the castle constantly flooded the adjacent garden and orchard. Of
foliage, save a few stunted willow trees, there was little
or none in sight; for when summer came round the sun's
heat soon parched up the rank grass in the courtyard,
and without, the dandelion and snapdragon which grew
upon its massive but dilapidated walls."

Such was the prison in which Abbot Feckenham was
destined to pass the last few years of his life. Even the
rigours of his detention and the dismal surroundings of
his prison-house were unable to extinguish his bene-
volent feelings for others. His last public work was the
repair of the causeway over the fens and the erection of
a market cross in the little town. He died in 1584, and
on the 16th of October he was buried in the churchyard
of the parish of Wisbeach.

I have very little more to add. Stevens, the continu-
ator of Dugdale, describes Abbot Feckenham as a man
of " a mean stature, somewhat fat, round-faced, beautiful

and of a pleasant aspect, affable and lively in conversation." Camden calls him "a man learned and good, who
lived a long time and gained the affection of his adver-
saries by publicly deserving well of the poor." To the
last he never forgot the poor of Westminster. In the
overseer's accounts of the parish of St. Margaret's it is
recorded in 1590: "Over and besides the sum of forty
pounds given by John Fecknam, sometime abbot of
Westminster, for a stock to buy wood for the poor of
Westminster, and to sell two faggots for a penny, and
seven billets for a penny, which sum of forty pounds doth
remain in the hands of the churchwardens." He also left
a bequest to the poor of his first monastic home of
Evesham.

Such is a brief outline of a man, who in his day delighted in doing good to others. In spite of difficulties
which would have crushed out the energies of most men
he persevered in his benefactions. Amongst other places
that benefited by his love for the poor is this great city
of Bath which may well revere his memory and inscribe
his name upon the illustrious roll of its worthies.

VII

CHRISTIAN FAMILY LIFE IN PRE-REFORMATION DAYS [1]

M Y subject is one of great and enduring interest— " The Christian Family Life." Looking back across my own more than half a century of experience, I see—or shall I say seem to see?—that a great change has taken place in the family life of Catholics, and that to-day—speaking broadly—it is not what it was fifty years ago. Did I not know that there is apparently a natural tendency as men get on in life to disparage the present in comparison with the past, I should be inclined to say that the ideals of the Christian family as we recognise them to-day have as a whole greatly deteriorated, and that some have been dropped altogether as unsuited for the days in which we live. In the task that has been assigned to me it is perhaps fortunate, for myself, that I am not in any way called upon either to establish this deterioration as a fact, or to endeavour to ascertain the cause, if it be a fact; or yet, again, to suggest possible remedies. My comparatively easy task is to set before you at least the broad outlines of Catholic home life in pre-Reformation days. It may, however, be useful for me to preface that story with a few words upon the general question as it appears at the present day.

The Catholic life depends in great measure for its

[1] A paper read at the Catholic Conference at Brighton, 1906.

existence and its growth upon the Christianity of the family life. I take this to be an axiom. For although it may be allowed that the grace of God may so act upon the individual soul as to produce the flowers of virtue amid the most chilling surroundings and in the mephitic atmosphere of a bad home, still in His providence the ordinary nursery of all God's servants is a home presided over by pious parents, who themselves practise the religion they teach their children. The father, mother, and children together make up the sacred institution of God called the family. Without the parental influence, example, and teaching, the child will hardly have a chance of acquiring even the mere elements of religion or the first principles of an ordered life. The child is for the most part the creation of its surroundings, and no amount of schooling in the best of "atmospheres," or of religious instruction from the most capable of teachers, can supply the influences which are lacking in the home life. On parents rests the responsibility—a heavy responsibility of which they cannot divest themselves—of training their offspring in habits of virtue—of seeing, for example, that they say their prayers, attend church, receive the Sacraments and, as their minds expand, are properly instructed in their duty to God and their fellow-men. The knowledge that their example will almost inevitably be copied by those they have brought into the world should act upon parents as a restraint upon word and action, and they should share personally in all the prayers and acts of religion they inculcate as necessary. There is much, no doubt, in surroundings and circumstances, but there is no home so humble that it may not be a school of sound, solid, practical Catholic life; there are no surroundings and circumstances, however hard

Q

and difficult, in which the Christian family, recognising its obligations, cannot practise the lesson taught by the Holy Household at Nazareth. Of course it is religion which must bind the members of the family together, and no ties are secure, or will bear the stress of life, which are not strengthened by prayer and the faithful practice of religious duties.

FORGETFULNESS OF THE FAMILY TIE

In these days—when the State so frequently steps in to usurp parental rights and to give relief from parental duties; when the Church, in its anxiety to secure some kind of religious knowledge, is looked upon as freeing the parent from its duty of imparting it; and when the well-meaning philanthropist urges free meals and free boots as the necessary corollary of compulsory education —the whole duty of man and woman to those they have brought into the world, and the family tie binding parents and children together, are in danger of being forgotten. The State regulations for secular education claim children almost before they can toddle, and gratuitously instruct them in all manner of subjects, some no doubt useful, but many more wholly unnecessary if they are not positively harmful. The parent is almost a negligible quantity in the matter, and, by way of a set-off against this treatment, he is not called upon to contribute a penny towards his child's education, although in the greater number of cases, as was shown by the experience of years, he is fully able to do so. The priest has to see to the religious side of education. His experience is that the parent seldom troubles much about this side of his duty, and that it is with difficulty that he can be got to take an active interest in his child's moral training, or even to second the priest's efforts for the eternal welfare of the child, for whom, by every principle of natural and divine law, he is responsible. When the notion of responsibility for education goes from the parental mind, with it departs in most cases the sense of duty to the religious obligations incumbent on every parent in regard to the soul of his child. Unless, therefore, the priest taught the children to pray and instructed them in their faith and duty, unless he prepared them for the Sacraments, unless he saw that they approached them regularly, unless he drilled them to come to Mass on the Sundays and Holydays, no one else would do so. Hence the priest has to go on trying to fulfil much of the responsibilities of parents, in spite of the danger that the child, as it grows in age and knowledge, may come to look upon all this religious training as a mere detail of school work from which age emancipates it—a disaster which will be all the more certain if the religious lessons given are not enforced by the example of its parents in the home life, and by their obedience to the practical obligations of religion.

All this raises questions of the utmost importance, and in the opinion of many priests of experience, no greater service to religion at the present day could be effected than some crusade that would bring home to Catholic parents the necessity of returning in their home lives to the traditions and example of their ancestors in the Faith. As a small contribution, I propose to set out as briefly as may be what the life was that was lived in England and in English Christian homes in pre-Reformation days, in order that we may have some measure of comparison.

Early Rising

In the fifteenth and sixteenth centuries our fore-fathers were early risers, and probably the usual time for the household to bestir itself was not later than six. Hugh Rhodes' *Book of Nature* teaches:

> Ryse you earely in the morning,
>   For it hath propertyes three:
> Holynesse, health, and happey welth
>   As my father taught mee.
> At syxe of the clocke, without delay
>   Use commonly to ryse,
> And give God thanks for thy good rest
>   When thou openest thyn eyes.

This same hour of six was ordered by the Bishop of Rochester for the officers of the household of his pupil Prince Edward, afterwards King Edward V, to hear their morning Mass. The King, in appointing Earl Rivers and the Bishop tutors to his son in 1470, en-joined that he should not be allowed to lie in bed, but that he should rise "every morning at a convenient hour."

The *Prymer* of 1538 (the first English one, though printed at Rouen) in its " Maner to lyve well, devoutly and salutaryly every day, for all persones of mean estate," says: " Fyrst rise at six in the morning in all seasons and in doing so thank God for the rest He has given to you."

Morning Prayers

This brings us to the first daily morning exercise on which our ancestors set such store. *The School of Vertue* for little children says:

First in the mornynge when thou dost awake
To God for his grace thy peticion then make
This prayer folowynge use dayly to say
Thy harte lyftynge up; thus begyn to pray:
O God, from whom all good gifts procede,
To Thee we repayr in tyme of our need.

And so through a prayer for grace to follow virtue and
flee from vice, and for God's special protection during
the day which is then beginning, which the child asks
may be spent:

To thy honour and joy of our parentes
Learninge to lyve well and kepe thy commandmentes.

Richard Whytford—" the Wretch of Syon "—in his
*Werke for Housholders, or for them that have the gydyng
or governaunce of any company,* thus sets out a form of
early mornin_ exercise which is specially intended for
the use not of recluses or cloistered religious, but of
those having to live an ordinary Christian life in the
world :

" As soon as ye do awake in the morning to arise for
al day [he writes] first sodeynly tourne your mind and
remembrance unto Almighty God; and then use (by a
contynual custom) to make a cross with your thombe on
your forehead or front, in saying of these wordes: *In
nomine Patris;* and then another cross upon your mouth
with these words, *Et Filii;* and then a third cross upon
your breast, saying *Et Spiritus Sancti, Amen.*

" And if your devotion be thereto ye may again make
one whole cross from your head unto your feet and
from your lyfte shoulder unto your right saying altogether, *In nomine Patris,* &c. That is to say, ' I do
blesse and marke myself with the cognysaunce and
badge of Christ, in the Name of the Father, &c., the

Holy Trinity, three persons and one God.' Then say or thynke after this form: 'Good Lord God, my Maker and my Redeemer, here now in thy presence, I (for thys tyme and for all the tyme of my hole lyfe) do bequeath and bytake or rather do freely give myselfe, soule and body,'" etc.

The *Prymer* before named speaks of the first prayer of the day as to be said at once on rising:

"Commende you to God, to our Blessyd Lady Sainte Mary and to that saint that is feasted that day and to all the saints of heaven. Secondly, Beseech God that he preserve you that day from deadly sin and at all other tymes, and pray Him that all the works that other doth for you may be accept to the laud of his name and of his glorious Mother and of all the company of heaven."

So, too, in *The Young Children's Book*, a version of an earlier set of rhymes, the child is told to—

> Aryse be tyme out of thi bedde
> And blysse thi breast and thi forhede.
> Then wasche thi hondes and thi face
> Keme thi hede, and aske God grace
> The to helpe in all thi werkes;
> Thou schall spede better what so thou carpes.

HEARING MASS

So much for the early morning exercise; we come now to the question of the morning Mass. I do not think that there can be much doubt that all in pre-Reformation days were not satisfied that they had done their duty if they did not hear Mass daily if they were able to do so. Of course it is obvious that very many would be prevented by their occupations and business from going to the church on the week-days, but even for these the prevalence of the custom in cities and towns of having an early Mass at four, five, or six o'clock in the morning, which was known as the "Morrow Mass" or the "Jesu Mass," is an indication that people were anxious to have the opportunity of attending at the Holy Sacrifice. This is all the more certain, as this Mass was generally offered as the result of some special benefaction for the purpose or by reason of the stipend found by the people of a parish, "gathered wekely of the devotion of the parishioners," as one foundation deed declared, in order that "travellers" or "those at work" might know that they could hear their Mass without interfering with the necessary business of their lives. Even when actual presence was impossible, the mediaeval Catholic was taught to join in spirit in the Great Sacrifice when it was being offered up on the altar of his parish church. According to some antiquaries, the origin of the low side-window to be found in many churches was to enable the clerk or server at Mass to ring a hand-bell out of it at the "Sanctus" in order to warn people at work in the neighbouring fields and elsewhere that the more solemn part of the Mass had begun. We can hardly doubt that this practice did really exist, in view of a Constitution of Archbishop Peckham in 1281. In this he orders that "at the time of the elevation of the body of our Lord (in the Mass) a bell be rung on one side of the church, that those who cannot be at daily Mass, no matter where they may be, whether in the fields or their own homes, may kneel down and so gain the indulgences granted by many bishops" to such as perform this act of devotion.

Andrew Borde, in his *Regyment*, incidentally gives testimony to the practice of hearing daily Mass on the part of those whose occupations permitted them so to do. After speaking of rising and dressing, he says:—

"Then great and noble men doth use to here Masse, and other men that cannot do so, but must apply [to] theyr busyness, doth serve God with some prayers, sur-rendrynge thanks to hym for hys manyfold goodness, with askyng mercye for theyr offences."

The Venetian traveller who at the beginning of the sixteenth century wrote his impressions of England, was struck with the way the people attended the morning Mass:—

"They all attend Mass every day [he writes], and say many Paternosters in public. The women carry long rosaries in their hands, and any who can read take the office of our Lady with them, and with some companion recite it in church, verse by verse, in a low voice, after the manner of churchmen."

Some years later another Venetian wrote that, when in England, every morning "at day break he went to Mass arm-in-arm with some nobleman or other."

King Edward IV, in the rules he drew up for the household of his son, says that: "Every morning (after rising) two chaplains shall say Matins in his presence, and then he shall go to chapel or closet and hear Mass," which shall never be said in his chamber except for "some grave cause." "No man to interrupt him during Masse time."

In the Preface to *The Lay Folkes Mass Book* Canon Simmons gives ample authority for the statement that in Catholic times all who could were supposed to hear daily Mass, and that unless prevented by necessary work or business they in fact did so very generally. In Wynkyn de Worde's *Boke of Kervynge* the chamberlain

is instructed " at morne " to " go to the church or chapell
to your soveraynes closet and laye carpentes and cuye-
shens and put downe his boke of prayers and then draw
the curtynes." And so in the same way Robert of
Gloucester says of William the Conqueror, reflecting no
doubt the manners of the age in which he himself wrote:
" In churche he was devout ynou, for him non day [to]
abyde that he na hurde masse and matyns and even-
son[g] and eche tyde." On which quotation Canon
Simmons remarks: " That the rule of the Church was
not a dead letter is perhaps unmistakeably shown by the
matter-of-course way in which hearing Mass before
breaking fast is introduced as an incident in the every-
day life of knights and other personages in works of
fiction which, nevertheless, in their details were no
doubt true to the ordinary habits of the class they were
intended to portray."

As a matter of course, in *The Young Children's Book*
the child is taught when his morning's exercise has been
done:—

> Than go to the chyrche and here a Masse
> There aske mersy for thi trespasse.

And in an old set of verses called *The Dayes of the Weke
Moralysed*, for Monday, the first work day, the following
advice is given:—

> Monday men ought me for to call
> In wich, good werkes ought to begyn
> Heryng Masse, the first dede of all
> Intendyng to fle deadly syn, etc.

With regard to attendance at Holy Mass it is important to observe that the people were fully instructed in
the way they ought to behave in church during the

sacred rite, and, indeed, at all times. Myrc, in his *Instructions*, bids the clergy tell their people that on coming into God's house they should remember to leave outside "many wordes" and "ydel speche," and to put away all vanity and say *Pater noster* and *Ave*. They are to be warned not to stand aimlessly about in the church, nor to loll against the pillars or the wall, but they should kneel on the floor

> And praye to God wyth herte meke
> To give them grace and mercy eke.

So, too, Seager in *The School of Vertue* says:—

> When to the church thou shalt repayer
> Knelying or standynge to God make thy prayer:
> All worldely matters from thy mynde set apart
> Earnestly prayinge to God lyfte up thy hart
> A contrite harte he wyll not dispyse,
> Whiche he doth coumpt a sweet sacrifice.

Richard Whytford, speaking to householders of their duty to see that those under their charge come to the Sunday Mass, writes:—

"Take the pain what you may to go forth yourself and call your folk to follow. And when you ben at the church do nothing else but that you come for. And look oft time upon them that ben under your charge that all they be occupied lyke (at the least) unto devoute Chrystyans. For the church (as our Saviour saithe) is a place of prayer not of claterynge and talking. And charge them also to keep their sight in church close upon their books or bedes. And while they ben younge let them use ever to kneel, stand or sit, and never to walk in church. And let them hear the Masse quietly and devoutly, moche part kneeling. But at the Gospel, at

the Preface and at the Pater noster teach them to stand
and to make curtsey at the word *Jesus* as the priest
dothe."

When the bell sounds for the Consecration, says
another instruction, all, " both ye younge and olde," fall
on their knees, and holding up both their hands pray
softly to themselves thus :—

> Jesu ! Lord, welcome thou be
> In form of bread as I thee see :
> Jesu ! for thy holy name
> Shield me to-day from sin and shame ;

or in some similar way such as the *Salve, lux mundi* :
" Hail, light of the world, word of the Father ; Hail,
thou true victim, the living and entire flesh of God made
true man "—or in the words of the better known *Anima
Christi sanctifica me.*

Grace at Meals

After morning Mass comes the first meal, which comes
before the occupations of the day begin. At this and at
every meal children were taught to bless themselves by
the sign of the Cross, and to follow the head of the
family as he called down God's blessing upon what His
providence had provided for them. At dinner and at
supper there was apparently some reading in many
families, which was at any rate a means of teaching
some useful things, and of avoiding, as one account
says, " much idle and unprofitable talk." In 1470 it is
ordered that at meals Prince Edward should have " read
before him such rolls, stories, &c., fit for a prince to
hear " ; and Whytford thinks that meal-time in a Christian family could not be spent better than upon incul-

cating the religious duties and knowledge which parents are bound to see that their children know. In the scheme of instruction he sets forth he says:—

"Ben such thynges as they been bounde to knowe, or can saye, that is the Pater Noster, the Ave Maria, and the Crede, with such other things as done follow. I wolde therefore you should begin with [those under your care] betimes in youth as soon as they can speak. For it is an old saying: 'The pot or vessel shall ever savour and smell of that thing wherewith it is first seasoned,' and your English proverb sayeth that 'the young cock croweth as he doth hear and lerne of the old.' You may in youth teche them what you will and that shall they longest keep and remember. You should therefore, above all thynges, take heed and care in what company your chylder ben nouryshed and brought up. For education and doctrine, that is to say bringing up and learning, done make ye manners. With good and vertuous persons (sayth the prophet) you shall be good and vertuous. And with evil persons you shall also be evil. Let your chylder therefore use and keep good company. The pye, the jaye, and other birds done speak what they most hear by [the] ear. The plover by sight will follow the gesture and behaviour of the fowler, and the ape by exercise worke and do as she is taught, and so will the dog (by violence) contrary to natural disposition learne to daunce. The chylder, therefore, that by reason do farre exceed other creatures, will bear away what they hear spoken; they should therefore be used unto such company where they sholde heare none evil, but where they may hear godly and Chrystyan wordes. They wyll also, in their gestures and behaviour, have such manners as they use and behold in other persons so will they do. Unto some craftes or occupations a certain age is required, but virtue and vice may be learned in every age. See therefore that in any wyse you let them use no company but good and vertuous. And as soon as they can speak let them first learn to serve God and to say the Pater, Ave, and Crede. And not onely your chylder, but also se you and prove that all your servants what age so ever they be of, can say the same, and therefore I have advised many persons and here do counsel that in every meal, dynner, or souper one person should with loud voice saye thus," etc.

Whytford then gives a long explanation of the Our Father, etc., in which may be found set forth, as in the many similar tracts written in the Middle Ages, the full teaching of the Church on faith and practice.

GUARD OF THE TONGUE

The foundations of the Christian virtues have to be laid early in life, and the parent or head of the family is warned constantly of his obligation of seeing that this is being done, and of rooting out every tendency to evil in those of whom they have charge. Bad language is to be specially guarded against, and the first indication of the formation of a habit to be noted and means taken to put a stop to its growth. Richard Whytford suggests that children should be made to repeat the following lines:—

> Yf I lye, backebyte or stelle,
> Yf I curse, scorne, mocke or swere
> Yf I chyde, fyght, stryke or threte
> Good mother or maystresse myne
> Yf ony of these myne

I trespace to your knowyng
With a new rodde and a fyne
Early naked before I dyne
Amende me with a scourgyng.

and then, continues the writer:—

"I pray you fulfil and performe theyr petition and request, and think it not cruelly, but mercyfully done. . . . Your daily practice doth show unto you that yf you powder your flesh while it is newe and sweet, it will continue good meet, but yf it smell before it be powdred all the salt you have shall never make it seasonable. Powder your children, therefore, betyme and then you love them and shall have comfort of them."

Correction, however, should not be done in anger, and all are to understand that the pain of him who administers the rod is greater than his who receives the punishment. Before children the greatest care is necessary not to do anything that they may not imitate. All idle expressions and vain oaths should be avoided, for such habits are catching, and the young are to be taught to say with respect "Yea, father," "Nay, father," or "Yea, mother," "No, mother," and not to get into the habit of making use of such expressions as "by cocke and pye," "by my hood of green," etc.

WORK

It is unnecessary to go through the day in any well-constituted family in Catholic England. Work was everywhere insisted upon as necessary in God's service, and work was savoured, so to speak, by the remembrance of God's presence. The two orders of the natural and supernatural were not so separated as they are generally supposed to be to-day. Of course there are many in our

day who no doubt keep themselves in God's presence,
but whilst I believe that most will allow that this is the
exception, in the ages of faith it was apparently the
rule; and if we may judge from the books of instruction
and other evidence, God was not far removed from the
threshold of most Catholic families in pre-Reformation days. Of course there were exceptions, and many
perhaps led as wicked lives as now, but there is obviously something about the family life of that time which
is lacking in this. There was the constant recognition
of God's sanctifying presence in the family. Of this I
have spoken, and over and beside this there were those
common religious practices of prayer and religious self-
restraint and mutual encouragement to virtue of which,
alas, the modern counterpart of the old English home
knows so little. On the faith of those simple and generally unlettered people there was a bloom—I know of no
better word to express what I see—which perished as
one of the results of the religious revolution of the sixteenth century.

I have said that the family exercised themselves in
prayer in common. It has been doubted whether people
really did attend their churches for the liturgical services,
such as Matins and Evensong on Sundays and feast
days. The evidence that they did so very generally is
to me conclusive. But beyond that, we know that many
who could read made a practice of saying the Little
Office day by day, thus joining in the spirit of the
canonical hours ordered by the Church. I have pointed
out that Edward IV directed that the chaplains should
recite the "Divine Service" with the Prince his son
daily. The 1538 Prymer—intended, of course, for the
use of the laity—assumes that the "Office" is said by

all who can. In the directions it gives on the point for the Christian man's day it says: " As touching your service say unto Tierce before dinner and make an end before supper. And when ye may say Dirige and Commendations for all Christian souls (at least on Holy Days, and if ye have leisure say them on the other days) at the least with three lessons." I have noted how the Venetian traveller spoke of the practice of English people coming to say their "Office" together in church.

PARENTS AND CHILDREN

Priests are warned of their duty to instruct parents as to the necessity of bringing their children to the Sacraments and to the Mass and other services on the Sundays and feast days. Such fathers and mothers as may be found to neglect this duty are to be punished by fasting on bread and water, and the clergy are to make sure by personal examination that as children grow up they have been sufficiently instructed in their religion by their parents. Should the parents fail in this respect the godparents were held to be personally responsible. On the afternoons of the Sundays, when Evensong was over, the father was to " appoint " his children " thyr pastyme with great diligence and straight commandment." Whytford says that he " should assign and appoint them the manner of their disports, honest ever and lawful for a reasonable recreation . . . and also appoint the time or space that they be not (for any sports) from the service of God. Appoynt them also ye place, that you may call or send for them when case requireth. For if there be a sermon any tyme of the day, let them be there present— all that be not occupied in nedeful and lawful besyness,

"When ye are come from the church (in the early morning) [says the Rule of Life printed in 1538], take hede to your house holde or occupacyon till dyner tyme. And in so doing thynke sometyme that the pain that ye suffer in this worlde is nothyng to the regarde of the infinite glory that ye shall have yf ye take it meekly. . . . Shrive you every week to your curate unless you have very great lette. If ye be of power refuse not your alms to the first poor body that axeth it of you that day if ye think it needful. Take pain to hear and keep the word of God. Confess you every day to God without fail of such sins ye know ye have done that day. Consider often either day or night when ye do awake what our Lord did at that hour the day of his blessyd passion and where he was at that hour.

"Seek a good faithful friend of good conversation to whom ye may discover your mind secrets. Enquire and prove him well or ye trust in him. And when ye have well proved hym do all by his counsell. Say lytell: and follow virtuous company. After all work praise and thank God. Love hym above all things and serve hym and hys glorious mother diligently. Do to non other but that ye wolde were done to you: love the welth of another as your owne.

"And in going to your bedde have some good thought either of the passyon of our Lord or of your synne, or of the pains which souls have in purgatory, or some other good spiritual thoughts, and then I hope your lyving shall be acceptable and pleasing to God."

THE EVENING BLESSING

Most books of instruction for children insist much upon an old Catholic practice which still survives in

R

some countries, but which, I fear, has fallen much into disuse with us in these days, when the relations between parent and child are more free and easy than they used to be in pre-Reformation Catholic England. Speaking of the Fourth Commandment, Richard Whytford says:—

"Teche your children to axe blessing every night, kneeling before their parents under this form: 'Father, I beseech you of blessing for charity': or thus: 'Mother, I beseech you of charity give me your blessing.' Then let the father and mother holde up bothe ther handes and joining them both togyder look up reverently and devoutly unto heaven and say thus: 'Our Lord God bless you children,' and therewith make a cross with the right hand over the child, saying '*In Nomine*,' &c.

"And if any child be stiff hearted, stubborn and froward and will not thus axe a blessing, if it be within age, let it surely be whysked with a good rod and be compelled thereunto by force. And if the persons be of farther age and past such correction and yet will be obstinate, let them have such sharpe and grievous punishment as conveniently may be devysed, as to sit at dinner alone and by themselves at a stool in the middle of the hall, with only brown bread and water, and every person in order to rebuke them as they would rebuke a thief and traitor. I would not advise ne counsel any parents to keep such a child in their house without great afflic-cyon and punishment."

This mediaeval reverence for parents was much insisted upon by all writers. Hugh Rhodes' "Book of Nurture," printed in the *Babees Book*, for example, says to the child:—

When that thy parents come in syght doe to them reverence
Aske them blessing if they have been long out of presence.

In this regard no doubt we shall all call to mind what is told of the brave and blessed Sir Thomas More. Even when Lord Chancellor, morning after morning, before sitting in his own court to hear the cases to be argued before him, he was wont to go to the place where his father, Sir John More, was presiding as judge, and there on his knees crave his parent's blessing on the work of the day.

FILIAL REVERENCE

Another pre-Reformation writer warns children never to be wanting in due courteous behaviour to their parents: "What man he is your father, you ought to make courtesye to hym all though you should mete hym twenty tymes a daye." On his side the parent is warned frequently in the literature of the period "not to spoil his son" by neglecting a "gentle whysking" when it was deserved. He is to be watched, and incipient bad habits forthwith corrected during

> That tyme chyldren is moost apt and redy
> To receyve chastisement, nurture and lernynge.

For "the child that begynneth to pyke at a pin or a point will after pyke unto an ox, and from a peer to a purse or an hors, and so fro the small things unto the great." If a child, writes one educationalist of those days, is caught taking even a pin, let him be set with a note pinned to him: "This is the thief." Let this be done in the house, but should this fail to correct the habit let him carry his docket into the street of the city.

THE LESSON OF IT ALL

This brief indication of the characteristics of the Catholic family life in pre-Reformation days might be lengthened out almost to any extent. The main lines would, however, remain the same, and additional details would only show more clearly how close in those days the supernatural was to the natural—how God was ever present, and how the sense of this real though unseen presence affected the daily life of all in every Christian home. The proof lies on the surface of every record. The names of " Jesus and Mary " are found written on the top of almost every scrap of paper and every column of account ; the wills begin with the invocation of the Blessed Trinity and generally contain some expression indicative of gratitude to the Providence of God and of belief in the immortality of the soul and of the reward gained by a life of virtue; letters are dated by reference to some Sunday or festival and so on. One has only to turn over the pages of that wonderful collection of fifteenth-century epistles known as the Paston Letters, to see what the Church festivals and saints' days were to the people of those Catholic times, and how they entered into their very lives. A letter is frequently dated on the Monday, etc. (whatever day of the week it might be) *before* or *after* such or such a celebration. At times the date is taken from the words of some collect of the preceding Sunday, as when Agnes Paston heads a communication as " written at Paston in haste the Wednesday next after *Deus qui errantibus*." How many of us, with all the advantages we have in printed missals, would at once know, as this lady, and doubtless, too, her correspondent did, that this date was the Wednesday in the third week after Easter?

VIII

CHRISTIAN DEMOCRACY IN PRE-REFORMATION TIMES[1]

WE are all of us, I take it, interested in the social questions which nowadays are clamouring for consideration. In all parts of the civilised globe the voice of democracy has made itself heard; it has arrested the attention of rulers and statesmen, and has proved that the day when popular aspirations received sufficient answer in the *sic volo sic jubeo* of the autocrat is past; and, moreover, that the "masses" have at least as much right to be considered as the "classes." Perhaps fortunately for myself, I am not directly concerned to explain, much less to defend, the principles of what is broadly known as "Christian democracy." About all this matter opinions differ very widely indeed; and although, I suppose, we may all of us, in these days, claim to be socialists of some kind of type, there is obviously, even amongst us Catholics, such divergence of opinion that any preliminary attempt to clear the ground with a view to agreement even on first principles is not uncommonly productive of no small amount of heat and temper. My concern is happily with facts not with theories, with the past not with the present. I confess that personally I like to feel my feet upon the ground, and facts furnish

[1] A paper read at the Catholic Conference at Nottingham, 1898.

undoubtedly the best corrective for mere theorising which, at times, is apt to run away with all of us, and to give rise either to unwarranted hopes or unnecessary fears. In the belief that even " the dark ages " have their useful lessons for us whose lot has been cast in these times, I propose to lay before you briefly the teaching of the Church of England in pre-Reformation days, as to the relations which should exist between the classes of every Christian community, and to illustrate by a few examples the way in which the teaching was translated into practice by our Catholic ancestors.

THE RELATION BETWEEN RICH AND POOR

There can be no doubt as to the nature of the teaching of the English Church in regard to the relation which, according to true Christian principles, should exist between the rich and the poor. The evidence appears clear and unmistakeable enough in pre-Reformation popular sermons and instructions, in formal pronouncements of Bishops and Synods, and in books intended for the particular teaching of clergy and laity in the necessary duties of the Christian man. Whilst fully recognising as a fact that " the poor must always be with us "—that in the very nature of things there must ever be the class of those who " have " and the class of those who " have not " —our Catholic forefathers knew no such division and distinction between the rich and the poor man as obtained later on, when Protestant principles had asserted their supremacy, and pauperism, as distinct from poverty, had come to be recognised as an inevitable consequence of the policy introduced with the new era. To the Christian moralist, and even to the Catholic Englishman, whether

secular or lay, in the fifteenth century, those who had
been blessed by God's providence with worldly wealth
were regarded as not so much the fortunate possessors
of personal riches, their own to do with what they listed
and upon which none but they had right or claim, as in
the light of trusted stewards of God's good gifts to man-
kind at large, for the right use and ministration of which
they were accountable to Him who gave them.

Thus, to take one instance: the proceeds of ecclesiastical benefices were recognised in the Constitutions of
Legates and Archbishops as being in fact as well as in
theory the *eleemosynæ*, the *spes pauperum*—the alms and
the hope of the poor. Those ecclesiastics who consumed
the revenues of their cures on other than necessary and
fitting purposes were declared to be " defrauders of the
rights of God's poor " and " thieves of Christian alms
intended for them "; whilst the English canonists and
legal professors who glossed these provisions of the
Church law gravely discussed the ways in which the
poor of a parish could vindicate their right—*right*, mind
—to a share in the ecclesiastical revenues of their
Church.

This " jus pauperum," which is set forth in such a
text-book of English law as Lyndwood's *Provinciale*, is
naturally put forth more clearly and forcibly in a work
intended for popular instruction, such as *Dives et Pauper*.
" To them that have the benefices and goods of Holy
Church," writes the author, " it belonged principally to
give alms and to have the cure of poor people." To him
who squanders the alms of the altar on luxury and useless show the poor man may justly point and say: " It
is ours that you so spend in pomp and vanity! . . . That
thou keepest for thyself of the altar passing the honest

needful living, it is raveny, it is theft, it is sacrilege." From the earliest days of English Christianity the care of the helpless poor was regarded as an obligation incumbent on all: and in 1342 Archbishop Stratford, dealing with *appropriations*, or the assignment of ecclesiastical revenue to the support of some religious house or college, ordered that a portion of the tithe should always be set apart for the relief of the poor, because, as Bishop Stubbs has pointed out, in England from the days of King Ethelred "a third part of the tithe" which belonged to the Church was the acknowledged birthright of the poorer members of Christ's flock.

That there was social inequality goes without saying, for that is in the very constitution of human society, and may indeed be said to be a very law of human nature. In feudal times this obvious truth passed unquestioned as the divine law of the universe, and with the overthrow of the system in the thirteenth century there was created a chasm between the upper and lower classes which it was the interest of popular agitators and demagogues to widen and deepen. But even then, in theory at least, the claims of poverty were as fully recognised as the duty of riches. The verses of *Piers Plowman* and the *Canterbury Tales*, and even the words of "the mad preacher," John Ball, are not more clear as to the existence of the social difficulties of those days and the claims put forward in the name of justice to common humanity, than the language of the great and fearless orator, Bishop Brunton, as to the religious obligations of Christian riches. Again and again, in his sermons, this great preacher reminds his hearers of the fact that poor and rich have alike descended from a common stock, and that no matter what their condition of life may be, all Christians are members of one body and are bound one to the other by the duties of a common brotherhood.

Still more definite is the author of the book of popular instruction, *Dives et Pauper*, above referred to. The sympathy of the writer is with the poor, as indeed is that of every ecclesiastical writer of the period. In fact it is abundantly clear that the Church in England in Catholic days, as a *pia mater*, was ever ready to open wide her heart to aid and protect the poorer members of Christ's mystical body. This is how *Pauper*, in the tract in question, states the Christian teaching as to the duty of riches, and impresses upon his readers the view that the owners of worldly wealth are but stewards of the Lord: "All that the rich man hath, passing his honest living after the degree of his dispensation, it is other men's, not his, and he shall give full hard reckoning thereof at the day of doom, when God shall say to him: 'Yield account of your bailywick.' For rich men and lords in this world are God's bailiffs and God's reeves, to ordain for the poor folk and to sustain them." Most strongly does the same writer insist that no property gives any one the right to say "this is *mine*, and that is *thine*; for property so far as it is of God is of the nature of governance and dispensation," by which those who by God's Providence "have," act as His stewards and as the dispensers of His gifts to such as "have not."

The words of the late Pope Leo XIII as to the Catholic teaching, most accurately describe the practical doctrine of the English pre-Reformation Church on this matter: "The chiefest and most excellent rule for the right use of money," he says, "rests on the principle that it is one thing to have a right to the possession of money and another to have the right to use money as one pleases.

. . . If the question be asked, How must one's possessions be used? the Church replies without hesitation in
the words of the same holy Doctor (St. Thomas): *Man
should not consider his outward possessions as his own,
but as common to all, so as to share them without difficulty
when others are in need.* When necessity has been supplied and one's position fairly considered, it is a duty to
give to the indigent out of that which is over. It is a
duty, not of justice (except in extreme cases), but of
Christian charity . . . (and) to sum up what has been
said: Whoever has received from the Divine bounty a
large share of blessings . . . has received them for the
purpose of using them for the perfecting of his own
nature, and, at the same time, that he may employ
them, as the minister of God's Providence, for the
benefit of others."

THE CONDITION OF THE POOR

There is no need to dwell upon this point, as there
can be no doubt as to the practical teaching of the
Church in Catholic England on the subject of the duties
of the "classes" to the "masses." I pass at once to the
actual state of the poor in the times which preceded
what a modern writer has fitly called "the Great Pillage." It would be, of course, absurd to suggest that
poverty and much hardness of life did not exist in pre-
Reformation days; but what did not exist in Catholic
times was that peculiar product which sprung up so
plentifully amid the ruins of Catholic institutions over-
thrown by Tudor sovereigns — pauperism. Bishop
Stubbs, speaking of the condition of the poor in the
Middle Ages, declares that "there is very little evidence

to show that our forefathers in the middle ranks of life
desired to set any impassable boundary between class
and class. . . . Even the villein by learning a craft might
set his foot on the ladder of promotion. The most certain
way to rise was furnished by education and by the law
of the land. 'Every man or woman, of what state or
condition that he be, shall be free to set their son or
daughter to take learning at any school that pleaseth
him within the realm.'" Mr. Thorold Rogers, than whom
no one has ever worked more fully at the economic
history of England, and whom none can suspect of un-
due admiration of the Catholic Church, has left it on
record that during the century and a half which preceded the era of the Reformation the mass of English
labourers were thriving under their guilds and trade
unions, the peasants were gradually acquiring their lands
and becoming small freeholders, the artisans rising to
the position of small contractors and working with their
own hands at structures which their native genius and
experience had planned. In a word, according to this
high authority, the last years of undivided Catholic
England formed "the golden age" of the Englishman
who was ready and willing to work.

"In the age which I have attempted to describe,"
writes the same authority, "and in describing which I
have accumulated and condensed a vast amount of un-
questionable facts, the rate of production was small, the
conditions of health unsatisfactory, and the duration of
life short. But, on the whole, there were none of those
extremes of poverty and wealth which have excited the
astonishment of philanthropists, and are now exciting
the indignation of workmen. The age, it is true, had
its discontents, and these discontents were expressed

forcibly and in a startling manner. But of poverty which perishes unheeded, of a willingness to do honest work and a lack of opportunity, there was little or none. The essence of life in England during the days of the Plantagenets and Tudors was that every one knew his neighbour, and that every one was his brother's keeper."

THE REFORMATION AND THE POOR

This period was put an end to, in Mr. Rogers' opinion, by the confusion and social disorder consequent upon the introduction of the new principles of the Reformers, and the uprooting of the old Catholic institutions.

To relieve the Reformation from the odious charge that it was responsible for the poor laws, many authors have declared that not only did poverty largely exist before, say, the dissolution of the monastic houses, but that it would not long have been possible for the ancient methods of relieving the distressed to cope with the increase in their numbers under the changed circumstances of the sixteenth century. It is, of course, possible to deal with broad assertions only by the production of a mass of details, which is, under the present circumstances, out of the question, or by assertions equally broad: and I remark that there is no evidence of any change of circumstances, so far as such changes appear in history, which could not have been fully met by the application of the old principles, and met in a way which would never have induced the degree of distressing pauperism, which in fact was produced by the application of the social principles adopted by the Reformers. The underlying idea of these latter was property in the sense of absolute ownership, in place of the older and

more Christian idea of property in the sense of stewardship. In a word, the Reformation substituted the idea
of *individualism* as the basis of property for the idea of
Christian *collectivism*.

Most certainly the result was not calculated to improve the condition of the poorer members of the community. It was they who were made to pay for the
Reformation, whilst their betters pocketed the price.
The well-to-do classes in the process became richer and
more prosperous, whilst the " masses " became, as an old
writer has it, " mere stark beggars." As a fact, moreover, poverty became rampant, as we should have expected, immediately upon the great confiscations of land
and other property at the dissolution of the religious
houses. To take one example: Dr. Sharpe's knowledge
of the records of the city of London enables him to say
that: " the sudden closing of these institutions caused
the streets to be thronged with the sick and poor, and
the small parish churches to be so crowded with those
who had been accustomed to frequent the larger and
more commodious churches of the friars that there was
scarce room left for the parishioners themselves."

" The Devil," exclaims a preacher who lived through
all these troublous times—" the Devil cunningly turneth
things to his own way." " Examples of this we have
seen in our time more than I can have leisure to express
or to rehearse. In the Acts of Parliament that we have
had made in our days what godly preambles have gone
afore the same, even *quasi oraculum Apollinis*, as though
the things that follow had come from the counsel of the
highest in Heaven; and yet the end hath been either to
destroy abbeys or chauntries or colleges, or such like, by
the which some have gotten much land, and have been

made men of great possessions. But many an honest poor man hath been undone by it, and an innumerable multitude hath perished for default and lack of substance. And this misery hath long continued, and hath not yet [1556] an end." Moreover, "all this commotion and fray was made under pretence of a common profit and common defence, but in very deed it was for private and proper lucre."

In the sixty years which followed the overthrow of the old system, it was necessary for Parliament to pass no fewer than twelve Acts dealing with the relief of distress, the necessity for which, Thorold Rogers says, "can be traced distinctly back to the crimes of rulers and agents." I need not characterise the spirit which is manifested in these Acts, where poverty and crime are treated as indistinguishable; it was not the spirit of old Catholic days, but it was the spirit of "Protestant individualism" carried into the sphere of social economy.

Not the Good but the Goods of the Church

The fact is, as we are now beginning to find out, the change of religion in England was not effected so much by those who hungered and thirsted after purity of doctrine and simplicity of worship, who hated iniquity and what they held to be superstition, as by those who were on the look-out to better their own interests in a worldly point of view, and who saw in the overthrow of the old ecclesiastical system their golden opportunity. These "new men" looked not so much to the "good" as to the "goods" of the Church, and desired more the *conversio rerum* than any *conversio morum*. What Jansens long ago showed to be the case in Germany, and what Mr. Phillipson and M. Hanotaux declare to be certainly true of France, is hardly less clear in regard to England, when the matter is gone into—namely, that the Reformation was primarily a social and economic revolution, the true meaning of which was in the event successfully disguised under the cloak of religion with the assistance of a few earnest and possibly honest fanatics.

It is, to say the least, strange that the religious innovations synchronised so exactly with ruthless and wholesale confiscations of the old Catholic benefactions for the poor, and with the appropriation of funds intended by the donors for their benefit, to purposes other than the relief of distress. Putting aside the dissolution of the religious corporations, the destruction of the chauntries, the wholly unjustifiable confiscation of the property of the guilds, the heartless seizure of hospitals and almshouses, the substitution of the well-to-do for the poor as the recipients of the benefits coming from the foundation funds of schools and colleges, even the introduction of married clergy whose wives and children had to be supported on the portion of the ecclesiastical benefices intended for the relief of poverty, and much more of the same kind, are all so many indications of the new spirit of Individualism, which produced the great social revolution commonly known as the Protestant Reformation. It was a revolution indeed, but a revolution not in the ordinary sense. It was a rising, not of people against their rulers, nor of those in hunger and distress against the well-to-do, but it was in truth the rising of the rich against the poor, the violent seizure by the new men in power of the funds and property which generations of benefactors had intended for the relief of the needy, or by educational and other endowments to assist the poor man to rise in the social scale.

CONFISCATION OF GUILDS

It is, of course, impossible, within the narrow limits of this brief paper to go as deeply into the subject as it deserves. Fortunately the facts lie on the surface of the history of the sixteenth century, and whatever desire may have existed to cover them up, now that the sources of authentic information are open to all, they can no longer be denied. I will content myself here with a brief reference to the confiscation of the chauntries and guilds which took place, as all know, in the first year of King Edward VI, and I shall endeavour to illustrate what I have to say by examples taken mainly from this county of Nottingham.

It may at first sight, perhaps, not appear very obvious what the question of the *chauntries* has to do with the present subject. But this is simply because the purpose for which these adjuncts to parish churches existed has not been understood. We have been taught to believe that a "chauntry" only meant a place (chapel or other locality) where Masses were offered for the repose of the soul of the donor, and other specified benefactors. No doubt there were such chauntries existing, but to imagine that they were the rule is wholly to mistake the purpose of such foundations. Speaking broadly, the chauntry priest was the assistant priest, or, as we should nowadays say, curate of the parish, who was supported by the foundation funds of the benefactors for that purpose, and even not infrequently by the contributions of the inhabitants. For the most part their *raison d'être* was to look after the poor of the parish, to visit the sick, and to assist in the functions of the parish church. Moreover, connected with these chauntries were very commonly what were called "obits," which were not, as we have been asked to believe, mere money payments to the priest for anniversary services; but were for the most part money left quite as much for annual alms to the poor as for the celebration of the anniversary services. Let us take a few examples. In this city of Nottingham there were two chauntries connected with the parish church of St. Mary, that of Our Lady and that called Amyas Chauntry. The former, we are told, was founded "to maintain the services and to be an aid to the vicar, and partly to succour the poor," the latter to assist in "God's service," and to pray for William Amyas, the founder. When the commissioners in the first year of Edward VI came to inquire into the possessions of these chauntries, they were asked to note that in this parish there were " 1,400 houseling people, and that the vicar there had no other priests to help but the above two chauntry priests." I need not say that they were not spared on this account, for within two years we find the property upon which these two priests were supported had been sold to two speculators in such parcels of land —John Howe and John Broxholme.

Then again, in the parish of St. Nicholas, we find from the returns that the members of the Guild of the Virgin contributed to the support of a priest. In the parish there were more than 200 houseling people, and as the parish living was very poor, there was no other priest to look after them but this one, John Chester, who was paid by the Guild. The King's officials, however, did not hesitate to confiscate the property on this account. It is useless to multiply instances of this kind, some hundreds of which might be given in the county of Nottingham alone. I will, however, take one or two examples of "obits" in this part of the world: In the parish of South Wheatley there were parish lands let out to farm which produced eighteenpence a year, say from £1 to £1 4s. of our money. Of this sum one shilling was for the poor and sixpence for church lights, that is two-thirds or, say, 16s. of our money was for the relief of the distressed. So in the parish of Tuxford the church "obit" lands produced £1 5s. 4d., or more than £16 a year, of which 16s. 4d. was for the poor and 9s. for the church expenses. It is almost unnecessary to add that the Crown took the whole sum intended for the poor, as well as that for the support of the ecclesiastical services. Neither can we hold, I fear, that the robbery of the poor was accidental and unpremeditated. I know that it has been frequently asserted that although grave injury was undoubtedly done to the poor and needy in this way, it was altogether inevitable, since the money thus intended for them was so inextricably bound up with property to which religious obligations (now declared to be superstitious and illegal) were attached, that the whole passed together into the royal exchequer. I confess that I should like to consider that this spoliation of the sick and needy by the Crown of England was accidental and unpremeditated, but there are the hard facts which cannot be got over. The documents prove unmistakeably that the attention of the officials was drawn to the claims of the poor, and that in every such case these claims were disregarded, and a plain intimation is given that the Crown intended to take even the pittance of the poor.

The Guilds

I pass to the question of the Guilds. They were the benefit societies and provident associations of the Middle Ages. They undertook towards their members the duties now frequently performed by burial clubs, by hospitals, by almshouses, and by guardians of the poor. " It is quite certain that town and country guilds obviated pauperism in the Middle Ages," writes Mr. Thorold Rogers. "They assisted in steadying the price of labour, and formed a permanent centre for those associations which fulfilled the function that in more recent times trade unions have striven to satisfy." In these days, I fancy, no one would care to defend the abolition of these friendly and charitable societies and to justify the confiscation of their corporate property, which may be taken as for the most part representing the accumulated savings of the working classes. Moreover, in putting an end to the Guild system, the Reformers did a far greater injury than can be gauged by the amount of the money seized. A large proportion of the revenues of these societies was derived from the entrance fees and annual subscriptions of the existing members, and in dissolving them the State swept away the organisation by which these voluntary subscriptions were raised. In this way far more harm was done to the interests of the poor, sick, and aged, and in fact to the body politic at large, than was caused by the mere loss of their hard-earned savings.

I have here merely indicated some lines of inquiry, especially on the ecclesiastical side, into matters of fact which, if followed out, may help us to come to some sound knowledge of the principles which guided our

Catholic forefathers in these matters, and which I think may be safely called the principles of Christian Democracy, or Christian Collectivism. That Christian Democracy was, I think, manifested before the Reformation in this—that the community, parishes, trades, etc., did in fact show full appreciation of the principles of self-help and mutual assistance. Self-help and self-government showed themselves in popular efforts to carry out common objects as far as possible, and to secure the common good. The community possessed common interests in numberless things, had common lands, common cattle, and other stock: and, in a word, the tendency was to create a system of common property which owed its existence largely to the people themselves. Since the Reformation we need only look at the principles demonstrated by the laws: we see for generations that the bent of legislation was to do away with what was common—the principle of Tudor enclosure carried out to the fullest extent. It is evident that the idea of the " common " is opposed utterly to the idea of absolute property, whilst the root idea of Christian Democracy is that the social order is founded upon the principle, which is also the Christian idea, that property is of the nature of a trust and stewardship, rather than that of absolute, individual possession. I need not point out how the firm apprehension of this principle must influence our judgment on many of the schemes and practical proposals of the day.

IX

THE LAYMAN IN THE PRE-REFORMATION PARISH[1]

HISTORY relates that some years ago a Scotch Presbyterian, with serious religious difficulties and doubts, came for advice to a then well-known Catholic priest. In the course of the interview he asked to be informed as to what his position would be should the result of his inquiries lead him to join the Church. " Among us," he said, " I know exactly what the status and rights of the laity are, and I should like to know what is the exact position of a layman in the Church of Rome." "Your question," replied the priest, "is easily answered. The position of a layman in the Church of Rome is twofold: he kneels before the altar—that's one position; and he sits before the pulpit—and that's the other; and there is no other possible position." This brief statement, which illustrates one view of the question under discussion, cannot, of course, be taken as furnishing an adequate or accurate definition of the status of the Catholic layman of the present day. To begin with: he is always being invited to assume another, and, as things go, a most important position in regard to the Church, namely, that of putting his hand into his pocket for the money necessary to meet the thousand and one imperative wants

[1] A paper read at the Catholic Conference at Stockport, 1899.

incidental to the present circumstances of Catholics in England.

I am not called upon, however, to discuss the main question, having been requested merely to illustrate, as far as it is possible in a brief paper, the functions of the laity in the mediaeval parish. I am dealing with facts as I read them in pre-Reformation documents, and am not concerned to expose or advocate this or that theory, or suggest this or that solution of difficulties experienced at the present day. Whilst fully believing that the past has its many useful and suggestive lessons for us to-day, I am not such a *laudator temporis acti* as to suppose that we ought to imitate, or that we could imitate successfully, all we find flourishing in mediaeval Catholic England.

At the outset, I may remark that what strikes the observer most forcibly in dealing with the records of parochial life in pre-Reformation times, is the way in which priest and people are linked together as one united whole in Church duties. In these days the strong sense of corporate responsibility in the working of a parish, and the well-being of a parochial district with which our Catholic forefathers were imbued, does not exist. I am not concerned with the why and the wherefore, but with the fact, and of this there can be no doubt. The priest in modern times has, for the most part, to worry through his many difficulties in his own way and without much assistance from his flock as a body. No doubt, in the main, he has to look to them for the money with which he carries out his schemes, but money is not everything, and the real responsibility for all lies upon the priest himself, and upon the priest alone. All church building and beautifying, the providing of vestments and sacred plate, the furnishing of altars, the erection of

statues and pictures and painted glass, the establishment
and maintenance of schools, and the payment of debts
incurred in the many works and foundations necessary
for the due working of the district, have all to be initiated,
superintended, and maintained by the energy of the
priest himself. There are, it is true, generally many
volunteer labourers—all praise to them—who, for the
love of God and His Church, do their best to second the
efforts of their pastor. But then they *are* volunteers, and
herein mainly lies the contrast between the old Catholic
times and our own. To-day, at best, a priest can enlist
the sympathies and practical support of but a small
fraction of his flock in their parish; the rest, and by far
the greater number, take little or no part in the work—
regard it, even if they do not speak of it, as his parish,
his business, not theirs. It may be, and probably is, the
case, that most of these do not neglect the plain Christian
duty of supporting their pastors and their religion, and
that many actively co-operate in charitable works in
other places, and are even exemplary and regular members of flourishing sodalities or young men's societies
attached to other churches; but so far as their own parish
is concerned, it profits little or nothing by their support,
or work, or sympathy.

In pre-Reformation days such a state of things was
unknown and altogether impossible. The parish was
then an ever-present reality; the taking part in its affairs
was regarded as a duty incumbent on all, and so far as we
may judge by the somewhat scanty records which have
come down to us, the duty was well fulfilled in practice.
No doubt it is partly true that in these days there are
no parishes strictly so-called. Yet the canonical definition of an ecclesiastical district has little to do with the

matter: the need of co-operation is to-day clearly as
great, if not greater than in olden times, and if the law
as to the hearing of Mass, and the fulfilling of other
obligations in the church of the district, be now relaxed,
that ought not to be construed into freeing the parishioner from all ties of fellowship contracted by the mere
fact of dwelling in a particular district, or all duties connected with it. At any rate, whilst, no doubt, the stricter
enforcing of parochial rights in mediaeval times tended
to impress upon men's minds the other obligations of a
parishioner, there does not, in fact, appear to have been
much need to remind them of those common duties.
Everything seems to have been ordinated as far as possible to interest and enlist the practical sympathies of
all in the affairs of their parish. There was no question
of mere voluntary effort on the part of individuals, but
there is on all hands proof of the well-understood and
well-fulfilled duty of all. Let me illustrate one or two
characteristic features of pre-Reformation parochial life.

Our main sources of information are the various
churchwardens' accounts and the inventories of ecclesiastical parish plate and furniture which have survived
"the great pillage." From a general survey of the
ground, the observer must at once be struck with the
similarity of the evidence afforded by all these documents. They one and all so plainly tell the same tale,
that it is fair to conclude that the picture of parochial
life presented by these precious records that have survived the pillage of the sixteenth century and the neglect of subsequent generations, is practically true of
every parish in Catholic England. What they prove to
us, then, above all else is, that the people at large took
a personal and intelligent interest in building, beautify-

ing, and supporting their parish churches, and that the churches were, in a way that seems strange to us now, *their* churches—their very life may be said to be centred in them, and they, the people, quite as much as their priests, were intimately concerned in their working and management. Whatever had to be done to or for God's House, or in the parochial district of which it was the centre, was the common work of priest and people alike. It can, in absolute truth, be described as a "family concern," settled and carried out by the parson and his flock—the father and his children. Moreover, in those more simple times, traditions—family or parochial traditions—were sacred inheritances, and each piece of furniture and plate, every vestment and hanging of every parish church, had a history of its own, which was known to all through the publication on feast days and holidays of the names of these benefactors to the common good.

We will come to specific instances presently; but just let us fully understand how completely our Catholic forefathers were regarded, and regarded themselves, as the proud possessors of their various parish churches. Bishop Hobhouse, in an interesting preface to one of the Somerset Record Society publications, describes the parish thus: " It was the community of the township organised for Church purposes and subject to Church discipline, with a constitution which recognised the rights of the whole body as an aggregate, and the right of every adult member, whether man or woman, to advice in self-government; but, at the same time, kept the self-governing community under a system of inspection and restraint by a central authority outside the parish boundaries."

As Dr. Jessopp has well pointed out,[1] the self-government of a Catholic pre-Reformation parish was most
marked. The community had its own deliberative and
administrative assembly—the parish meeting. It elected
or appointed its own officers—sometimes men, sometimes women—who had well-defined duties, and were
paid for services out of funds provided by the parishioners. Such, for instance, were the parish clerk, the
gravedigger, watchman, keeper, and carrier of the parish
processional cross. These were in no sense either the
nominees or paid servants of the rector. They had
duties which were directed, no doubt, to him, but they
were paid by the parishioners themselves, and were " removable, when removable at all," by the rural dean or
archdeacon at their petition.

" The president or chairman of the church council or
parish meeting," writes Dr. Jessopp, " was the rector of
the parish, or his deputy; but he was by no means a
' lord over God's heritage.' There is no evidence—but
quite the contrary—to show that he initiated to any
great extent the subjects of debate, and the income
raised for parish purposes, which not infrequently was
considerable, was not under his control, nor did it pass
through his hands." The trustees of parish property
were the churchwardens. They, generally two in number, were elected annually, and were always regarded in
fact, as well as in theory, as the responsible representatives of the parish. Many instances could be given
where these wardens, either from parochial funds or
specific bequests they were called on to administer for
the common benefit, found the stipends for additional
curates to work the parish, paid the fees for obits and

[1] *Nineteenth Century*, January, 1898, p. 5.

other anniversary services to the parish priests and other ministers, or for clerical or lay assistance in the celebrations of some more solemn festivals. In some cases I have found them arranging the hours for the various daily Masses, which, in their opinion, would best suit the convenience of the people.

The parish possessions were considerable, and comprised all kinds of property—lands, houses, flocks and herds, cows, and even hives of bees. These were what may be termed the capital of the parish, which was constantly being added to by the generosity of generations of pious benefactors. Then, over and besides the chancel, which was the freehold of the parson, the body of the church and other buildings, together with the churchyard and its enclosure, and generally, if not always, the common church house, were then under the special and absolute control of the people's wardens. Then, if the law forced the parish to find fitting and suitable ornaments and vestments, it equally gave them the control of the ecclesiastical furniture, etc. of the church. Their chosen representatives were the guardians of the jewels and plate, of the ornaments and hangings, of the vestments and tapestries, which were regarded, as in very truth they were, as the common property of every soul in the particular village or district in which the church was situated. It is no exaggeration to say that the parish church was in Catholic times the care and business of all. Its welfare was the concern of the people at large, and it took its natural place in their daily lives. Was there, say, building to be done, repairs to be effected, a new peal of bells to be procured, organs to be mended, new plate to be bought, and the like, it was the parish as a corporate body that decided the matter, arranged the details, and provided for the payment. At times, let us say when a new vestment was in question, the whole parish might be called to sit in council at the church house on this matter of common interest, and discuss the cost, the stuff, and the make.

The parish wardens had their duties also towards their poorer brethren in the district. I have come across more than one instance of their being the guardians of a common chest, out of which temporary loans could be obtained by needy parishioners to enable them to tide over pressing difficulties. These loans were secured by pledges and the additional surety of other parishioners. No interest, however, was charged for the use of the money, and in cases where the pledge had to be sold to recover the original sum, anything over and above was returned to the borrower. In other ways, too, the poorer parishioners were assisted by the corporate property of the parish. The stock managed by the wardens " were," says one of the early English reformers, " in some towns (*i.e.*, townships and villages) six, some eight, and some a dozen kine, given unto the stock, for the relief of the poor, and used in some such wise that the poor ' cottingers,' which could make any provision for fodder, had the milk for a very small hire; and then, the number of the stock reserved [that is, of course, the original number being maintained], all manner of vailes [or profits], besides both the hire of the milk and the prices of the young veals and old fat wares, was disposed to the relief of the poor." [1]

The functions and duties of the mediaeval parishioners were determined by law and custom. By law, according to the statute of Archbishop Peckham in

[1] Lever, *Sermon before the King*, 1550 (Arber's reprint, p. 82).

1280,[1] which remained in force till the change of religion,
the parish was bound to find, broadly speaking, all that
pertained to the services—such as vestments, chalice,
processional cross, the paschal candle, etc.—and to keep
the fabric and ornaments of the church proper, exclusive
of the chancel. In 1305 Archbishop Winchelsey somewhat enlarged the scope of the parish duties, and the
great canonist, Lyndwood, explains that, very frequently,
especially in London churches, the parishioners, through
their wardens, kept even the chancels in repair, and, in
fact, found everything for the services, except the two
Mass candles which the priest provides.

To take some examples: first, of the way in which,
according to the custom of our Catholic forefathers, the
memory of benefactions to the parish was kept alive.
The inventory of the parish church of Cranbrook, made
in 1509, shows that the particulars of all gifts and donors
were regularly noted down, in order that they might
periodically be published and remembered. The presents
vary greatly in value, and nothing is too small, apparently, to be noted. Thus we have a monstrance of silver-
gilt, which the wardens value at £20, " of Sir Robert
Egelyonby's gift"; and the list goes on to say: " This
Sir Robert was John Roberts' priest thirty years, and he
never had other service or benefice, and the said John
Roberts was father to Walter Roberts, Esquire." Again,
John Hindeley " gave three copes of purple velvet, whereof
one was of velvet upon velvet with images broidered,"
and, adds the inventory for a perpetual memory, " He
is grandfather of Gervase Hindeley, of Cushorn, and
Thomas, of Cranbrook Street." Or again, to take one
more instance from the same, it is recorded that the

[1] Wilkins, ii, 49.

"two long candlesticks before Our Lady's altar, fronted with lions and a towel on the rood of Our Lady's chancel," had been given by "old Moder Hopper." So, too, in the case of St. Dunstan's, Canterbury, we have a wonderful list of furniture with the names of the donors set out. The best chalice, for instance, was the gift of one "Harry Boll." The two great latten candlesticks were a present from John Philpot, and "a kercher for Our Lady and a chapplet and pordryd cap for her son" came from Margery Roper.

I have said that the memory of these gifts was kept alive by the "bede-roll," or list of people for whom the parish was bound to pray, published periodically by the parson. Thus, to take one instance: At Leverton, in the county of Lincoln, the parson, Sir John Wright, presented the church with a suit of red purple vestments, "for the which," says a note in the churchwardens' accounts, "you shall all specially pray for the souls of William Wright and Elizabeth his wife" [the father and mother of the donor] and other relations, "as well them that be alive as them that be departed to the mercy of God, for whose lives and souls" these vestments are given "to the honour of God, His most blessed mother, Our Lady Saint Mary, and all His saints in Heaven, and the blessed matron St. Helen, his patron, to be used at such principal feasts and times as it shall please the curates so long as they shall last."[1]

In this way the names of benefactors and the memory of their good deeds was ever kept alive in the minds of those who benefited by their gifts. The parish treasury was not looked on as so much stock, the accumulation of years, of haphazard donations without definite history

[1] *Archæol.*, xli, 355.

or purpose; but every article, vestment, banner, hanging, chalice, etc., called up some affectionate memory both of the living and the dead. On high day and feast day, when all that was best and richest in the parochial treasury was brought forth to deck the walls and statues and altars, the display of parish ornaments recalled to the minds of the people assembled within its walls to worship God, the memory of good deeds done by generations of neighbours for the decoration of their sanctuary. "The immense treasures in the churches," writes Dr. Jessopp, "were the joy and boast of every man and woman and child in England, who, day by day, and week by week, assembled to worship in the old houses of God which they and their fathers had built, and whose every vestment and chalice, and candlestick and banner, organ and bells, and pictures and images, and altar and shrine they look upon as their own, and part of their birthright." [1]

It might reasonably be supposed that this was true only of the greater churches; but this is not so. What strikes one so much in these parish accounts of bygone days is the richness of even small, out-of-the-way village churches. Where we would naturally be inclined to look for poverty and meanness, there is evidence to the contrary. To take an example or two. Morebath is a small, uplandish, out-of-the-way parish of little importance on the borders of Exmoor; the population, for the most part, had to spend their energies in daily labour to secure the bare necessities of life, and riches, at any rate, could never have been abundant. Morebath may consequently be taken as a fair sample of an obscure and poor village. For this hamlet we possess full accounts from the year

[1] *Nineteenth Century*, March, 1898, p. 433.

1530, and we find at this time, and in this very poor, out-of-the-way place, there were no less than eight separate accounts kept of money intended for the support of different altars of devotions. For example, we have the "Stores" of the Chapels of Our Lady and St. George, etc., and the guilds of the young men and maidens of the parish. All these were kept and managed by the lay-elected officials of the societies—confraternities, I sup-pose we should call them—and to their credit are entered numerous gifts of money and specific gifts of value of kind, such as cows, and swarms of bees, etc. Most of them had their little capital funds invested in cattle and sheep, the rent of which proved a considerable part of their revenues. In a word, these accounts furnish abund-ant and unmistakeable evidence of the active and in-telligent interest in the duty of supporting and adorning their church on the part of these simple country folk at large. What is true of this is true of every other similar account to a greater or less degree, and all these accounts show unmistakeably that the entire management of these parish funds was in the hands of the people.

Voluntary rates to clear off obligations contracted for the benefit of the community—such as the purchase of bells, the repair of the fabric, and even for the making of roads and bridges—were raised by the wardens. Collec-tions for Peter's pence, for the support of the parish clerk, and for every variety of church and local purpose are recorded, and the spirit of self-help is manifested on every page of these accounts. To keep to Morebath. In 1528 a complete set of black vestments was purchased at a cost—considerable in those days—of £6 5s., and to help in the common work, the vicar gave up certain tithes in wool he had been in the habit of receiving. These

vestments, by the way, were only finished and paid for
in 1547, just before the changes under Edward VI rendered them useless. In 1538 the parish made a voluntary
rate to purchase a new cope, and the general collections
for this purpose produced some £3 6s. 8d. In 1534 the
silver chalice was stolen, and at once, we are told, "ye
yong men and maydens of ye parysshe dru themselves
together, and at ther gyfts and provysyon they bought
in another chalice without any charge of the parish."
Sums of money, big and small, specific gifts in kind, the
stuff or ornaments needed for vestments, were apparently always forthcoming when needed. Thus, at one
time a new cope is suggested, and Anne Tymwell, of
Hayne, gave the churchwardens her "gown and her
ring"; Joan Tymwell, a cloak and a girdle; and Richard
Norman, "seven sheep and three shillings and fourpence
in money," towards the cost.

These examples could be multiplied to any extent,
but the above will be sufficient to show the popular
working of a mediaeval parish. The same story of local
government, popular interest, and ready self-help, as well
as an unmistakeable spirit of affection for the parish
church as theirs, is manifested by the people in every
account we possess. Every adult of both sexes had a
voice in the system, and the parson was little more in
this regard than chairman of the village meetings, and,
as I have more than once seen him described, "chief
parishioner." In the management of the fabric, the service, and all things necessary for the due performance
of these, the people were not only called upon to pay,
but it is clear the diocesan authorities evidently left to
the parish a wise discretion. No doubt the higher ecclesiastical officials could interfere in theory; but in prac-

tice interference was rare. It would not be to my present purpose to describe the various methods employed to replenish the parochial exchequer. There was apparently seldom much difficulty in finding the necessary money, and it will be of interest to see how it was expended, by some further examples.

The church accounts of Leverton (six miles from Boston) have been printed in the *Archæologia*, and those that are interested in this subject may conveniently turn to them as illustrating it. The church, until the past three hundred years of neglect has disfigured it, must have presented a very beautiful appearance, when decked for a festival, in the hangings and ornaments which generations of the inhabitants had lovingly gathered within its walls. When first the accounts were opened in 1492, the parish was beginning to be interested—as, by the way, so many parishes were at this period—in bells. The people evidently made a great effort to get a new peal, and they contributed generously. The rector headed the list with ten shillings and sixpence, which was afterwards paid for him by a friend; but what I would remark is that the whole arrangement for the purchase and hanging of the bells was in the hands of the people's representatives, the churchwardens. They bought timber for the framework, and hired a carpenter to make it. They hired a cart to bring over the great bell from the neighbouring parish where it had been cast, and there are notes of the cost of the team of horses and other items of expense, not forgetting a penny for the toll of a bridge. We may judge, however, that the work was not altogether a success, as in 1498 the two wardens made a " move " to " the gathering of the township in the kirk," at which they gathered £4 13s. 10d. They forthwith set about the building of a new steeple, and ordered another peal of bells. The stone was given to them, but they had to see to the quarrying of it. Trees were bought in a neighbouring wood, and by direction of the wardens, were felled and cut into beams and boards, or fashioned roughly for scaffolding.

As the sixteenth century progressed, a great deal of building and repair was undertaken by the parish authorities. In 1503 the wardens ordered a new bell, and went over to Boston to see it "shott." The same year they took in hand the making of a new font, and a deputation was sent over to Frieston, about three miles from Leverton, to inspect and pass the work. The lead for the lining of the font was procured in pigs, and cast into a mould on the spot by a plumber brought over for the purpose. In 1517 extensive repairs were undertaken in the north aisle which necessitated much shoring up of the walls. Two years later, on the completion of the works, the church and churchyard were consecrated, the Bishop's fees, amounting to £3, being paid out of the public purse. In 1526 the rood-loft was decorated, and the niches filled with images. In that year one of the parishioners, William Frankish, died, and left a legacy to the churchwardens for the purpose of procuring alabaster statues to fill the vacant spaces. The wardens hired a man, called sometimes the "alabastre man," and sometimes "Robert Brook, the carver," and, in earnest for the payment, at the conclusion gave him a shilling. At the same time a collection was made for the support of the artist during his stay. Some of the parishioners gave money, but most of them apparently contributed "cheese."

I wish I had time to quote more fully from these interesting and instructive accounts. The serious building operations continued up to the very eve of the religious changes. They by no means satisfied the energies of the parish officials. If books required binding, a travelling workman was engaged on the job, and the leather, thread, wax, and other materials for the mystery of bookbinding were purchased for his use. Sometimes extra was paid to his wife for the stitching of leaves and covers, and the workmen were apparently lodged by one or other of the people, and this was accounted as their contribution to the common work. Then there were vestments and sur-plices and other linen bought, mended, and washed, and the very marks set upon the linen cloths are put into the accounts. So entirely was the whole regarded as the work of the people, that, just as we have seen that the parish paid for the consecration of their parish church and graveyard, so do we find the wardens assigning a fee to their own vicar for blessing the altar linen and new vestments, and entering the names of benefactors on the parish bede-roll.

I have said that the wardens often appear as arranging more than the ordinary material details. Thus, at Hen-ley-on-Thames they ordained that the Chaplain of Our Lady's altar should say Mass every day at six o'clock, and the chauntry priest of St. Catherine's at eight o'clock, as the hours most convenient for the majority of the people. At St. Mary's, Dover, the wardens paid the parson a stipend for regularly reading the bede-roll, and charged a fee for inserting any name upon it. They paid deacons, sub-deacons, clerks, and singing men and children on great days to add solemnity to the church festivals. Two priests were generally paid at Easter to help to shrive, and one year there were payments to

three priests "to help to shrive and to minister at
Maundy Thursday, Easter Even, and Easter Day." The
same year the parish paid for "a breakfast for such
clerks as took pain to maintain God's service on the
holidays"; and on Palm Sunday they expended three-
pence on "bread and wine to the readers of the Passion."

"How curious a state of things is revealed to us in
these documents!" says a writer who had been engaged
over these churchwardens' accounts. "We have been
taught to regard our mediaeval forefathers as a terribly
priest-ridden people, yet nothing of all this, but quite
the contrary, appears in all these parish papers."

What is seen so clearly in the parish accounts as to
the powers exercised by the wardens in the management
of the church property receives additional confirmation—
were that at all necessary—from the pre-Reformation
wills. We have only to turn over the leaves of the collection of Yorkshire wills, published by the Surtees
Society, to see how well understood was the intimate
connection between the parishioners and the parish
church; how people loved to leave some article of value
to the place where they had worshipped, in order to per-
petuate their memory; and how to the wardens was
entrusted the care of these bequests. Even where the
names of the popular representatives are not inserted in
the wills themselves, they, as the legal trustees for the
common church property, and not the parson of the
parish, trouble themselves in the matter. Did time allow,
I might quote some curious illustrations of the gifts and
bequests thus made for the common good. I wonder
what the authorities of some of our modern parish
churches would think of a bequest of dresses and gowns

to various images to make vestments, or even " 20 marks to buy 20 bullocks to find a priest to pray for my soul and the soul of my wife "? Yet in these interesting wills there are numerous examples of such donations, which to my mind appear to indicate, more than any other way can, the affection of our Catholic forefathers for their religion, and the real practical hold the Faith had over them. The local church was to them a living reality: it was theirs, and all it contained, in an absolute and sometimes almost a startling way. One instance comes to my mind. In the parish of Yatton, in Somerset, on the eve of the Reformation—about 1520, say—a difficulty arose as to the repair of certain sluices to keep back the winter floods. To make a long story short, in the end the parish were ordered to make good the defect. It meant money, and the wardens' accounts show that they had been spending generously on the church. It was consequently decided that to raise the necessary cash they should sell a piece of silver church plate, which had been purchased some years before by the common contributions of the faithful. " How monstrous! " I can hear some people say. Possibly: I am not going to try and defend what they did; but the instance furnishes me with a supreme example of the way in which the people of a mediaeval parish regarded the property of God's house as their own.

X

ST. GREGORY THE GREAT AND ENGLAND[1]

THE year of our Lord 604 is a date memorable in the history of the Church. On the 12th of March in that year, aged sixty-five, and in the fourteenth year of his Pontificate, died St. Gregory the Great, perhaps the most illustrious of the long line of Popes who have sat in Peter's Chair and governed the Church of Christ during the nineteen centuries of its existence. To Englishmen of any form of religious belief, the thirteenth centenary of that event, celebrated this year, should not be without interest. As early as A.D. 747, the Council of Clovesho ordered that the 12th of March, the feast of St. Gregory, should ever be kept solemnly, as well as that of the burial of St. "Augustine, Archbishop and Confessor, who was sent to the English nation by the said Pope and our Father Gregory to bring them the certainty of the Faith, the Sacrament of Baptism, and the knowledge of the heavenly kingdom."[2] For many hundreds of years our forefathers were mindful of all they owed, in the way of religion and of civilisation, to this great Pontiff, and they loved to call him their

[1] Published in the *Dublin Review*, April, 1904.
[2] Haddan and Stubbs, *Councils and Eccles. docts.*, iii, 368.

279

"master," their "teacher," the "preacher of their faith," their "doctor," their "father," and their "apostle." "By his labours," writes Bede in his *Ecclesiastical History of the English People*, "he brought our race, that is, the English people, from out of the power of Satan to the faith of Christ, (and so) we rightly can and must call him our Apostle." [1] "Gregory the holy Pope, the Apostle of the English nation," writes the author of the Anglo-Saxon homily for his feast, "on this present day, after manifold labours and holy studies, happily ascended to God's kingdom. He is rightly the Apostle of the English nation, for through his counsel and mission he withdrew us from the worship of the devil, and turned us to God." [2]

To us Catholics especially, who, after the lapse of thirteen centuries, still look to Rome and the Pope for guidance in the Faith which our Saxon ancestors received from Gregory, the celebration of this centenary should be something more than a bare commemoration of an interesting event which happened many long centuries ago. It should renew within us those deep feelings of grateful devotion and loyalty to the See of Peter felt and expressed by the English people for generations after the coming of the first Roman missionaries to our shores. "No other nation in the Christian world can claim a Pope for its Apostle," was the constant boast of the English people in Catholic days. For this reason England was admittedly bound to the successors of Peter by closer ties and more intimate relations than were the other peoples of Christendom. It is indeed

---

[1] *Hist. Eccl.*, lib. ii, c. 1.

[2] *The Homilies of the Anglo-Saxon Church*, ed. Thorpe, ii, p. 117.

remarkable how, for centuries after their conquest to Christianity by the missionaries of St. Gregory, the Saxon peoples turned to Rome. They looked to it for inspiration in their ecclesiastical buildings and their ecclesiastical ceremonies, as well as for authoritative guidance in the faith. To make the journey to Rome and, once in a lifetime at least, to visit the *limina Apostolorum*, was the ardent desire of multitudes of both women and men; and the letters of St. Boniface alone show that in his day the roads to Rome were well worn by the journeyings of English pilgrims of all sorts and conditions. The English loved to note down in their books the position and the very measurements of the sacred places in the Eternal City; and there is some reason for thinking that here in England, at Canterbury, on the greatest festivals, such as Christmas, they tried to copy the ceremonies of Papal Mass as far as possible, and even sang the two Epistles with the *Gradual* in Greek and in Latin. To use the words of the latest editor of St. Bede's *History*, all must allow that " the Church of England long retained a grateful sense of what she owed to St. Gregory." [1] This devotion of the English to their " Apostle " and to the Popes who followed him was recognised even beyond the limits of their country. Thus, the author of the *Gesta Abbatum Fontanellensium*, A.D. 743-753, speaks of " the men of Britain, that is the English, who always remain the most faithful servants of the Apostolic See "; [2] whilst the chronicler Thietmar writes: " I have time without number noted that the Angles, called so either because of their angelical faces, or because they occupy an angle

[1] *Baedae Opera Historica*, ed. C. Plummer, ii, p. 67.
[2] Pertz, *Mon. Germ.* ii, 289.

of this earth," are oppressed by the Danes and made to pay tribute to them, though "they were tributaries of the Prince of the Apostles, Peter, and the spiritual sons of their father Gregory." [1]

On occasion of this centenary, then, it needs no excuse to recall those well-known facts which brought St. Gregory into such close connection with our race, and which left in the minds and hearts of the English people so deep a sense of gratitude to him and his successors, that it lasted on, in spite of changes of dynasty, social upheavals and conquests, for more than eight centuries.

Tradition brings St. Gregory into connection with England for the first time in the story of the "fair-haired youths" in the market-place at Rome. The anecdote is, indeed, one of our cherished national possessions, and like so many of the tales which have centred round the great personality of the Saint, and now form almost necessary chapters in his life, this story is, we may be happy to think, of English origin. John the Deacon, who wrote the longest biography of the Pope, about the year 827, plainly says that the instances he gives about St. Gregory's wonder-working powers are those which are commonly read to the people in the English churches. [2] Whatever their exact historical value, these stories must, at least, be regarded as certain evidence of the love and affection of the first Christian missionaries—Augustine, Mellitus, Paulinus, and the rest—for the Pope who had sent them hither and had encouraged them in the serious and difficult work of converting the far-distant land of England. They speak, too, of the eagerness of our first

---

[1] Pertz, *Mon. Germ.*, iii, 847-8.
[2] Migne, *Patr. lat.*, lxxv, col. 105.

Christian ancestors to know all they could about Rome, and especially about him whom they had come to revere and love as "their father and apostle."

Until comparatively recent times it was believed that St. Bede's *Ecclesiastical History* was the source from which St. Gregory's later biographers, the deacons Paul and John, had drawn many of the facts they relate about him. But the discovery of an earlier life of the Saint, made by Professor Ewald in a manuscript in the library of St. Gall, has thrown new and unexpected light upon the origin of several of the anecdotes related in these biographies.[1] The MS. in question (No. 567) is of the eighth or ninth century, and, according to the high authority of its finder, it is certainly the earliest known life of St. Gregory, anterior to the account given in St. Bede's *History*, and consequently, of course, to the two lives by the deacons, John and Paul. In his introductory essay to the portions of this manuscript that he has printed, Ewald shows that this, the earliest life, is undoubtedly English in origin, is the work of a Northumbrian, and almost certainly of a monk of Whitby, since he calls Whitby *nostrum coenobium*. The account given of the work of St. Paulinus in the north; the knowledge manifested of King Edwin and of the burial of his remains in the church of St. Peter, prince of the Apostles, "with the bones of our other kings, at the north of the altar sanctified in the name of the most blessed Apostle Peter, and to the east of that, which in the same church is consecrated to St. Gregory"[2] all help to connect the

---

[1] It is now nearly three centuries since attention was called to the work, but in such a way as to frighten off every later enquirer, cf. *Downside Review*, July, 1886, p. 271.

[2] Paul Ewald, *Die älteste Biographie Gregors I* in *Historische*

writer clearly with the northern part of England, and in some way with Rome through St. Paulinus, St. Gregory's immediate disciple. Of the writer's own personal love and devotion to St. Gregory there is ample testimony in this new life. To him the great Pope is " Papa noster "; " Apostolicus noster "; " doctor noster "; " noster Gregorius " (*our* Gregory), and the English race are his special Apostolate. And the setting of the scenes recall the north and St. Paulinus in particular. Even in his day, St. Bede tells us, and he knew that part of the country well, the memory of Paulinus, the Apostle of the north, and of his preaching, was still fresh and green among the people of Northumbria. In the northern Cheviots, too, at Kirk-Newton, the dedication of a church to St. Gregory, and the existence of a " Gregory hill " and a " Gregory well," in a place where local tradition still points to the spot where stood the royal house of Edwin, and where still runs the stream in which Paulinus is said to have been engaged for six-and-thirty days in baptising his new converts, seems to show, were proof needed, the ancient devotion and veneration of Paulinus for Gregory. Is it too fanciful, therefore, to suggest that many of these stories told about St. Gregory the Great, and which have now been shown by the discovery of Professor Ewald to have had an English, and a northern English origin, may have fallen from the very lips of St. Paulinus himself, and having been treasured as cherished traditions by the first Christians of the northern

Aufsätze dem Andenken an Georg Waitz gewidmet, 1886, p. 63. I have, since this essay was written, published the entire text of this precious MS., entitling it: *A Life of Pope St. Gregory the Great, written by a Monk of the Monastery of Whitby (probably about A.D.* 713), Westminster, Art and Book Co., 1904.

parts, were preserved to us by this monk of Whitby? The writer, indeed, professes to record what is commonly spoken of among the people; for instance, he prefaces his account of the story of the English youths in Rome by the phrase, " est igitur narratio fidelium "—" it is a tale told among the faithful." [1] The story, too, it must be remembered, has a real northern setting: *Deira* was Northumbria, and Aelli, the king, was the father of Edwin, by whose conversion, as the writer of this early life takes care to note, Gregory's prophecy was fulfilled.

What is true about the origin of the "market-place" story is true also of several of the other well-known anecdotes connected with the life of St. Gregory. The miracle of the woman who had doubts as to our Lord's presence in the Holy Eucharist at the time of Communion,[2] for example: the cloths sent to St. Gregory; the story of the Tyrant and his approach to Rome; that of Trajan, and in fact all that are related by Paul the deacon in six chapters [3] of his life of the Saint, are taken almost certainly from this early English life, and may thus be said to have had an English origin. Perhaps it would be more correct to represent these tales as having been returned to Italy whence they came, after having been told to the new converts in England by their first missioners, treasured up in the memories of the grateful neophytes and repeated from mouth to mouth, as perhaps teaching them, in a way they could understand, more about the

---

[1] Paul Ewald, *Die älteste Biographie Gregors I* in *Historische Aufsätze dem Andenken an Georg Waitz gewidmet,* 1886, p. 48.

[2] Migne, *Patr. lat.,* lxxv, col. 52. Told in the life by Paul the deacon.

[3] Cap. 23 to 29.

real personality of Gregory, and warming their hearts more towards him, than could any dry statement of facts and dates. In regard to the Trajan story, harder perhaps to believe in those days even than in our own, it has been remarked that it is instructive "to see how the Englishman (the writer of this early life) very explicitly throws the responsibility of it on the Romans," adding, "some of our people say that the tale is told by the Romans."

Sometimes, no doubt—perhaps often—the stories of the wonders worked by their great father and apostle of their race would, in process of time, tend to grow in the telling as all such stories do. One such instance is afforded us by an English addition to the anecdote of the Emperor Trajan, who was said to have been delivered from hell by the prayers of St. Gregory. The story itself, as already pointed out, is first known in this earliest life of the great Pope by the northern monk. In a later version, given in an English collection of anecdotes intended to enlighten the tedium of ordinary parochial discourses, or to emphasise the point of some doctrinal teaching, there is a somewhat curious explanation of the constant sickness that almost overwhelmed St. Gregory in the last years of his life, which is brought into connection with the Trajan story. "In the life of St. Gregory," the writer says, "we read that after he had liberated the soul of the Emperor Trajan from hell by his prayers, an angel appeared to him and said: 'Since you have prayed for this man who was lost, and obtained what you asked, you have now to choose one of two things: you must either pass the space of two days in Purgatory, or be afflicted with pain and sickness during the rest of your life.' The Saint made choice of the life-long sufferings;

and he got what he asked, as may be read in the story
of his life." [1]

According to the English tradition, then, St. Gregory
first came into contact with the English in the Roman
forum, and the incident first made him dream of becoming the Apostle of our race. This event must be placed
somewhere about the year 585—that is, after his return
from Constantinople, whither he had gone to represent
Pope Pelagius II at the Imperial Court. Although
Gregory had thought to escape from all contact with
worldly affairs by taking refuge in the cloister as a
monk, the Pope had other views in his regard, and made
him one of the seven regionary deacons of the City of
Rome. In one of his official rounds, he is supposed to
have first come upon the English youths. The story will
be well known to everyone, but it may perhaps be allowed
to find a place here, as it is given in the early life spoken
of above, which, be it remembered, represents the earliest
English tradition as to the incident, and that which
almost certainly St. Bede subsequently utilised. Although in its main features the story is the same that
we know so well, there are one or two interesting differ-
ences, which make it perhaps worth while to give it at
length in the words in which, as the Whitby monk says,
"it was told among the faithful."

"Before his (*i.e.*, St. Gregory's) pontificate," says the
writer, "there came to Rome some men of our nation
with fair faces and light hair.[2] When he had heard of

---

[1] B. Mus. Add. MS. 11284, f. 76. The writer refers the reader
to the Preface of the *Dialogues* for St. Gregory's account of his
sufferings. This is a mistake for the Introductory letter to the
Morals of the Book of Job. Migne, *Patr. lat.,* lxxv, col. 615.

[2] It will be noticed that this earliest account of the incident

their arrival, he desired to see them, and was struck by the sight of their light colour, and his attention was arrested by their novel and unwonted appearance. What is more than this, being inwardly moved by God, he was led to inquire to what nation they belonged. (Some say that they were handsome boys, some call them curly-headed and graceful youths.)[1] When (in reply to his question) they had answered: ' The people to whom we belong are called Angles,' he exclaimed: ' Angels of God.' Then said he again: ' And what is the name of the king of that people?' To which they replied, ' *Aelli.*' Upon this he exclaimed again: ' *Alleluia*, for in that place ought God's praises to be sung.' Once more he asked what was the special name of the tribe to which they belonged. They told him: ' *Deira* '; on which he exclaimed: ' *de ira Dei* '—those who are flying from God's wrath to the Faith." [2]

The author of this early life then describes the attempt made by St. Gregory himself before becoming Pope to journey over into England as our Apostle. The account of this, as given by St. Bede,[3] is very brief, and the special incidents related in the two lives of the deacons John and Paul do not appear at all in his version. They are, however, to be found fully recorded in this early life, which is thus again recognised as the source of these narratives. We there learn of Gregory's secretly setting out from Rome, with the permission he had with diffi-

does not speak of the *pueros venales* of St. Bede. The other lives of the deacons Paul and John follow Bede in saying that these youths were *slaves*, which St. Bede introduced with the phrase, "Advenientibus nuper mercatoribus."

[1] This passage Ewald notes as an addition.
[2] P. Ewald, *Die älteste Biographie Gregors I, ut supra*, p. 48
[3] *Hist. Eccl.*, lib. ii, cap. 1 (ed. Plummer, i, p. 80).

culty extorted from Pope Benedict I, and of the determination of the Roman people to bring him back[1] again to the city. From this source also comes the incident, not to be found in St. Bede, but which appears in the two later lives, of the jingling cries invented by the Romans in their endeavour to force the Pope to recall the Saint: " Petrum offendisti; Romam destruxisti; Gregorium dimisisti "—" Thou hast offended Peter and ruined Rome in letting Gregory go." In this life likewise is to be found the story, again not to be found in Bede, but which is in the later lives, of the locust which is said to have settled upon Gregory's book as he was resting during a mid-day halt in his flight from Rome. The incident is well known from one of those plays upon words, which through the *non Angli sed angeli* story we are used to attribute to St. Gregory. In this case, repeating to himself the name of the insect—*locusta*—he interpreted it as signifying *locus-sta*, or *sta-in-loco*—" remain in the place "—which play of his fancy was immediately realised by the arrival of the messenger, whom the Pope had been forced to send, to recall Gregory to the Eternal City. It is at least curious and worth noting that this story, as well as the *non Angli* incident, which so well represent St. Gregory's playful nature, and which we English at least have learnt to regard as typical of our Apostle, have both an English origin.

It may here, perhaps, be permitted to give a translation of another passage from the old life, which deals

[1] See in Migne, *ut sup.*, cols. 51, 52 (Paul the Deacon's Life), and col. 72 (John the Deacon's Life). We may note that it is from this early English life that John the Deacon got the correct name of the Pope, Benedict I. Bede omits it, and Paul the Deacon erroneously gives the name of Gregory's immediate predecessor, Pelagius II.

U

with the fulfilment of St. Gregory's old prediction as to
the conversion of the people of Deira. Nothing of the
kind has found a place in the later lives, although from
his connection with the north we might almost have expected that St. Bede would have given something of the
same kind as we find in the Northumbrian monk of
Whitby, especially when we can be almost certain that
he had this account before him. The author of the early
life writes: "By these (*i.e.*, the Kentish missionaries,
Augustine, Mellitus, and Laurence) Ethelbert, the first
of all the English kings, was brought to the faith of
Christ, and washed by His baptism, was made glorious
with all His people. After this, in our own nation, which
is that of the Northumbrians, Edwin, the aforesaid son
of Aelli, whom deservedly we remember in the prophecy
of the *Alleluia* of divine praise, ruled both with singular
wisdom and with the sceptre of that royal authority
(which had existed) ever since the English peoples
landed in this island.

"O! how excellently well and how fitly did not all
these things happen. Thus, the name *Angle*, if one letter
e be added, becomes *Angel*: certainly the people who are
called by this name are meant to praise God for ever in
Heaven. . . . And the name *Aelli* is composed of two
syllables. If from the first of these the letter *e* is removed,
and in the second syllable an *e* is put in place of the
(final) *i*, the word is *Alle*, which in our language means
absolutely 'everyone.' And this it is that our Lord says:
Come to Me *all ye* that labour,"[1] etc.; as, indeed, the
whole people did when they lovingly embraced the Faith
at the bidding of their Apostles.[2]

[1] Paul Ewald, *ut supra*, p. 50.
[2] "In his loyalty to the royal house of Deira, the founders and

In spite of Gregory's flight from Rome to avoid the
burdens and the responsibilities of the papacy, he surrendered himself finally to God's will, and was consecrated
Pope on September 3rd, A.D. 590. He had not forgotten,
and did not forget even in the multitude of affairs which
now claimed his attention, the far-off English peoples
whose Apostle he had desired to be. As Supreme Pontiff,
the zeal of former years came back to assist him in carrying out what he, from his office of common father of all
nations of the earth, now regarded as a duty and responsibility. He had evidently determined upon and planned
the mission of Augustine long before he was in a position
to accomplish it, for in a letter written after the first
English conversions had been made, and after Augustine
had received consecration as first Bishop of the English
at Arles, the Pope says as much to Syagrus of Autun.[1]
At first it was evidently his intention to obtain English
youths and to educate them in Rome, so that they might
subsequently return as missionaries to their native
country. In the early days of his Pontificate the Pope
wrote to Candidus, the agent for the patrimony of the
Church in Gaul, to act for him in this matter. He bade
him use the money he received from this source to
furnish clothes for the poor, or to obtain "English youths

patrons of his own monastic house at Whitby, he (the author of the
old life) gives Edwin, the sainted first Christian king of Northumbria, a splendid character. . . . Of St. Paulinus, his ecclesiastical hero, he gives an account filling four sections (14-17). The
two next relate what is wholly new—the translation of the body of
St. Edwin from Hatfield, near Doncaster, to Whitby, some time
between the years 695-704; here we incidentally learn that in the
monastery church there, there was an altar under the dedication of
St. Gregory."—*Downside Review*, July, 1886, p. 273.

[1] Ep. ix, 108, Migne, *Patr. lat.*, lxxvii, col. 1035.

of seventeen or eighteen, who may be dedicated to God
and brought up in monasteries for His service. As, however, such youths will be pagans, I desire," he says, "that
a priest be sent with them in case they fall ill on the
journey, so that he may be able to baptise them should
he see they are likely to die."[1] It can hardly be doubted
that these directions were carried out; and that, although
there is no direct evidence on the matter, some of the
missionaries who subsequently came to England were
natives of the soil, educated and prepared for their work
in this way. Indeed, by reason of a suggestion made by
some ancient Welsh writers, it has been supposed by
some that St. Paulinus, the Apostle of Northumbria, was
of British birth and had been taught in St. Gregory's
monastery in Rome; but this is a mere supposition, and,
in view of the traditional description of his person given
by St. Bede,[2] seems to be improbable, if not quite un-
tenable.

By the spring of 596, St. Gregory's preparations for
despatching his long-contemplated mission to England
were complete. For that difficult and perilous work he
naturally turned to men of his old monastery of St. Andrew
on the Cœlian, some of whom had been his companions
in the abortive attempt he had made some years before
to become himself the Apostle of England. It is impossible for any Englishman to read without emotion the
marble record in the Church of S. Gregorio on the
Cœlian hill in Rome, which to-day commemorates the
setting forth from that spot of the mission of St. Augustine and his companions, more than thirteen centuries
ago. It requires little stretch of imagination to believe

[1] Ep. vi, 7, Migne, *Patr. lat.*, lxxvii, col. 799.
[2] *Hist. Eccl.*, lib. ii, c. 16.

that St. Gregory himself had trained them in his own spirit and zeal for souls, and in his entire self-sacrifice to prepare them for the work. The actual progress of this mission on its way to England and what they accomplished does not immediately concern us, except in so far as it has relation to St. Gregory's own action. Leaving Rome, then, in A.D. 596, the travellers rested awhile at the celebrated monastery on the island of Lerins, then a great centre of Christian learning, which had furnished many illustrious rulers to the churches of southern Gaul. From Lerins they passed on to Aix; where, troubled by rumours of the difficulties which lay before them, it was determined to stay awhile and to send Augustine back to Rome for advice, and even, it would seem, to suggest to the Pope the necessity of their recall and the entire abandonment of their mission.

To this appeal to be allowed to return, St. Gregory turned a deaf ear. He, however, seems to have recognised the need of increasing the authority of the leader of the mission, and he sent Augustine back as the Abbot of the little community. By him he sent letters of thanks to those who had shown kindness to his missionaries on their way, and the following letter of exhortation and good advice to the monks themselves.

" To the brethren on their way to England. Gregory, the servant of the servants of God, to the servants of Our Lord Jesus Christ. It is right, my dearest children, that you should make every effort to finish the good work which, by God's help, you have begun, because it were better not to undertake good works, than to think of withdrawing from them, when once they have been commenced. Let not the hardships of your journey, nor the tongues of evil-speaking people frighten you, but carry

out what you have undertaken at God's inspiration, with
all eagerness and fervour, knowing that the reward of
eternal glory is secured by great labours. Humbly obey
Augustine your prior, whom on his return to you we
have appointed your Abbot, in all things. Remember
that whatever you do according to his directions will
always be profitable to your souls. May God Almighty
shield you with His grace, and may He grant that I
may see the fruits of your travail in our everlasting
country, so that although I cannot myself labour along
with you, I may share in the joy of your reward, because, indeed, had I my wish, I would join in your
work. May God, my beloved sons, take you into His
safe keeping." [1]

At the same time St. Gregory wrote to Virgilius of
Arles, and sent the letter by the hands of Augustine, to
" whose zeal and ability " he bears testimony. He informs
the Bishop of Arles that he has sent the bearer " with
other servants of God " on a mission " for the benefit of
souls to a place he (Augustine) will tell " him about. In
this work he writes: " You must give him the assistance
of your prayers and other help. If need shall arise, aid
him by your encouragement and refresh him, as is right,
with your paternal and priestly consolation; so that if,
whilst accompanied by the helps of your holiness, he
shall gain anything for Our God, which we anticipate he
will, you also, who have assisted the good work devotedly
by the abundance of your prayers, may likewise have
your reward." [2]

The Pontiff likewise wrote at the same time to Theo-
doric, King of Orleans and Burgundy, who then held his

[1] Ep. vi, 51, Migne, *Patr. lat.*, lxxvii, col. 836.
[2] *Ibid.*, 53, Migne, *Patr. lat.*, lxxvii, col. 837.

Court at Châlons-sur-Saône; to his brother, King Theodebert, and to their grandmother, Brunhild, who lived
with the latter at Metz, asking them to assist in the good
work. "We have heard," he says to the two first-named,
"that the English nation has been led by the mercy of
God, eagerly to desire conversion to the faith of Christ,
but that the priests near by are negligent and do not
fan the flame of desire by their exhortations." "For this
reason, I have," he continues, "despatched Augustine
and his companions, and have instructed them to take
with them some priests of the neighbouring country,
by whose assistance they may ascertain the disposition
of this people, and encourage their good intentions by
their preaching, as far as God allows." Then after be-
speaking the goodwill of the two rulers for his missionaries, he concludes: "Since souls are at stake, may
your influence protect and aid them, so that God Almighty, who knows with what devoted heart and pure
zeal you render this assistance in His work, may take
all your affairs into His merciful charge, and lead
you through earthly sovereignty into His Heavenly
kingdom." [1]

Encouraged by Gregory's earnest exhortations, the
missionaries again set out on their journey through Gaul
towards unknown England. Help and hospitality were
accorded to them by the bishops to whom the Pope had
written on their behalf. They were received by Theo-
doric and Theodebert, and by Clothair II, who was
then ruling in Paris under the tutelage of his mother,
Queen Fredegond. Their journey was slow, and they
had to winter in Gaul, so that it was not till Easter
time, 597, that they landed in England, and the harvest

[1] Ep. vi, 58, Migne, *Patr. lat.*, lxxvii, col. 842.

of souls so eagerly looked for by St. Gregory began to be gathered into the granaries of the Church.

The delight of the Pope found expression in many of his letters at this time. In fact, during the eight years which passed between the coming of the English mission and the death of St. Gregory, in writing to Patriarchs, Bishops, Kings, Queens, and others, the Pontiff refers to the success of the Gospel in this country some six-and-twenty times, so full is he of the work. To his friend Eulogius, Bishop of Alexandria, for example, he wrote, asking him to share in his great joy: " I know well, that even in the midst of your own good tidings (which you send me), you can rejoice at those of others, and so I will repay your news by announcing tidings not very dissimilar. The English, a nation occupying a little angle of the world, have been up to this time without the Faith, and have retained the worship of stocks and stones. Now, however, through your prayers, God put it into my mind to send thither a monk of my own monastery to preach the Gospel to them. By my licence he has been consecrated bishop by the bishops of Germany, and by their assistance he reached the above-named nation at the extremity of the world; and now, news has just reached me of his safety, and of his wonderful doings. Either he or those that were sent with him have been so conspicuous amongst this people by the great miracles they have worked, that they seem to have the power of the Apostles in the signs they have wrought. On the feast of Our Lord's Nativity . . . as I hear from our same brother and fellow bishop, more than ten thousand English were baptised. I mention this so that you may know what has been done through your prayers at this farthest extremity of the world, whilst you are talking to me about the people of Alexandria. Your prayers bear fruit in places where you are not, while your works are manifest in the place where you are."[1]

"To him" (that is, to St. Gregory), writes Venerable Bede, "must be attributed, as a work of affection and justice, that by preachers whom he sent our nation was set free from the jaws of the old enemy, and made to share in eternal liberty."[2] And in proof of the venerable Pontiff's joy at the success of his endeavours, St. Bede quotes a passage from St. Gregory's work, the *Morals on the Book of Job.* "God Almighty," he there says, "has opened the midst of the sea to the sunlit clouds, for He has brought even the ends of the earth to the Faith by the renowned miracles of His preachers. For, behold, how He has already touched the hearts of all nations! Behold how He has joined the east and west in one faith! Behold how the British tongue, which knew only how to utter savage cries, has already begun to sing the Hebrew Alleluia in the divine praises! Behold how the swelling ocean already submits to carry the feet of the saints; how its rough waves, which earthly princes could not tame by the sword, are through the fear of God made captive by the simple words of His priests! Behold how those who, whilst they had not the Faith, never knew fear for any bands of fighting men, now amongst the faithful obey the word of humble men. For, indeed, the heavenly message being once understood, and miracles also attesting it, the grace of the knowledge of God is poured out upon that people; it is restrained by fear of the same divine power, so that

---

[1] Ep. viii, 30, Migne, *Patr. lat.*, lxxvii, col. 931.
[2] *Hist. Eccl.*, lib. ii, c. 1 (ed. Plummer, i, p. 78).

it dreads to do evil, and with every best desire longs to attain to the grace of eternal life." [1]

In less than a year from the time of the first landing of the missionaries, Augustine found it necessary to send two of his monks, Laurence and Peter, back to Rome to obtain assistance and advice. They left England, probably in the spring of 598, taking to the Pope a full account of the prosperous state of his mission, and putting before him certain difficulties which required his supreme direction. Though it is said that Gregory did not delay to reply to the questions proposed to him, the messengers did not leave Rome again on their return before June 22nd, 601, when Laurence and Peter took with them fresh labourers for the work that had to be done in England. Amongst them were three names afterwards prominent as missionaries in the country, Paulinus, Mellitus, and Justus. They carried with them fresh letters of recommendation from the Pope to bishops and rulers, asking their aid for the missionaries, and manifesting the great joy of St. Gregory at the tidings of the first successes by which God had blessed the undertaking.

"By the grace of our Redeemer," he writes in one of these communications, " so great a multitude of the English nation is converted to the Christian Faith, that our most reverend common brother and fellow-bishop Augustine declares that those that are with him are not sufficient to carry on the work in every place. We have consequently determined to send him some (more) monks with our much-loved sons, Laurence the Prior, and Mellitus the Abbot." [2]

---

[1] Migne, *Patr. lat., ut supra;* also *Moralium*, lib. xxvii, c. 11, Migne, *Patr. lat.*, lxxvi, col. 410.

[2] Ep. xi, 58, Migne, *Patr. lat.*, lxxvii, col. 1176.

By this same mission Gregory sent letters to King Ethelbert of Kent, and his Queen, Bertha. To the former he writes words of encouragement and paternal advice. " Almighty God," he says, " raises up certain good men to govern His people, so that through them He may distribute the gifts of His mercy to all under their sway. Such, we understand, has been the case in regard to the English nation, over which Your Magnificence has been placed, so that the heavenly gifts may be bestowed upon the people under your rule through the favours granted to you." He then exhorts him to persevere in helping on the conversion of the English people, and holds up to him as a model the example of the Emperor Constantine. He then proceeds: " Our most reverend brother Augustine, Bishop, is proficient in the monastic rule, filled with a knowledge of the Holy Scripture, and by God's grace endowed with good works. Give a willing ear to his admonitions, carry them out devotedly, and store them carefully in your memory. If you give heed to him when he speaks to you in Almighty God's name, Almighty God will the more speedily hearken to him when he prays for you. If, which God forbid, you disregard his words, how shall Almighty God hear his pleadings for you, when you refuse to hear his for God. . . . I have forwarded you a few trifling tokens of esteem, which, however, you will not look on as trifles when you remember that they come to you with the blessing of blessed Peter the Apostle."[1]

To Queen Bertha, the Pontiff wrote in the same encouraging strain. " Our most beloved sons, Laurence the priest, and Peter the monk," he says, " on their

[1] Ep. xi, 66, Migne, *Patr. lat.*, lxxvii, col. 1201.

return, told us how graciously Your Highness received
our most reverend brother and fellow-bishop, Augustine,
and of the great consolation and affection you have
shown him. We have blessed Almighty God that in
His mercy He has deigned to reserve the conversion of
the English nation as your reward. For even, as by
Helena, mother of the most pious Emperor Constantine
of precious memory, the Faith of Christ was enkindled in
the hearts of the Roman people; so also we trust that
through your zeal His mercy has been working in the
English nation." The Pope then mildly rebukes Bertha
for having failed to try and convert her husband before,
but encourages her to strengthen her consort in the
fervour of his conversion. " Your name," he adds, " has
reached not only the Romans, who have prayed fer-
vently for your welfare, but divers parts of the world,
and even Constantinople and the ears of the most Serene
Prince. As the consolation of your Christianity has
given us joy, may the angels in heaven rejoice at the
completion of your work."[1]

St. Gregory's letter to Augustine himself, written at
this same time, allows us to see at once the fulness of his
joy at all he had heard, and at the same time his fear
lest, perhaps, the soul of his disciple should be in any
way harmed by any unwise exaltation at the swift success that had attended his mission. He writes: "Glory
be to God in the highest, and on earth peace to men of
good will; for the grain of wheat which fell into the
earth is dead, and so He, by whose weakness we receive
strength, by whose pains we are freed from suffering,
should not reign solitary in Heaven. For love of Him,
we seek in Britain the brethren whom we know not, and

[1] Ep. xi, 29, Migne, *Patr. lat.*, lxxvii, col. 1141.

by His favour we have found those whom we sought without knowing them. Who can describe the joy that filled the hearts of the faithful here, because by Almighty God's grace and through the labours of your fraternity, the English nation has had the clouds of error dispersed and is flooded by the light of holy Faith? . . . Whose work is this, but His who saith: *My Father worketh until now, and I work.* To show that He converted the world, not by the wisdom of men, but by His own power, He chose illiterate men to send into the world to preach. This has He done also now, for He has deigned to perform feats of strength among the English people by means of weak instruments.

" In that heavenly gift, dearest brother, there is that which should inspire exceeding great fear. I know well, beloved, that God Almighty hath through you wrought great miracles in the nation that He hath deigned to select. In that heavenly gift, however, there is that which should make you fear while you rejoice. You can be glad, indeed, because the souls of the English are drawn to interior grace through exterior means. Yet you must also fear lest, amidst the signs that are wrought by you, your weak mind should be presumptuously lifted up by its powers, and through vain glory should fall from within according as it is exalted in honour from without. . . ." [1]

One point settled by St. Gregory at this time is worthy of some notice. In his letter to Ethelbert the Pope had urged the King to destroy the pagan temples in his kingdom, but he subsequently modified this view. After the second band of missionaries had left Rome, he despatched a letter to overtake Mellitus on the journey,

[1] Ep. xi, 28, Migne, *Patr. lat.*, lxxvii, col. 138.

by which to correct his first judgment on this matter. In this second letter he says: "After the departure of our brethren with you, we were in great anxiety since we heard nothing of the success of your journey. When Almighty God shall have brought you to our most reverend brother, Augustine, tell him that I have long deliberated over this point in regard to the English: (and have come to the conclusion) that the temples of idols in that country should not be demolished, but the idols therein destroyed. Bless water, sprinkle the temples with it, erect altars and deposit relics in them: for if these temples have been well built, they should be transferred from the worship of idols to the service of the true God. When the people see that the temples are not destroyed, and, putting error from their hearts, come to know and worship the true God, they will the more readily resort to the places that are familiar to them. Moreover, as it is their practice to slay numbers of oxen in the service of their devils, substitute some similar solemnity for this: on the day of the dedication of the church, or of the martyrs whose relics are deposited therein, let them construct bowers of the branches of trees near these churches into which the temples have been converted, and let them celebrate their solemnities with religious rejoicings. Let them no longer sacrifice animals to the devil, but kill them for their own use, to the glory of God, and let them render thanks for their abundance to the Giver of all things. In this way, while some form of external rejoicing is preserved to them, they may be the more inclined to appreciate interior consolations; for it is undoubtedly impossible to cut off everything from their rude minds at once. He who would climb a height ascends by steps or paces, not by vaulting."[1] It was upon the directions laid down in this letter that St. Augustine acted when he purified the heathen temple at Canterbury and dedicated it as a Christian church, under the patronage of St. Pancras. If we are to believe in a subsequent tradition preserved at Canterbury itself, the choice of the patron was dictated by a wish to take this martyred Roman youth as patron, so as to be a memorial of the fair-haired Saxon boys whose presence in Rome had first suggested to St. Gregory the need of converting England to the faith.[1] Very possibly, also, some of the monk missionaries may have come from the monastery which St. Gregory had established at the Roman Church of St. Pancras in order that the Saint's body might be kept with honour, and the unbroken liturgical services be offered to God above his tomb.[3]

It is unnecessary here to say much about the formal letter to St. Augustine sent by the Pope in reply to questions as to discipline and ecclesiastical management proposed to him. St. Gregory answers with great care and minuteness, and the document evidences his interest in the state of the country, his grasp of the situation, and his broad-minded consideration. In this "little book," as St. Bede calls this document, we may understand the spirit of him whom we glory in revering as our Apostle. What evidently characterises the *Responsions* of St. Gregory throughout, is the wise discretion which knows how to relax as well as how to maintain the strictness of rule; how, by condescension, to adapt even outward circumstances into means for securing the very end de-

---

[1] Ep. xi, 76, Migne, *Patr. lat.*, lxxvii, col. 1213.
[2] *Hist. Mon. S. Augustine Cantuar.* Rolls series, p. 80.
[3] Ep. iv, 18, Migne, *Patr. lat.*, lxxvii, col. 687.

sired, and how to admit of the good from whatever
quarter derived, so long as it was "the good" and could
be made to serve God's work and God's glory.

The last act of St. Gregory for the English Church
was to make provision for its government. He established the Metropolitan Sees at London (afterwards
transferred to Canterbury) and at York; the latter to
enjoy archiepiscopal rights only after St. Augustine's
death. According to this original plan each Metropolitan was to preside over twelve suffragans, and to
each Archbishop he proposed to give the pallium. He
then exhorted the newly-established Church of the English people to concord and unity: " Let all things that
are done for the zeal of Christ," he says, " be arranged
with common counsel and united action: let all determine what is right to be done unanimously, and carry out
what they determine without differing one from another."[1] This important direction as to the administration of the Church of England was sent off at the end of
June, 601, and although St. Gregory lived for nearly
three years after this, he did not, of course, live to see
his entire plan for the organisation of the Church carried
out; and part of it was subsequently found to be unworkable in practice.

Something must now be added to what has already
been said about the love and reverence with which
St. Gregory was always regarded by the English people.
Churches were dedicated to God under the patronage
of his name, and from the earliest times altars were set
up in his honour. Of the latter, two may be named:
that erected in the Church of the blessed Apostles Peter
and Paul at Canterbury, at which, in St. Bede's day,

[1] Ep. xi, 65, Migne, *Patr. lat.*, lxxvii, col. 1200.

every Saturday a priest celebrated the divine mysteries in memory of the archbishops who had succeeded Augustine in the charge committed to him by St. Gregory:[1] and that "in the porch of Pope St. Gregory," built by St. Oswald at the Church of "the blessed Apostle Peter" at York, in memory of the great Pope "from whose disciples he had received the word of life."[2]

Throughout the whole Church, and in a particular manner in England, the works of St. Gregory became the foundation of the moral, theological, and spiritual teaching during centuries after his death. It is not too much to say that his *Morals on the Book of Job* and his treatise on the *Pastoral Charge* long formed the storehouses from which generations of spiritual writers drew their inspirations, their ideas, and frequently their very words. Amongst the books that St. Augustine brought with him was the tract *De Cura Pastorali* of the Saint, which was long treasured at Canterbury by those who loved to be called the "*discipuli beati papae Gregorii*" —the disciples of the blessed Pope Gregory.[3] Pope Honorius, in his letter to King Edwin, after his baptism in the north by St. Paulinus, urges him to study the works of St. Gregory, "your teacher."[4] In the language of St. Aldhelm, the great Pope was "our watchful shepherd and teacher, who saved our ancestors from the dark errors of paganism and brought to them the grace of regeneration."[5] St. Bede gives a catalogue of

[1] *Hist. Eccl.*, ii, cap. 3 (ed. Plummer, i, p. 86).
[2] *Ibid.*, cap. 20.
[3] *Ibid.*, *Praef.* (ed. Plummer, p. 6).
[4] *Ibid.*, lib. ii, c. 17.
[5] Migne, *Patr. lat.*, lxxix, col. 155.

X

St. Gregory's works, and Alcuin says that whatever the Pontiff wrote was in the library at York.[1] Writing, too, in 797 to an English Bishop, Speratus, on the office of a bishop, he says: " Often read, I beg of you, the book of our teacher Saint Gregory on the *Pastoral Charge*. In it you will see the dangers of priestly office, and not forget the reward of the faithful servant who has worked. Often keep the book in your hands; imprint its meaning deep upon your memory, so that you may know how anyone should receive the dignity of the priesthood; and having received it, with what intention he should preach; and, indeed, he (St. Gregory) has described with the greatest discretion what is proper for each one." [2]

Lastly, to take one more example: among the books which King Alfred translated for the use of his people was the *Pastoral Book* of St. Gregory. He sent a copy of this translation to each bishop in his kingdom, that it might be placed in his cathedral church. With it he sent a precious " aestel," or marker, and ordered that " no one should remove the aestel from the book, or the book from the minster," unless it were wanted by the Bishop. In his letter to the Bishops of the kingdom, which accompanied the book, the King says: " I began, among the various and manifold troubles of this kingdom, to translate into English the book called *Pastoralis*, or in English, *Hirdeboc*, sometimes word for word, and sometimes according to the sense, as I had learnt it from Plegmund my archbishop, and Asser my bishop, and Grimbald my Mass-priest, and John my Mass-priest; and when I had learnt it as I best could understand it,

---

[1] *Historians of the Church of York* (Rolls series), i, p. 395.
[2] Migne, *Patr. lat.*, c, col. 242.

and as I could most nearly interpret it, I translated it into English." [1]

The Popes are always to be found in subsequent ages, even after the Conquest, constantly reminding England of its debt to their predecessor St. Gregory the Great. For instance, to give some examples only after the Normans were established in the land: Paschal II, writing to Henry I, refers to the necessity of keeping the laws and directions received " from Blessed Gregory, the Apostle of the English race." Pope Calixtus II, in a letter to the same king, uses the expression: " Pope Gregory, that renowned propagator of the Christian faith in your kingdom." In the same way the debt of gratitude is fully acknowledged on the part of the English. Ralph, Archbishop of Canterbury, for instance, in 1199, speaks of the close relations which have ever existed between Rome and Canterbury, " from the time when the Holy Father Gregory sent the saintly and venerable man Augustine to preach the Faith." Throughout this letter the great Pontiff is *pater noster Gregorius* —" our father Gregory,"—and the Archbishop declares that it is for this reason that Canterbury has always shown " the greatest obedience to the supreme and chief See, that of the blessed Peter." The Metropolitan rights, about which the Archbishop was then appealing to the Pope, were really safeguarded from the earliest times, because they had been established by St. Gregory. Alcuin declared this in one of his verses: " It was," he says, " because Gregory the Bishop had decreed thus or old, when from the City of Rome he sent the seed of life to the English nation."

The feelings of our Saxon forefathers towards the

[1] W. Hunt, *Hist. of the English Church*, i, p. 281.

great Pontiff are well expressed in the words, written as
a Northumbrian, by the old English monk in the earliest
life of St. Gregory: " O most loving Father, Lord God
Almighty, though we did not deserve to have the actual
presence of the blessed Gregory amongst us, nevertheless
we have ever to give Thee thanks that it was through
him we had our teacher Paulinus."

We may conclude by the relation of an incident recorded as having happened after the death of our great
Apostle, which is partly fact and partly, possibly, legend
embroidered upon the groundwork of reality by the devotion and reverence of subsequent generations. Gregory's death, we are told, was immediately followed by
a display of the proverbially fickle character of a mob,
and of a Roman mob, perhaps, in particular. The Pope
had lived for the people, he had taught them, he had fed
them and cared for them, but his death synchronised
with a time of great scarcity and distress. A rumour,
rising no one knew from whence or from whom, and
spreading, no one knew how, among the half-starving
people, attributed their troubles to the fact that Gregory
had dissipated the patrimony of the Church, which they
had come to regard as their own. The mob surrounded
the papal palace, and determined to destroy all the
works of the saint, whom they had suddenly come to
regard as their worst enemy. This catastrophe was
averted by a tragic occurrence which was long the talk
of Rome. Peter, the deacon, as all readers of St. Gregory's
Dialogues know so well, had been the constant attendant
of the Pope, and his amanuensis in the composition of
his works. Fearing that the threats of the mob might
really result in the destruction of the works he regarded
as so precious, Peter came forward, and offered in his

person to stand the test of their worth. He promised to take an oath upon the Gospels that these works were inspired by the Spirit of God, and that it would be a grievous offence against the Almighty to destroy what had thus been written. He offered consequently to take this oath as to the truth of what he was going to relate, and to take the consequences of what St. Gregory had foretold would happen, namely his death, if he ever revealed what his intimate relation with the Pope had made known to him. Having told them this, Peter, it is said, mounted some steps, took an oath upon the Gospels, and related the following incident in the life of the dead Pontiff to which he could testify. Whilst dictating to him it was frequently St. Gregory's custom to place himself behind a curtain screened from the sight of his scribe. One day Peter moved by curiosity at the curious pauses the saint had been making in speaking, raised the curtain and looked behind, when he beheld the semblance of a dove—the emblem of God's Holy Spirit—hovering round about St. Gregory's head and, as the Saint paused, approaching him and appearing to whisper in his ear as if directing him. Upon the holy Pontiff finding out that the faithful Peter had surprised his secret, he warned him never to reveal it to anyone, and declared that in the hour that he did so, he would die. This was the supreme test to which Peter the deacon submitted himself, to save the works of his beloved master from destruction. The proof was in favour of the works, for, as the story goes, as his relation of this incident concluded, he expired suddenly in the sight of all.

Lastly, it is impossible to celebrate the memory of this event, which happened thirteen hundred years ago,

without reflecting upon the historical influence exercised
by the mission of Gregory upon "the making of England." Perhaps no single life in the entire period from
that day to this, has been so productive of such lasting
fruit, and to no single individual does England owe
so much. The historian Green has fully discerned this,
and has well described what the genius of Rome and
the genius of Pope Gregory effected for this country's
good. " Nothing is more characteristic of Roman Christianity," he writes, " than its administrative organisation.
Its ordered hierarchy of bishops, priests, and lower
clergy, its judicial and deliberative machinery, its courts
and its councils, had become a part of its very existence,
and settled with it on every land that it won. Gregory,
as we have seen, had plotted out the yet heathen Britain
into an ordered Church, and although the carrying out
of this scheme in its actual form had proved impossible,
yet it was certain that the first effort of the Roman See,
now that the ground was clear, would be to replace it
by some analogous arrangement. But no such religious
organisation could stamp itself on the English soil without telling on the civil organisation about. The regular
subordination of priest to bishop, of bishop to Primate
(and, we may add, of Primate to Pope), in the administration of the Church would supply a model on which
the civil organisation of the State would unconsciously,
but irresistibly shape itself. The gathering of the clergy
in national synods, would inevitably lead the way to
national gatherings for civil legislation. Above all, if
the nation in its spiritual capacity came to recognise
the authority of a single Primate, it would insensibly
be led in its temporal capacity to recognise a single
sovereign. . . . The hopes of such an organisation rested

in the submission of the English States to the Church of Rome."

This was the work St. Gregory did for England, and if to some the words of the historian of *The English People* may appear somewhat far-fetched, it is impossible to read the records of those early times without seeing that the influence of Rome and Roman ways made for unification. Without St. Gregory and his monk-missionaries, the welding of the peoples, and even nations, in this land into the one English folk might have been indefinitely postponed.

INDEX

313

Y